Psychotherapy
With Sexually
Abused Boys

Interpersonal Violence:
The Practice Series

Jon R. Conte, Series Editor

Interpersonal Violence: The Practice Series is devoted to mental health, social service, and allied professionals who confront daily the problem of interpersonal violence. It is hoped that the knowledge, professional experience, and high standards of practice offered by the authors of these volumes may lead to the end of interpersonal violence.

In this series...

Psychotherapy With Sexually Abused Boys

An Integrated Approach

William N. Friedrich

Interpersonal Violence:
The Practice Series

SAGE Publications
International Educational and Professional Publisher
Thousand Oaks   London   New Delhi
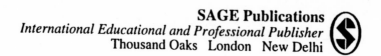

For information address:

SAGE Publications, Inc.
2455 Teller Road
Thousand Oaks, California 91320
E-mail: order@sagepub.com

SAGE Publications Ltd.
6 Bonhill Street
London EC2A 4PU
United Kingdom

SAGE Publications India Pvt. Ltd.
M-32 Market
Greater Kailash I
New Delhi 110 048 India

Printed in the United States of America

Library of Congress Cataloging-in-Publication Data

Friedrich, William N.
    Psychotherapy with sexually abused boys : An integrated approach /
William N. Friedrich.
        p.   cm. — (Interpersonal violence, the practice series ; 11)
    Includes bibliographical references and index.
    ISBN 0-8039-5694-0 (acid-free paper). — ISBN 0-8039-5695-9 (acid-
free paper : pbk.)
        1. Male sexual abuse victims—Mental health. 2. Child
psychotherapy. 3. Boys—Abuse of—Psychological aspects.
4. Sexually abused children—Mental health. I. Title. II. Series:
Interpersonal violence ; v. 11.
RJ507.S49F753   1995
618.92'85860651—dc20   95-3736

This book is printed on acid-free paper.

96 97 98 99 00 01 10 9 8 7 6 5 4 3 2

Production Editor: Tricia K. Bennett   Typesetter: Christina M. Hill

Contents

Dedicated to the boys,
who have gifted me with their stories.

Preface

The craft of therapy coupled with clinical writing combines two very important dimensions in my professional practice. I am a clinical child psychologist who has specialized in the treatment of sexually abused children and their families. Both therapy and writing exercise different aspects of my self and help me remain balanced.

My book, *Psychotherapy of Sexually Abused Children and Their Families* (Friedrich, 1990), reflected my first attempt to bring together theory and practice in this field. I view recovery from trauma as a coping process, and the book was grounded in coping theory. However, the longer I work in this field, the more my thinking has evolved. The theory that increasingly organizes my perspective is developmental psychopathology (Rolf, Masten, Cicchetti, Nuechterlein, & Weintraub, 1990; Sroufe, 1989). Coping is important, but I view it as one step removed from three basic, interpersonal, and clearly developmental processes. These include attachment, dysregulation, and the formation of the self. These three concepts are tentatively laid out in *Casebook of Sexually Abused Children* (Friedrich, 1991a), where the various cases illustrate different aspects of these dynamics.

So here I am writing a new book, a book driven by my learning from the children and families I continue to see daily. There are a number of excellent books on therapy with sexually abused children (Cunningham & MacFarlane, 1990; Gil, 1991; James, 1989; Mandell & Damon, 1989; Trepper & Barrett, 1989), to which I refer frequently. Over the past years, my practice has increasingly focused on male victims. These boys range from the preschooler to the adolescent, and my work typically includes their families. At least half of the boys are victims of incest, and the majority of them are from significantly troubled families. This may include several generations of victimization, chemical dependency, parental depression, low income, and marital problems. Sexual abuse is usually only one of the forms of maltreatment that they have experienced. Consequently, my perspectives and the clinical examples that are laced throughout the book may be different from the cases of practitioners who have fewer referrals from protective services.

I wrote this book as well for a number of additional reasons. They are the boys, the Jasons, Jareds, and Justins of the world. The boys who populate this book—each of them reflects a reason. Each of them has an untold story. By their telling, I hope to empower therapists to work with boys in a sensitive, complex, and committed way.

One Jason was plagued with problems of identity and sexual confusion because of his sexual abuse by a male perpetrator. When I first saw him, he was binding his genitals because he was ashamed of his sexual self.

Jared's physical abuse seemed as bad as the sexual abuse he experienced. The aggression and sadism that he initially exhibited were increasingly apparent and dangerous. His anger masked a tremendous amount of dependency as well as depression that had no voice. He also had accompanying language delays that made him more vulnerable to excessive aggression.

Justin was a boy whose sexually abused mother had never liked him. Her emotionally distant and covertly rejecting posture made him vulnerable in at least two ways: the first was to the sexual abuse he experienced, and the second was that the abuse impact was magnified because of his earlier neglect.

Each of the above features—sexual identity; the added burden of physical abuse, language delay, and subsequent aggression; and alienation from mother due to her issues with males—is extremely powerful. They shape the course, nature, and context of treatment and are quite pertinent to therapy with sexually abused boys.

My experience has taught me to be both pragmatic and directive. Therapy is rarely viewed positively by boys. They prefer not to talk in ways that make them feel vulnerable. The time necessary to engage the boy and to develop rapport is frequently brief. I feel an urgency to create safety and to seize a therapeutic moment before the family is caught in another crisis. At times, I am working harder than anyone else in the family. The approach to therapy I describe is for advocates who are fierce about children, but who also know how to balance their lives in other ways. Writing is one form of balance for me.

I don't know that my suggestions constitute the most effective strategy for working with boys. I feel some chagrin in writing out an approach to treatment that is largely untested and has not been empirically validated. However, I believe my most important contribution with this book is to help therapists learn a more organized way to think about sexual abuse—a way that respects the trauma but also borrows from rich clinical theory and from several empirically validated approaches, including goal-setting (Kiresuk & Sherman, 1968), trauma-focus (Lanktree & Briere, 1992), and cognitive-behavioral therapy (Deblinger, McLeer, & Henry, 1990).

This is a book about males, but I'm convinced that the theory works as well for females. However, there are reasons to think that trauma can have a differential impact relative to gender. I try to make that case in Chapter 1. The case examples are all male, and each example has been disguised to protect the boy and his family.

I am indebted to many people who have guided my personal and clinical development and have enabled the writing of this book. Blair Justice first made me excited about the area of child maltreatment. My first reading of the attachment literature was prompted by another professor, Jim Clark. I identified with him to such an extent that I attempted to read every book in his office. His two volumes by Bowlby on attachment and separation caught my eye during a visit to his office, and my reading and rereading of them over the years has been enormously instructive. John Tyler, Pat Brady, and Donna Copeland were additional professors or supervisors who modeled compassion and a commitment to the hurts of others.

I am indebted as well to the larger group of individuals that forms the American Professional Society on the Abuse of Children. I am truly privileged to be part of an organization that values children unconditionally and that has as its mission better and more effective protection and services for victims. There are particular people within the organization—Barbara Boat, Barbara Bonner, Judy Cohen, David Corwin, Mark Everson, Kathleen Faller, David Finkelhor, Eliana Gil, Cheryl Lanktree, Julie Lipovsky, Anthony Mannarino, John Myers, Theresa Reid, Ben Saunders, and Linda Williams—whose personal spirit and professional writings have both been inspirational. Other friends and colleagues with whom I have bounced these ideas around include Lucy Berliner, John Briere, Paul Gerber, and Sandra Hewitt. There are also fellows, residents, and trainees who have worked with me during my first years at Mayo and who agreed to see "just one more kid." I also deeply appreciate the work and collegiality I share with child protection workers at Olmstead County Social Services in Rochester, Minnesota.

I also owe a great deal to my remarkably competent secretary, Gloria Mensink. Not only does she frequently have to deal with my patients over the phone, but she also very ably typed yet another book for me. I don't know what I would do without her.

Finally, this book could not have been written without my family. My wife and children are my primary attachments and built-in selfsoothers. Their affection for me has allowed me to evolve into a better person. With their help, I have a much more positive and accurate sense of who I am as person, father, husband, and therapist.

1

Introduction to the Model

*Children who have spent their lives in a state of chronic depression
report . . . a sense of not being connected to the experiences of
childhood, a feeling that life has been lived behind a screen, within an
envelope which protects the child from trauma or from neglect.*

—DeSalvo, 1989, p. 103

Two equally true and contradictory points remain evident regarding
sexual abuse. The first is that over the past decade, the previously
unacknowledged area of child sexual abuse has become such a well-
accepted phenomenon as to be routine in clinical practice. The second
point is that we still do not know very much about sexual abuse.
Studies on impact are typically cross-sectional or retrospective. We
have a rudimentary knowledge about what constitutes good treatment, and even less is known as to whether treatment is effective.

There are a number of reasons for these two, seemingly opposite,
yet valid positions. One reason why we know so little about sexual
abuse is also a reason why abuse occurs: The victims are children. Children, their behavior, and treatment simply are not studied as carefully
or with as much vigor as are adults. Another reason is that the majority
of sexual abuse treatment professionals are primarily clinicians by

1

training and lack research skills. The so-called premier mental health professions of psychology and psychiatry have not been the movers and shakers in this field the way I feel they should have been.

Another reason is sociocultural in nature. Both the scope of the problem of child sexual abuse and its sensationalistic aspects have polarized the field. We have moved from never thinking about sexual abuse in children, to thinking that sexual abuse in children is everywhere and that it is the source of most problems, and finally to questioning whether or not it exists at the rates determined by several nationwide prevalence studies. These wide vacillations reflect, in part, our limited tolerance for painful and complex issues.

Although a variety of contributors could explain the seemingly opposite opening statements in this chapter, there are at least three related issues that cloud our treatment efforts. The first is the fact that sexual abuse is not simply an overt act. The abuse-of-sexuality model has broadened my perspective to think of more than sexual acts (Bolton, Morris, & MacEachron, 1989). The abuse of sexuality includes evasiveness about sexuality, lack of exposure to knowledge about sexuality, overpermissiveness, negativity about sexuality, seductiveness by caregivers, and, finally, the overtly sexual environment, or what is traditionally thought to be sexual abuse.

A second issue is that sexual abuse does not result in a consistent cluster of symptoms (Kendall-Tackett, Williams, & Finkelhor, 1993). The same acts, in different children, can be manifested in seemingly disparate immediate and long-term sequelae. With one child, depression and impaired self-esteem seem primary. With another, sexual behavior problems are predominant. Children cannot be adequately understood unless they are appreciated as developing organisms who must be evaluated and treated in the context of their family. Both of these issues make the effect of sexual abuse difficult to sort out as well as to treat.

The potential enormity of the impact of sexual abuse has made the traumatic aspect the focus of much of the research to date. I know that therapists are often gripped by the trauma. We respond to sexual abuse by asking either too much or too little about it. We hear warnings that unless the child talks about everything, he will not move forward. On the other hand, we hear precautions that the child should talk about the victimization in due time and should not be rushed for fear of being revictimized and overwhelmed. There is considerable confusion about how central to make the actual victimization in the therapy.

The field of child sexual abuse needs to move beyond a simple focus on the trauma. It needs to do this not only because trauma exists along a continuum ranging from minimal to extremely severe but also because a simple focus on trauma creates blinders (Cicchetti, 1989). Victims must be defined by more than their victim history. Not to do so is to belittle them. Not to do so also removes us from the numerous useful theories that can drive our research and therapy so that we can become better informed and more effective practitioners.

Clinical practice must be driven by both theory and research findings. Currently, the majority of sexually abused children do not receive treatment. Those children who are treated may be seen by therapists who (a) may not appreciate the unique impact of sexual abuse; (b) have little broad-based clinical training and thus are not aware of a wide variety of empirically validated treatment techniques; and (c) have so little idea of how and what to treat that they may follow approaches that are too brief, not directed at the system the child is living in, or even traumagenic.

❏ Case Example

A case can illustrate the integrated model to be presented and emphasize the clinical relevance of the theory. A 5-year-old boy reports that he has been sexually abused by a relative outside his nuclear family. He is interviewed by a child protection worker in combination with a police officer. His report is deemed valid. Because of his age, the county prosecutor chooses not to go to trial. After some urging by the child protective service worker, the child comes to you. The parents are vague in their description of the boy's behavior. They also express concern about their relationship with the offender, expressing the hopes that he is not upset with them and that their relationship will not be disrupted.

Typically, your therapy approach is nondirective play therapy. You believe this strategy enables you to be the most sensitive to the needs of the child. It is your preferred method to establish rapport and develop a working alliance. As the therapy is progressing, however, you have become aware of certain features, although none of them have been addressed specifically. For example, the father appears uninvolved. You have not observed any eye contact or signs of closeness between the boy and his mother when she brings him to his appointments. The brief contacts you have had with the mother certainly suggest that she is visibly distressed. She has a difficult time talking about her son's behavior and about the circumstances around his victimization. You are aware as well that your client is having problems sleeping. He has difficulty falling asleep and comes into the parents' bed halfway through the night, prompting anger from the father. In addition, he is unable to finish a human figure drawing. After seven appointments over a 10-week period, including two cancellations, the parents call to terminate treatment. They state that the therapy has done little to help and is no longer needed.

Have these seven sessions been helpful? As a reader, do you believe the therapist acted in a knowledgeable manner? Had he established any specific therapeutic targets? Had he tried to address the larger family issues? Every reader probably wonders what could be done to make the therapy both more goal-oriented and helpful to the child.

This case is not atypical. Clinical practice should be driven by theory and research findings; the various models that have been suggested to understand the impact of sexual abuse, however, do not necessarily lend themselves to adaptation for treatment. Research into treatment efficacy with children is only now emerging (Deblinger et al., 1990).

❏ Current Theories

Three theories, the posttraumatic stress disorder model (PTSD) (McLeer, Deblinger, Atkins, Foa, & Ralphe, 1988), the traumagenic factors model (Finkelhor & Browne, 1985), and the information-processing of trauma model (Hartman & Burgess, 1993), have been instrumental in understanding the impact of sexual abuse on children. Each of them has a primary focus on the nature of the trauma and thus ignores the larger world of the child. The PTSD model is the one that directly lends itself to treatment practice. The PTSD model emphasizes the traumatic nature of sexual abuse in a fairly constant set of behavioral and cognitive effects, including intrusive thoughts, numbing, hyperarousal, and the avoidance of triggering events. Treatment techniques derived from the PTSD formulation include anxiety reduction strategies as well as cognitive restructuring. There is evidence that this approach is useful in reducing anxiety in sexually abused children (Berliner, 1991; Deblinger et al., 1990).

The PTSD model would be much more useful if the majority of sexually abused children presented with PTSD as a diagnosis. In a recent review of the literature on the impact of sexual abuse on children, the percentage of sexually abused children ($N = 151$ children from four studies) with general PTSD symptoms ranged from 20% to 77% (Kendall-Tackett et al., 1993). A frequent ancillary PTSD symptom, nightmares, was studied in a larger number of children, but the percentage of sexually abused children with nightmares ranged from 18% to 68%, depending on the study. Nightmares also seemed to be more common in preschool children than in school-age or adolescent children.

The traumagenic factors model has less direct relevance to treatment practices, although it is an elegant explanation of abuse impact (Finkelhor & Browne, 1985). The authors have suggested that sexual abuse is deleterious because of four traumatic factors: betrayal, stigmatization, powerlessness, and traumatic sexualization. Each of these traumagenic factors has a potential impact on both overt behavior and internal psychological processes, including cognitions. This model is extremely helpful in identifying the broad, at times overwhelming, range of possible treatment needs, but it does not directly suggest interventions.

The information-processing of trauma model is a complex neuropsychosocial model that emphasizes the hyperarousal inherent in the trauma (Hartman & Burgess, 1993). It posits that the limbic system of the brain is overwhelmed by the incoming trauma. Consequently, key processes in the construction of memory for the event and in subsequent learning are disrupted. This gives rise, for example, to dissociation.

These theories are not completely separate but overlap somewhat. For example, all three models include a belief in the traumatic nature of sexual abuse and all posit a wide range of sequelae that are either acute, long-term, or both.

Another problem with the above theories is their focus on the individual victim. Although Hartman and Burgess (1993) describe a Phase 1 (the victim's social context), the key elements of their model are the individual, neurophysiological outcomes.

A theory that appreciates both individual impact and family context is truly needed to guide the treatment of sexually abused children. This is even more the case given the fact that children are embedded within a larger developmental and family context (Kegan, 1982).

The sexually abused child cannot be considered outside a family context. Although there is no denying the traumatic potential of sexual abuse, research increasingly points to family variables, including support for the child, as strongly associated with the effect of abuse (Friedrich, 1988; Friedrich, Beilke, & Urquiza, 1987). Other clinical literature describes the PTSD-like reactions that some parents have regarding their child's sexual abuse (Newberger, Gremy, Waternaux, & Newberger, 1993; Uherek, 1991). These facts do not negate the unique impact of sexual abuse. However, I believe that individually based theories on impact are not sufficient either to understand the impact or to guide the type of broad-based treatment that is needed.

Another feature, and one that makes this book most relevant, is the growing realization that gender differences in the impact and treatment needs of sexually abused children must be considered. I have only to look at my own evolution as a therapist with sexually abused children to fully appreciate this fact. I began by being unaware of male victims. Then, when they did burst into my consciousness, I tended to ignore them because there were already far too many female victims to treat. When I was finally forced to take notice of them, I was initially struck by how angry and out of control boy victims appeared in comparison to girl victims. However, the more time I have spent with sexually abused boys, the more I have appreciated that, for boys, the impact of sexual abuse and the resulting treatment needs are extremely diverse and do not lend themselves to simple categorization or reductionism. Depression and feelings of inadequacy can be as common as anger in male victims. These feelings can have as profound a lifelong impact as I have seen in female victims.

The preceding brief summary strongly suggests a need for treatment that is contextual and derived from theoretical formulations that are more unifying and empirically validated than the three models suggested earlier. In addition, we need specific treatment techniques that are unique to sexual abuse but whose generic utility and validity have been broadly established. Finally, I believe we need approaches that can work with boys.

❏ An Integrated Contextual Model

What I am proposing as the framework of this book is an integrated model that borrows from three well-developed theoretical perspectives. These include attachment theory (Alexander, 1992), behavior/emotion regulation (Dodge & Garber, 1992), and self-perception/development (Crittenden, 1994; Harter, 1988). The effects of sexual abuse are reflected in each of these three broad domains. Of even more clinical importance is the fact that specific treatment approaches, pertinent to individual, group, and family treatment, can be derived from this model.

The integrated model subsumes the traumagenic factors, information-processing, and the PTSD models and provides an additional developmental and family context. For example, the traumagenic factor of betrayal (Finkelhor & Browne, 1985) has both psychological and behavioral effects. These include distrust of others and an impaired ability to form close relationships. Both of these effects are clearly relevant to attachment theory. Stigmatization and powerlessness have behavioral and psychological sequelae that include reduced self-efficacy and a distorted view of self. Each of these is directly related to how the child or adolescent perceives himself. Finally, the traumatic nature of sexual abuse affects the child's ability to regulate his emotions, thoughts, and behaviors, leading to some of the specific symptoms outlined in the PTSD and information-processing models and is suggestive of dysregulation. In addition, sexual abuse is the abuse of the relationship, and the degree to which it influences prior attachments or is reflective of problematic prior attachments makes its effect pertinent to attachment theory as well. See Table 1.1 for a summary.

The book is organized into three large domains of attachment, dysregulation, and self. Within each domain, I will suggest strategies to treat effects. These strategies will include individual, group, and

Table 1.1 Integrated Model

Model	Attachment	Dysregulation	Self
PTSD		++	
Traumagenic Factors:			
Betrayal	++		
Powerlessness			++
Stigmatization			++
Traumatic Sexualization	+	++	
Information Processing		++	

family therapy approaches. Because understanding the boy is critical to good therapy, I suggest evaluation techniques as well for each domain.

❑ Why Focus on Boys?

The integrated treatment model outlined above is certainly applicable to both male and female victims. However, there are a number of gender differences that are pertinent, for clinical as well as sociocultural reasons (Elliott & Briere, 1992; Hunter, 1989; Struve, 1990).

PHYSICAL ABUSE HISTORY DIFFERENCES

Several studies have identified the fact that sexual abuse of boys is more often accompanied by physical abuse than is a similar level of victimization of girls (Finkelhor, 1984). This particular combination of aggression and sexuality adds to the degree of powerlessness that the male victim might experience. In addition, the longer this combination persists, the more likely the boys are to view aggression and sexuality as naturally coexisting processes. This combination can also result in reduced empathy for victims and other people over whom they have control.

EXTERNALIZING VERSUS INTERNALIZING

There is a considerable body of research that indicates male children exhibit behavioral difficulties more often in an externalizing (or aggressive and oppositional) manner than do females, whose behavioral distress seems to be more frequently of the internalizing variety (including depression and anxiety) (Kendall-Tackett et al., 1993; Watkins & Bentovim, 1992; Zahn-Waxler, Cole, & Barrett, 1992). This finding has implications both for treatment and for long-term outcomes. Because the boy is communicating via his anger and this is getting him into difficulties, therapy may emphasize establishing greater control over this behavior, effectively limiting communication about the boy's distress. This can also have the effect of holding the therapist at arm's length, reducing the amount of support the boy victim might receive. Of long-term importance is the fact that the earlier a significant pattern of aggression is developed, the more likely that the boy will have significant problems, such as anger and getting into difficulty with the law as he gets older (Patterson, 1993). Internalizing behaviors at a young age do not have the same predictive power as externalizing behaviors.

MATERNAL SUPPORT DIFFERENCES

A mother with a victimization history might find it difficult to support a child of either gender, because of how it triggers her feelings related to her victimization (Burkett, 1991). However, the mother's avoidance of the child may be more rejecting when the child is a male victim. It is very difficult to feel close to someone of the same sex who victimized you. Another mother may have an overly close, quasi-erotic relationship with her son. This adds to the boy's vulnerability for abuse and makes it more difficult for him to know how to respond either to victimization or to therapy. Boys are also routinely seen as needing less support and protection (Watkins & Bentovim, 1992). Of importance to the therapy is determining the nature and quality of the mother-son interaction prior to the abuse so that underlying themes can be identified and worked with in therapy.

I believe that therapists of either gender can work with male and female victims. But the greater prevalence of female therapists more often allows a female victim abused by a male to be seen by a female therapist. Presumably, the girl is less likely to feel apprehension with a gender pairing of this type. By default, male therapists are more often paired with male victims of male perpetrators. I am aware of numerous instances in which male therapists were actively resisted and even "victimized" by male victims. The aggressive distancing of these boys certainly got in the way of either beginning the therapeutic relationship or focusing on victimization issues. In those situations, referral to female therapists seems to be an important and necessary step. However, these boy victims may not have the opportunity to learn that men can differ from each other.

LANGUAGE AS A MODERATOR

Language is one of the most important moderating processes available to us (Mussen, 1975). Maltreatment clearly has an inhibiting influence on academic performance (Eckenrode, Larid, & Doris, 1993) and on language development (Friedrich, Einbender, & Luecke, 1983). In fact, maltreated toddlers already exhibit less capacity to talk about themselves or their feelings (Beeghly & Cicchetti, 1994). Language is a key element in social skills and self-control. Once an individual has begun to think about his feelings and his behavior and to explore options in a language-moderated manner, the likelihood of his behaving more appropriately increases. There are developmental data suggesting that language acquisition in males is not as rapid as it is in females, thus giving rise to greater levels of early dyscontrol in boys (Maccoby & Jacklin, 1974). Because of their earlier use of language, language is a more adaptive, appropriate, and well-used function in females. Therapy is usually language based, and using language when treating boys to the same degree as with girls requires some examination.

SOCIALIZATION FOR GROUP WORK

In the same way that language development seems to occur somewhat earlier for females, peer relationships and interpersonal socialization also seem to be a more natural process for females (Maccoby & Jacklin, 1974). Group therapy with girls takes on a different quality than group therapy with boys; it reflects the greater propensity for undersocialization and impaired peer relationships in boy victims (Friedrich, Berliner, Urquiza, & Beilke, 1988).

FEELINGS IDENTIFICATION

The identification of feelings is something that parallels language and socialization (Maccoby, 1980). If both language and socialization are somewhat less rapidly developed for boys, the common emphasis in therapy of helping the abused child identify his feelings will likely be more difficult with boys.

CONVERSATION AS POSTURING VERSUS LISTENING

There is fascinating literature on the difficulties men and women have in communicating (Tannen, 1990). An underlying theme often suggested is the fact that language in conversation is used by men for posturing rather than for more genuine interaction. I think, for example, about how I greet boy victims as opposed to girl victims. The short "yo" or "dude" greeting to a boy is far less a "How are you doing?" or "How has your week been?" or "How are you feeling?" than it is a greeting that underscores how tough, capable, and competent we each feel we are.

The degree to which these gender differences interfere with the therapeutic process depends on some combination of the boy-therapist mix. The degree to which you as a therapist have some control over how you deal with each of the above issues is important; the more you can reliably counter each of these potential difficulties, the more likely it is that a useful therapeutic process can be undertaken.

DIFFERENCES IN SEVERITY OF ABUSE

Watkins and Bentovim (1992) exhaustively reviewed the available literature on differences in severity of abuse between males and females. Although boys more often have to deal with the perception of homosexuality (an abuse effect), the current data do not support any clear statements regarding one gender experiencing more severe abuse overall than the other.

GENDER DIFFERENCES IN SEXUALITY

There is a widespread belief that gender differences exist in sexuality, an issue particularly pertinent to sexual abuse. Chodorow (1978) wrote that these differences are rooted in early family experiences, where both male and female children typically form their earliest and most intense emotional attachment to a woman. Both Chodorow (1978) and Gilligan (1982), who derived some of her thinking from Chodorow, suggest that as a consequence of this early, intense attachment, men have little training for a deep relationship with a man.

Social learning theory would make at least two predictions about gender differences (Oliver & Hyde, 1993). First, gender differences will change as social norms change. In addition, the double standard predicts that men will be rewarded for numerous partners and casual sex. A meta-analytic review of research on gender differences found two large differences—the incidence of masturbation and attitudes toward casual premarital sex (Oliver & Hyde, 1993). In addition, lesser but still significant differences were noted regarding greater permissiveness, lower age at first intercourse, and a greater incidence of homosexual behavior. All of the differences favored less inhibited sexual behavior in males.

What are the implications of this for sexually abused boys? Sexual behavior is commonly affected by sexual abuse, and empirical research has indicated that greater levels of sexual behavior are seen in sexually abused boys, when contrasted with sexually abused girls, particularly during the ages 7 to 12 years (Friedrich et al., 1992). Sexually abused boys are more often implicated in sexual aggression as well (Friedrich & Luecke, 1988; Gil & Johnson, 1993). All of this would suggest that sexual behavior is likely to be a more frequent treatment target for boys than for girls.

In fact, the three sexual abuse effects thought to be more or less unique to male victims are each related to some aspect of sexual behavior (Watkins & Bentovim, 1992). These are "1) confusion/anxiety over sexual identity, 2) inappropriate attempts to reassert masculinity, and 3) recapitulation of the victimizing experience" (p. 216).

❏ Preconditions to Treatment

Before developing the integrated model, there are four broad preconditions to psychotherapy with a sexually abused child that need to be considered. These include the safety of the child from further victimization, the need for therapy to be focused and directive, the use of a goal-oriented approach to make the therapy specific to the child and parent, and, finally, that all the players are known by the therapist (Faller, 1988).

A paramount requirement for a sexually abused child is the assurance of safety (Trepper & Barrett, 1989). Although this certainly includes safety from further sexual abuse, it also includes safety from further loss and separation. If the offending party continues to have access to the child, or the child cannot be assured of his safety because of the offender's proximity, the basic precondition for successful individual therapy is not met. A boy who does not feel safe at home cannot turn his emotional energies to the formation of a therapeutic relationship. It is critical that the child feels that he has a "secure base" (Bowlby, 1969) in his home and that his parents support the disclosure. Unsupervised or premature visitation and contact, foster placement that is nonsupportive, and other factors may contribute to the absence of a "secure base." The child will feel unsafe if he is aware that his statements can either interfere with his being allowed to return home or place family members at risk for further punishment. Rarely have I found individual therapy to be helpful with a child who is wary of what he says to me or who has been told directly or indirectly not to talk to me. If the child perceives himself not to be safe, or if he is acting as if his safety cannot be guaranteed, it is critical to determine whether or not he can be assured of safety by the nonoffending parent. The assurance of safety and the permission to disclose may need to happen concretely for therapy to proceed. For example, I try to always include the nonoffending parent early on in the therapy process for the purpose of giving the child permission to talk about victimization, regardless of the outcome. If that cannot be done, one's best efforts may be directed at consultation with the foster parents and advocating for the child with the caseworker.

A second issue pertains to the directed and focused nature of sexual abuse treatment. Although nondirective, child-oriented play therapy has a very long and respected history in generic child treatment approaches, there are a number of factors that limit its utility with children who have been traumatized (Reams & Friedrich, 1994). The child may be acutely embarrassed or ashamed, may have dissociated the events, or may fear revivification of the trauma if it is mentioned. Typically, insecurely attached children who are avoidant are not going to voluntarily disclose, regardless of the warmth of the therapist. All of these issues argue against the child being forthcoming about what has occurred. It is my belief that the abuse usually needs to be articulated. The child needs to be given a number of chances to directly or indirectly reveal the nature of the abuse, or treatment effectiveness is reduced. The unspoken distress that accompanies the abuse has to be articulated in order for it to be integrated with the cognitions of the child in such a way that fragmentation or dissociation is circumvented in favor of integration (Zimbardo, LaBerge, & Butler, 1993). Therapy that is directive and abuse-specific can help the child know what to expect and what to do in therapy. Incestuous families do not train their children to talk about feelings, nor are these boys taught to link trauma with feelings and thoughts. This becomes the necessary task of the child's therapist.

Increasingly, the therapist must be sensitive to how to foster disclosure, due to concerns of aiding the child in reformulating his memory of the event (Ceci & Brunk, 1993). Although this should be a consideration, however, it should not be used to prevent the child from giving a voice to his trauma, which is a necessary step in reducing dysregulation and reworking the child's self-image.

Third, the therapist typically needs to demonstrate the relevance of treatment to the psychotherapy-naive parent. This is enhanced by developing specific goals that are based on a careful and developmentally appropriate assessment of the child and parent. In the case presented at the beginning of the chapter, the parents were hesitant to bring their son. When therapy did not have an immediate payoff in terms of what they thought was important, it became easier for them to drop out. However, if they were made partners from the beginning in helping the child deal with an agreed-upon goal of working with his sleep difficulties, the necessary therapeutic alliance with the "child-parent" might have been developed. A version of goal attainment scaling (Kiresuk & Sherman, 1968) is useful even with young children in terms of establishing acceptable and optimal levels of outcome for a number of different behaviors. This has been explicated specifically for sexually abused children (Friedrich, 1990).

Finally, the therapist needs to know and remain in contact with the child, parents, foster parents, the caseworker, and the perpetrator's therapist. The therapist also needs to have familiarity with any ongoing or necessary legal proceedings. The therapist should be aware as well of the status of the offender, and there must be permission to communicate with other therapists involved. These are not cases that occur in isolation from other, large, interlocking systems. The work involved often feels like case management, and I often envy the training of my social worker colleagues, who seem better prepared to handle this.

❑ The Importance of Assessment

I believe it would be inappropriate to write a book about therapy without including suggestions to measure the effectiveness of intervention. Elsewhere I have written about good therapy being a balance of heart and mind (Friedrich, 1990). It is also a balance of the clinical with the analytical, and that is where assessment comes into play. Determining whether what you are doing is working is clearly on the analytic end of the continuum. In this book, I will attempt to indicate those approaches that have some empirically demonstrated utility. I will also include suggestions on how you can determine the effectiveness of your interventions. This will allow you to practice in a more integrated way and learn from your failures as well as successes.

To further this, I provide in this book two ways to assess outcome. The first is goal setting and measuring the degree to which children and their parents achieve the goals you help them establish early in the therapy. Goal setting not only helps to focus the therapy, it makes all parties accountable to each other.

The second method is more traditional psychological assessment. In Chapters 2, 6, and 10, measures are briefly described and listed in tables. My goal is to make it easier for clinicians to select a number of measures or procedures across the three areas of attachment, dysregulation, and self-representation. These measures can be used at intake, termination, and follow-up. The data can argue for the child in a variety of ways. Children who improve convincingly when removed from the abuse situation can help the therapist argue for continued safety. Children who deteriorate when they have contact with the perpetrator argue in a similar manner for the need for safety. Children who are identified as inattentive or depressed across several settings can be referred for a child psychiatric evaluation. Children with academic problems make apparent the need for a school conference to determine what can be done for the child in that setting. Abuse-specific issues, such as PTSD, dissociation, and sexual behavior problems, can also be determined and targeted for therapy. Therapists who do not carefully assess across these domains are not serving the child as well as they could.

I also have a social policy argument for assessment. How can we ever be in a position to argue for what is needed for some families and children if we do not take pains to quantify our efforts? For example, in an agency study, we needed 6 to 8 months of therapy to be successful with the majority of boys (Friedrich, Luecke, Beilke, & Place, 1992). The Health Maintenance Organization (HMO) gives you 8 weeks to treat a child who presents in worse shape than a child you saw 1 year earlier who did not begin to engage until 12 or 14 weeks, by your recollection. But because you never measured this, not just for this child but for many others, you are in a weak position to argue with the therapy allotment. Careful assessment and accountability is critical to good treatment, not just for the child you are now seeing, but for future children as well.

PART I

Attachment

2

Attachment: An Overview

A mouth opens inside his chest and forms a word without a sound. . . .
What is the word that cannot be said?

—Caddy, 1989, p. 45

Attachment is a word, like self-esteem, that becomes less clear the longer it is used and popularized. The apparent simplicity of the word *attachment* actually conveys a complex theory and an area of research that has profound implications for therapy.

Developmental psychologists, and John Bowlby and Mary Ainsworth in particular, did child clinical practice an enormous service with their distillation of John Bowlby's concept of attachment into a quantifiable dynamic. As attachment theory was becoming articulated in England by Bowlby, the notion of mother-child bonding was also becoming popularized by the pediatricians Klaus and Kennell (1976). Although these concepts share some features, attachment and bonding are not interchangeable terms. Bonding is suggestive of an instantaneous event, whereas attachment is a complex, developing process (Karen, 1994). It is attachment and the theory and research that has developed around it, and not "bonding," that has relevance to this book and to our practice.

What is meant by attachment? Several excellent papers that I recommend are those by Patricia Crittenden and Mary Ainsworth (1989) and by Pamela C. Alexander (1992). Alexander's paper focuses more specifically on sexual abuse. She summarized two lines of evidence on why we have to consider the nature of the child's family relationships to understand the impact of sexual abuse. The first pertains to the fact that many of the risk variables that potentiate the negative impact of sexual abuse are family and relationship based. These include the lack of maternal closeness, the presence of a stepfather, and disruptions in the mother-child relationship (Paveza, 1988). Fathers are also implicated in attachment problems that predate abuse. For example, many incestuous fathers have not been involved in normal socialization processes with their children (Parker & Parker, 1986; Williams & Finkelhor, 1992). This presumably makes them more vulnerable to seeing their child inappropriately and then to sexually transgressing with the child.

The second line of evidence is even more direct and is based on research with children (Friedrich, 1988) and adults (Elliott, 1994; Harter, Alexander, & Niemeyer, 1988; Peters, 1988; Springs & Friedrich, 1992). These researchers have identified such variables as family cohesion, maternal support and warmth, and the absence of family conflict as related to the short-term and long-term impact of sexual abuse occurring in childhood.

These studies do not negate the unique and independent impact of sexual abuse (Briere & Elliott, 1993). They do point to the fact that there are a number of environmental variables that can act in a protective manner, either to cut short the sexual abuse or to ameliorate the impact once it has occurred. For example, Elliott (1994) found that an abuse variable (the frequency and chronicity of abuse) and a moderator variable (interpersonal relationships, including the relationship with the mother) were important predictors of outcome.

A study very pertinent to sexually abused boys was completed by Jane Gilgun (1989), who interviewed men with a history of sexual abuse, some who later went on to either rape or molest children. The differences between those who behaved in an antisocial manner and

those who did not depended on the availability of environmental sup-
ports, particularly confidants. This corresponds directly with Alexander
(1992), who described attachment theory as a key concept in understanding the nature of the abuse and its impact.

Attachment difficulties predate the abuse in the vast majority of the
families in which maltreatment is evident (Crittenden & Ainsworth,
1989). This is even more true when the abuse is incestuous, but it is
also frequent when the abuse is extrafamilial, particularly if it is of
some duration and frequency. Estrangement in interpersonal relationships will almost always be a treatment consideration in families with
a sexually abused child.

Attachment theory subsumes much of the interpersonal aspects of
sexual abuse. It is descriptive not only of the overt nature of the relationship between the boy and offender, but also of the relationship
the boy has with the nonoffending parent. Attachment-based research
has shown that how children develop and distort their feelings and
thinking about people is related to the early security of their key interpersonal relationships. Attachment theory has been used to understand the antecedents and consequences of physical abuse (Egeland,
Jacobvitz, and Sroufe, 1988), and, more recently, the antecedents and
consequences of sexual abuse (Egeland, 1994).

Attachment undergoes a number of developmental transformations
as a child gets older. Crittenden's (1992) excellent paper describes the
complex attachment and cognitive transformations from infancy
through the end of preschool. However, even into childhood and, most
likely, adolescence as well, a number of guiding features continue to
persist. With secure attachment, the primary attachment objects will
maintain protection of the child, the child-parent dyad will maintain some level of proximity, and the outcome of the proximity will be
that the child perceives himself to be secure (Cicchetti, Cummings,
Greenberg, & Marvin, 1990). Consider a 9-year-old boy who has been
living in a foster home and showing reasonable stability in his behavior. He begins to act out when he hears that he must start visiting his
mother. Behaviorally, this suggests ambivalence about proximity.
Likely, he does not perceive security in her presence.

❑ Key Features of Attachment

The concept of attachment is a central element in almost all of the contemporary theories of child psychopathology and child treatment (Ainsworth, 1989). For example, research has shown that children's prosocial inclinations are governed primarily by the quality of their relationships with their parents (Sroufe & Fleeson, 1986). That may be hard to believe in this day and age of reductionism, where everything is reduced to biochemical agents and genes, but the complex interpersonal process of attachment has profound implications for the emergence and quality of peer relationships, aggression, and social skills.

Bowlby (1969) stated that attachment is an instinctual, biologically based bond with a caregiver. He believed that "attachment behavior is in some degree preprogrammed and therefore ready to develop along certain lines when conditions elicit it" (Bowlby, 1984, p. 13). Attachment behavior, including remaining close to the caregiver, is important to survival and hence is seen more overtly in the young in times of stress. However, attachment behavior is evident throughout adult life as well. The parent is used by the child as a *secure base*, a key term in the attachment literature.

Another central tenet in attachment theory is Bowlby's (1973) concept of the *internal working model*. This is an internalized, cognitive process that is relationship-bound and forms the basis of the personality. It is derived over time from the repetitive experiences of two processes: (a) the child's role in relationships (e.g., "Am I desirable and worthy of support or not?") and (b) the caregiver's role in relationships (e.g., "Can I count on this person to be accessible and caring or not?"). The internal working model is the ongoing distillation of an enormous amount of information into a manageable subset. It guides the child in accommodating to individuals, including caregivers and peers. These models can be constricting to the child (e.g., he learns to behave in either inhibited or exaggerated ways) or they can be adaptive (i.e., the child has a broad range of interaction styles and is not locked into a more narrow mode). Bowlby's (1980) later writings suggested that the child constructs two models—one cognitive, one affective—of the self for each relationship. Bretherton and Water's (1986) suggested a third—behavioral—model.

It can be seen from this formulation that based on expectations there is an automatic, cognitive process that forms the basis of the relationship. The child learns quickly to interact in predictable ways based on prior experiences that have shaped his expectations of interactions with the caregiver. In addition to these internalized cognitive and behavioral expectations, there is also a significant affective component, which governs how emotions are perceived and processed. Although there is a great deal of stability to the internal working model, the therapist can ascertain from these facts that it is an interpersonal process, which is critical to the formation of the self. It is not an intrapersonal process, as has been the basis of so much therapy to date.

❏ Styles of Attachment

Research utilizing the Strange Situation paradigm (Ainsworth, Blehar, Waters, & Wall, 1978), which has been used to explore attachment in infants and toddlers, has led to an awareness that attachment varies from dyad to dyad. The results suggested that children were either securely or insecurely attached. Briefly, the Strange Situation places the mother and child together in a strange environment that contains toys. A stranger comes in while the mother is present, and then the mother leaves the child with the stranger. The mother then returns and the stranger leaves. The mother then leaves the child alone. The stranger comes back in and attempts to comfort the child. The mother then finally returns for the last reunion. A total of eight episodes occur in less than 30 minutes. The Strange Situation has received some criticism. However, it is a remarkable developmental assessment with great predictive power. An excellent review of the origins of attachment theory and its validity as a concept (including the Strange Situation) is available for the educated lay reader (Karen, 1994).

A securely attached child has an internal working model of caregivers as consistent, supportive in times of stress, attuned to his needs, and reciprocal. Secure attachment with both parents is predictive of the most optimal outcome (Main & Weston, 1981). Early security in attachments is related to greater peer competence, resilience in the face of stress, empathy for others, resourcefulness and persistence, and popularity among preschoolers (Sroufe, 1988).

Insecure attachment falls into three categories, including resistant/ ambivalent, avoidant, and disorganized (Alexander, 1992). Basic to the internal working models of insecurely attached children is an awareness that caregivers are insensitive, inconsistent, and nonsoothing.

Resistant preschoolers, who are also labeled ambivalent or reactive, exhibit reunion behavior with their caregiver that is a mixture of both contact-seeking and angry resistance (Sroufe, 1988). Although they may appear clingy at times, they also seem always wary of impending separations. This creates distance in the midst of clinginess, a very confusing admixture. The caregivers exhibit role reversal with the child, for example, by seeking rather than providing nurturance. This role reversal is perceived as intrusive and disrespectful of the child's personal or emotional boundaries. The caregivers may be attentive but not attuned or in sync with their child; consequently, they behave inconsistently with the child. See Tables 2.1 and 2.2 for a summary of behaviors in the different types of attachments.

Avoidant children exhibit reunion behavior that often amounts to snubbing or avoiding the mother (Sroufe, 1988). They do not seek their mother consistently more than they seek a stranger, and they may exhibit spontaneous aggression to the mother at home. This pattern of attachment seems to be related to caregiving experiences that are insensitive and to mothers who are often emotionally unavailable. Such mothers may express little emotion, may avoid touching their infant, and may express little joy in the child's company. The child internalizes a set of expectations that the caregiver is avoidant of them and that interactions should be guarded against.

Attachment research has shown that categories of attachment are relatively stable across settings, including with teachers and other caregivers (Alexander, 1992). Of importance to therapists is the finding that early security of attachment is related to emotional openness with an interviewer at age 6 (Main, Kaplan, & Cassidy, 1985). In fact, there is evidence that children securely attached to both parents are the most confident and competent (Main & Weston, 1981). This is particularly striking for empathy. There are always exceptions, and security of attachment to mothers does not necessarily mean security of attachment

Table 2.1 Attachment Classifications and Attendant Behavior by Caregivers

Secure	Avoidant	Resistant
Warm	Emotionally unavailable	Unpredictable
Sensitively attuned	Dislikes neediness	Insensitively responsive
Consistent	Favors precocious autonomy	Not attuned
Reliably soothing		Hyperactive to baby's fear
Unconditional		Intrusive

Table 2.2 Attachment Classification and Attendant Behavior by Very Young Children

Secure	Avoidant	Resistant
Initiates interaction	Little preference for caregiver	Difficulty separating
Affective sharing	Mixes avoidance with proximity	Wary
Readily comforted	Little affective sharing	Mixes contact seeking with resistance
Energy to explore		

to fathers. But, from this literature, it could be suggested that the avoidantly attached child may eventually adopt a stance viewed as self-protective, or defended (Crittenden, 1994). Also, resistant children may eventually be more coercive with caregivers, including therapists.

The final, generally agreed-on category of insecurely attached children is the disorganized subset (Main & Solomon, 1990). This category emerged because of difficulty in sorting some children into one of the three categories already discussed. The disorganized child does not exhibit a consistent attachment pattern or interpersonal strategy. This seems to be related to the fact that the attachment figure is both the source of the child's distress as well as the potential soother and comforter. On reunion with the parent in the Strange Situation, the disorganized child behaves in contradictory and even stereotyped ways. Some researchers have reported that the child appears dazed and disoriented (Alexander, 1992).

Crittenden (1994) has suggested that this behavior is more related to the child's trauma experience than to the attachment classification. In fact, the parents of the disorganized child are typically dealing with their own unresolved trauma. Not only may they be abusive and neglectful of the child, but their own agitation or depression may be anxiety provoking and disorganizing to the child. The parents may also become frightened by the behavior they exhibit with their child; they may then switch to a mode of interaction that is too intrusive in their efforts to undo their previous actions. Such behaviors add to the child's confusion and further interfere with the internalization of a consistent, stable model.

The traumatized mother of the child exhibiting disorganized attachment behavior is constantly yearning for the love and care she never had, but she has no confidence that she will ever receive what she needs (Alexander, 1992). She is wise to distrust any offer of support and affection. As a mother, she often has no reserves to enable her to mother her own child. She looks to the child to mother her, and when the child naturally fails and demands his own attention, she becomes impatient and rejecting.

In the natural history of insecurely attached parent-child dyads, actual, physical disruptions in caregiving are not necessary. In fact, DeLozier (1982) found that threats of abandonment (not actual separations) were more common in the attachment histories of assaultive mothers. Bowlby (1973) stated that repeated threats to abandon, ranging from subtle to overt, are as pathogenic as actual separations, and probably more so.

There have been a number of attacks on the attachment paradigm because of its attribution to the mother of such a primary responsibility in the child's rearing and personality organization (Gavey, Florence, Pezaro, & Tan, 1990; Karen, 1994). These precautions do not take away from attachment theory's enormous clinical and heuristic utility, nor do they demand that the therapist either blame or act punitively with the mother of an insecurely attached child. Most parents want to have a better relationship with their child, and insecurity usually is indicative of what occurred in their relationship with their primary caregiver. To blame parents is to confirm the internal working models of parents who have likely been maltreated themselves.

❑ Attachment and Maltreatment

OVERVIEW

Maltreated children fall more often into the insecurely attached groupings (Carlson, Cicchetti, Barnett, & Braunwald, 1989); insecure attachment averages 85% among maltreated children (Karen, 1994). Whether that is the case with sexually abused children has not been empirically determined. However, incestuous family dynamics, with concomitant role reversal and intrusiveness, are inconsistent with secure attachment. This is congruent with a study by Burkett (1991), who found that sexually abused mothers were more self-focused, rather than child focused, compared to nonabused mothers. Mothers with an abuse history were also noted to rely more on their children for emotional support. Elliott (1994) also found in a study of adult professional women that an impaired relationship with her mother was more predictive of sexual abuse than any other relational factor.

Alexander's (1993) research also points to the implications of attachment-related processes in long-term outcome of incest. She found that the quality of current relationships predicted avoidant, dependent, self-defeating, and borderline personality disorders in these adults.

Other studies have found that mothers of sexually abused children have MMPI profiles characteristic of greater inconsistency and anger. Although this certainly does not characterize all mothers in these situations, for those with whom it did, one would expect that both of these would spill over into the parenting process (Friedrich, 1991b; Scott & Stone, 1986). However, personality differences between mothers of abused and nonabused children are not universally noted (Peterson, Basta, & Dykstra, 1993; Smith & Saunders, 1994). My contention is that observation of interaction, the most direct form of assessment, will be the arena in which differences are noted.

In a recent study of 118 incestuous fathers matched with fathers who were nonabusive, an important finding was that incestuous fathers fell into five distinct types (Williams & Finkelhor, 1992). Each type has direct implications for the father's parenting and indirect implications for the attachment security of the child. The types include (a) sexually preoccupied, (b) adolescent regressives, (c) instrumental sexual gratifiers, (d) emotionally dependent, and (e) angry retaliators. As a group, these fathers had unresolved rejection and trauma when younger and were less socially adroit. Secure attachment with the mother is related to both support by the father and marital quality (Belsky, Youngblade, & Pensky, 1989). The fathers described by Williams and Finkelhor (1992) clearly did not measure up to these prerequisites. Consequently, children in incestuous families are at risk for insecure attachment.

Boundary permeability in parents has been studied along with its attachment ramifications (Sroufe, Jacobvitz, Mangelsdorf, DeAngelo, & Ward, 1985; Sroufe & Ward, 1980). In their 1980 longitudinal study, Sroufe and Ward examined a subset of children for the Mother-Child Project. Mother-child interaction was captured on videotape in which some dyads exhibited elements of sexualized and intrusive contact, including extended kissing, groping inside each other's clothes, and sexualized conversation. Most of the dyads were mother-son. The behavior in these boys was characterized by inattentiveness, overactivity, and overarousal. Think of an internal model that predicts, "If I turn to mom, I not only won't get what I need, I'll get taken from." The working model of these children was that caregiving was overly arousing, confusing, and sexualized. Follow-up with these children found that several had been sexually abused by their mothers (Sroufe et al., 1985). In fact, as a group, they were some of the most disturbed children in the study.

What do children do when they are overwhelmed by a distressing event, in this case, sexual abuse? Main (1990) identified primary and secondary strategies. When attachment is threatened by victimization, the primary strategy is to reestablish contact with the attachment figure. Main (1990) labels this primary because the child can reduce attachment discrepancies and turn his energies to other matters. This happens when the child is securely attached. Secondary strategies are less effective and operate in insecurely attached children. Secondary strategies take two basic forms, deactivation or hyperactivation of the attachment system. If the child's internal working model predicts that he will be rejected when he seeks connection and support, deactivation of attachment provides a way of minimizing potential conflict with the attachment figure. What if the internal working model of the boy forecasts inconsistency, a common style with chaotic and highly stressed families? The boy may hyperactivate the attachment system, mixing higher than usual levels of contact seeking with anger. The parent in this situation comes into your office and says, "Dammit Doc, he's been following me into the bathroom, he won't give me a moment's peace, and now he's picking on his little sister. I don't have time to deal with this crap. This therapy shit is making it worse." The parent's behavior in this situation is a mirror image of the child's.

SPECIFIC PROCESSES

Alexander (1992) has identified three attachment-related features that frequently characterize sexually abusive families. These include rejection, role reversal/parentification, and fear/unresolved trauma. Within these three characteristics are many of the elements that characterize the origins of insecure attachment.

Rejection

Although rejection is more often associated with avoidant attachment in the preschool child, it is a feature common of all three types of attachment difficulties. The rejected child is left feeling unloved and unwanted. In the case of the sexually abused child, the rejection may be true of both the incestuous parent and the absent or unsupportive nonoffending parent.

The rejecting parent does not "know" the child and is not attuned to the child's needs. The incestuous father creates his own "knowledge" of his son, viewing the boy as existing for his own intimacy needs. The rejecting mother has several years of history with her son that have reinforced her unavailability for support. She is not the confidant the boy needs, and the boy is left with no one to talk to about his abuse. The absence of appropriate physical support and touch in the rejecting family can make the abuse more confusing and harder to discriminate from other touch he may have experienced.

It is critical to realize that this rejection can be both overt and easily detectable, as well as covert and extremely subtle. Consider the sexually abused mother of a sexually abused boy. As an adult, she has subsequent difficulties with males and with physical touch. Very understandably, she walls herself off from the hurts of relationships. Despite her best efforts to be a different mother from the way she was mothered, the boy is nonetheless left with vague, unspeakable feelings that there is something wrong with him, with his maleness. This dyad now sits across the office from you. The only overt manifestations of rejection may be that they are turned away from each other and they have few shared experiences. But multiply that by years of interaction and you can see the profound consequences.

I think it is even more pernicious when the rejection is mixed with occasional support. The child hears support when the family is out in public with the therapist. Two sessions later they come in and you find out that in the last two days the mother has threatened to send the boy off to the grandfather, the same man who abused her. The language used by the family with you is discrepant from their behavior to the child. Repeat this situation often enough and the boy has no way of accurately describing his feelings to you.

Before we blame the nonabusive mother too much, there is evidence that parental distance and inaccessibility is often associated with sibling incest, particularly if the nonabusive father is the distant one (De Jong, 1989). The father can also influence the child's attachment to the mother (Belsky et al., 1989).

I have also witnessed subtle rejection of the boy victim by his nonabusive father. After the abuse has become known, the father becomes avoidant of his son. The son's vulnerability and increased needs for support clash with the father's own internal model that he react to requests for support with distance of his own. For example, an 11-year-old, Chad, was molested by his teenage maternal uncle, who provided much of Chad's child care after his parents divorced. His father's fairly regular, twice monthly visitation dropped off to no contact in the 6 months prior to Chad's first appointment with me. Chad did not react to the loss of his father quietly, and the overburdened mother was besieged by him. This caused even more rejection on her part and gave his father an excuse to remain distant. "I'll just mess him up further. Look at the problems he's having now," was the father's statement to me.

Rejection is not unique to incestuous families. The fact that sexual abuse is rarely a random event should make us look at what family and child-rearing features make the child at risk for extrafamilial abuse. Let's consider an example. Two boys, one 8 and the other 9, were molested when they were on a bike trail. The 8-year-old told his single mother the evening it happened. This woman first called me to set up an appointment and then called the mother of the 9-year-old, who had not told his mother. For 3 months, the 9-year-old and his mother never discussed the abuse other than that the mother told her son he would have to talk to a detective who would be coming to the house.

The mother and her 9-year-old son are now in your office because, in the intervening 3 months, the boy became much more angry and difficult to manage. He even held a knife to his chest and told her that he wanted to die. When the boy and the mother are with you, their passivity is striking in contrast to what the mother reported about the boy's anger. Each of them had been walking around the issue, avoiding it in the same way that the mother had circumnavigated her son from a distance all his life. The benign neglect about which she is so ashamed may only emerge in later sessions with you and then only if you think about victimization in the context of attachment.

Here's an example from the mother of David, a 12-year-old molested by the mother's boyfriend. It only came up near the end of a several month course of therapy.

Mom   He's had a tough life.
Therapist   You mean with the abuse.
Mom   Yeah, that too, but I haven't been the nicest to him either. I've never been able to get close to him. He'll go around thinking women don't like him. And with Bruce doing that to him, he'll think only men like him.

Therapist That scares you.

Mom Well, I don't want him to be a homo either.

Therapist You don't want David to be a homo but you know how hard it is to like him. To let him know that you or women can like him.

Mom Doesn't he just drive you nuts when you're with him?

Therapist He can at times.

Mom Good. I didn't want to be the only one.

Sometimes the rejection occurs primarily after the abuse. Prior to the trauma, these parents were reasonably supportive and committed to the boy. The act of abuse made them feel like a failure to their son. How the parents interpret the victimization will be very important, as well as what the parents do with their affect. If they feel betrayed by their son, for not telling or for "putting himself in that situation," then this feeling of betrayal needs to be articulated in order for acceptance to replace it. This is discussed in Chapter 5.

Role Reversal/Parentification

The second phenomenon discussed by Alexander (1992) also cuts across the insecure types of attachment and is manifested in different ways for both the resistant and avoidant types. You may think that role reversal is a phenomenon true primarily in incestuous families or with female victims, but it is widespread. Oldest children, whether male or female, or those who activate some internalization in the parent are susceptible to role reversal. Avoidant boys, for example, may be very good at getting dependency needs met indirectly by being very attuned to parental moods (Crittenden, 1994). Their pseudomature behavior reflects their not having been given permission to be a child.

A variety of family therapists have made role reversal a part of their theories. A very clear example is structural family therapy with its concept of parental hierarchy (Minuchin, 1974). Basically, the child is expected to fulfill instrumental or emotional tasks usually fulfilled by the parent. Child care is an instrumental task. Counting on the boy to provide emotional support, including sexualized contact, is an example of an emotional role reversal.

There are several deleterious consequences to role reversal. The boy is now more susceptible to adult manipulation, and he is more likely to focus on meeting other people's emotional needs rather than on attending to his own developmental needs. In the case of a sexually abused boy, his being given a caregiving role with younger family members can result in sibling incest.

How many of us routinely think to check on whether the sexually abused boy is sleeping with his parents and inappropriately meeting their intimacy needs? For example, a mother who complained about her 9-year-old son, Adam, grabbing her breasts and who worried about his future as a sexual pervert was also sleeping with him nightly. In fact, she slept with Adam rather than sleeping with the equally distressed and younger sister. A behavioral program I instituted too early in the therapy, which was designed to reduce Adam's grabbing of her breasts during the day, did not work. It was only by accident that I understood the reason for failure when she brought up that she was tired because he was kicking her all night.

Therapist So what did you do?
Mom Kicked him back.
Therapist So now he'll stay in his own bed.
Mom No, I suspect he'll be there again tonight, won't you?
Adam I don't know.
Therapist So you get to sleep in her bed every night?
Adam Yeah.
Therapist Do you ever grab at your mom then? Her breasts?
Adam I don't know.
Mom He does, but only when we're tickling each other.
Therapist I think I know why Adam's having such a tough time figuring out what's wrong about grabbing you. He still thinks he's tickling you.
Mom No, he grabs real hard. Pinches even.
Therapist Well, to help Adam out, let's make a rule. No grabbing, anywhere, even when tickling. That way it'll be clear.
Mom I knew it should be stopping. At his age and all. But it's so hard.
Therapist So it seems like you know it needs to stop. His grabbing at you.
Mom Yeah.

Therapist The last time we tried something you had to do all the work. Maybe we should figure out a system where Adam has to have responsibility of his hands and you have responsibility of enforcing the rules.

Mom Yeah, it can't just be me.

The most ruinous aspects of role reversal are when the child is not allowed to be himself and when he is not allowed to be competent in the role he is supposed to assume. This gives rise to conflicted enmeshment, the family therapy equivalent of ambivalent attachment. For example, the boy is expected to meet either emotional or instrumental needs but is not given the support he needs to do the job.

Fear/Unresolved Trauma

Alexander's (1992) last theme is also compelling. Think about how a family would act if they could never use a large portion of their "house," but rather were restricted to one or two rooms and lived in constant fear of what lurked behind the glowing door. That is analogous to families living with unresolved trauma and remaining in that trauma-laced state of anxiety that colors victims who have not been able to resolve the trauma. Researchers who have studied the disorganized attachment classification have written that the parents frequently are struggling with their own abuse (Bowlby, 1984; Main & Solomon, 1990). Selma Fraiberg and colleagues' (Fraiberg, Adelson, & Shapiro, 1975) paper, "Ghosts in the Nursery," describes the haunting effects of lingering trauma. A depressed and agitated parent has a very difficult time reading cues coming from the child. How can a parent with unresolved trauma, whose language for feelings is inaccurate, be attuned to the child? The emotional burden of trauma also interferes with the parent's natural wish to provide consistent support.

Unresolved trauma is not unique to sexual abuse. I believe that the more we can point to the links between abuse, trauma, and other psychiatric conditions, the better. Psychologists have written about lingering effects of the Holocaust that show up in Holocaust survivors (Fox, 1994). Walsh (1978) found that children born within 2 years of the death of a relative with whom the parent had a conflicted history were more likely to have psychiatric disorders. Several researchers as well have suggested that an etiologic factor in the emergence of at least some eating disorders appears to be unresolved trauma in the parent (Root, Fallon, & Friedrich, 1986).

The stories of triumph over unresolved trauma are what add to the richness of my work. Mothers who are aware of their issues often force themselves to deal with their abuse because they realize that can help their child to have a better chance. One mother said, "Every time I try to use time out at bedtime it makes me remember my own abuse. I know why he won't go to bed. I couldn't sleep either after my dad did that to me. I have to get into that group you keep telling me about."

The contents of this chapter will interweave with and magnify all the content in the remainder of the book. The interpersonal world of the child is critical to every additional formulation, as well as to all treatment interventions. The added advantage of attachment theory is the concept of the internal working model, which has applicability to issues of self-regulation and self-representation.

PSYCHOLOGICAL CONSEQUENCES

Because the child is an interpersonal being, attachment disorders color each aspect of thinking and relating. An individual listing of problems would require the remainder of this book; it has been articulated better in the eloquent paper by Benjamin (1993) titled "Every Psychopathology Is a Gift of Love." As a way to orient yourself to thinking about the consequences of attachment difficulties, you may want to review some of the problems mentioned in Table 2.3.

The behavior problems briefly elaborated in Table 2.3 could be organized along dimensions of affiliation and autonomy (Benjamin, 1993). This is a central dialectic that will return again and again in this book. Disorders of affiliation include behavior problems reflecting dependency, indiscriminate affection seeking, remaining in victimizing relationships, and ambivalence about closeness. Aggression will frequently be part of the relationship, either as a target or proponent.

The attachment literature provides insight into decades of misconceptualizations in the psychiatric diagnostic literature. Take, for example, masochism or the category of self-defeating behavior (American Psychiatric Association, 1994). For too long, clinicians have viewed phenomena such as masochism as residing in the individual.

Table 2.3 Behavioral Effects of Attachment Difficulties

1. Indiscriminate affection seeking

2. Anxiety at reunions

3. Anxiety at leavetaking

4. Aggression that is directed at the primary attachment figure

5. Withdrawal directed at the primary attachment figure

6. Reduced number of friends

7. Inability to be soothed in the presence of the primary attachment figure

8. Victim/victimizing in relationships

It has not been viewed as a product of interpersonal difficulties, nor do we attribute equal responsibility to the sadist. The masochist was perceived as maximizing the pleasure principle. The masochist liked it, so must have deserved it. The large percentage of women who get raped after incest (Russell, 1986) do not want to be raped. A more interpersonal perspective is that their internal working model has been so distorted that future relationships are also victimizing and self-care is relegated to the back shelf. Always think about where he came from before blaming the victim or engaging in revictimizing behavior with him.

It used to be automatic for me to evaluate a mother, write a critical report that she heard about only from her caseworker or attorney, and then believe I had discharged my professional duty. I eventually realized that this was also revictimizing, and if I could not discuss my findings with her directly, then I was not taking an opportunity to be truly human with her.

The other pattern of difficulties related to attachment problems exists along another pole, autonomy, and is interpersonal as well. Benjamin's (1993) model anchors this dimension with enmeshment on the least autonomous end and with differentiation on the most autonomous end. An avoidantly attached child would capture many of the problems inherent in too much autonomy. These include loneliness, inability to use others, and, over longer periods of time, thinking that becomes too idiosyncratic due to being cut off from corrective input.

Attachment theory is based largely on work with mothers and infants or toddlers. Only now is work being extended beyond that to include adolescence and young adulthood (Egeland, 1994). Each cognitive and social developmental transaction can bring about new energies and new opportunities to work through earlier problems. Think about these transactions as constituting critical periods. Preschool, early adolescence, late adolescence, and early adulthood can all represent opportunities for change. With each passing year, early histories of insecure attachments will have increasing permutations. Notions of sexually abused children being fixated at early stages are thus erroneous and certainly not as hopeful as the concept of critical periods and fluidity. Development will always continue, albeit on different, but certainly meaningful, pathways (Calverly, Fischer, & Ayoub, 1994).

Attachment is critical to understanding all aspects of interpersonal behavior, but there are other relevant developmental processes as well, including cognitive development, family stability, and parenting style. Each of these can wield its own influence. In fact, the security of attachment and parental behavior appears to be only minimally related (Rosen & Rothbaum, 1993). This finding underscores the need to examine for rejection, role reversal, and unresolved trauma.

❏ Assessment of Attachment

The typical clinician cannot use the Strange Situation in his or her practice. The measures I will suggest are less direct in their assessment of the attachment relations. Interpretating the results clearly demands more inference. For those of you who want to learn the observational/interview approaches to attachment assessment, brief courses are available at the Institute of Child Development at the University of Minnesota, and with Patricia Crittenden at the University of Miami and Mary Main at the University of California at Berkeley.

Some additional clinician friendly suggestions are contained in Table 2.4. Unresolved trauma in the parent, for example, can be assessed with the Trauma Symptom Inventory (TSI) (Briere, 1994).

Table 2.4 Assessment Measures That Can Indirectly Determine Attachment

---

I. Parent-Completed Measures

  A. Generic
1. Adult Attachment Interview (George, Kaplan, & Main, 1985)
2. Social support
3. Family Environment Scale (Moos, 1979)
4. Negative projection (Friedrich & Reams, 1994)
5. Observation of parent-child interaction
6. Social Competence Scale from CBC (Achenbach & Edelbrock, 1983)

  B. Abuse-Specific
1. Untreatable Family Checklist (Friedrich, 1990)
2. Parental Support Questionnaire (Mannarino & Cohen, 1994)
3. Trauma Symptom Inventory (Briere, 1994)

II. Teacher-Completed Measures

  A. Teacher Report Form (Achenbach & Edelbrock, 1986)
1. Social competence
2. Withdrawal

III. Child-Completed Measures

  A. Generic
1. Kinetic Family Drawing (Burns & Kaufman, 1972)
2. Family Relations Test (Bene & Anthony, 1976)
3. Rorschach-Human Content (COP, AG, Penetration) (Exner, 1974)
4. Attachment stories (Bretherton, Ridgeway, & Cassidy, 1990)

  B. Abuse-specific
1. CITES–R (Wolfe et al., 1991)
    a. Negative reactions from others
    b. Social support

Rejection and role reversal can be assessed with the Parental Support Questionnaire (Mannarino & Cohen, 1994), and input from the child's perspective can be extrapolated from the Children's Impact of Traumatic Events Scale–Revised (CITES–R) (Wolfe, Gentile, Michienzi, Sas, & Wolfe, 1991). As you can see, these are all abuse-specific measures, which I believe to be the most appropriate for use with sexually abused children and their parents. Table 2.4 contains more generic measures as well, because a comprehensive evaluation would contain information from at least one caregiver, from the child, and on a range of measures.

3

Attachment: Individual Therapy

Some dramatic crumbling of inner walls, an earthquake in the heart of my solitude.

—Auster, 1989, p. 94

Crittenden (1992) provides a perspective on the task of the individual child therapist with her statement, "The central developmental problem that anxiously attached children experience is coping with unusually complex interpersonal circumstances in the context of unusually little support from attachment figures" (p. 575). From this quote flow two questions: (a) whether or not therapists can become attachment figures, and (b) how can we provide support that is perceived and accepted by the child.

A basic assumption of play therapy is that children can use the therapy relationship to learn that there are people in this world who can be supportive and nonabusive. The therapist provides conditions of warmth, nonjudgmental acceptance, and respect. Play therapy thus becomes not a treatment per se but an opportunity for growth (Shirk & Saiz, 1992). The child is then supposed to generalize this learning to other relationships.

From an attachment perspective, a chink hopefully appears in the child's internal working model because the therapist does not fit the child's perceptions of adults. We all want to make a difference to a child. That is why we are in this business. That is why we say things such as, "He needs a new role model, a male who is accepting but doesn't violate boundaries." We work with children because this is the age when these attachments are so critical.

But are these legitimate assumptions? First of all, there is little, if any, empirical basis for that assumption. Child therapy outcome studies are relatively rare and do not have attachment as an outcome variable. Other studies generally fail to measure peer and social relationships as an outcome; when they do, lasting differences are not found (Reams & Friedrich, 1994). Effecting the security of attachment is a lengthy process, not addressed in brief therapy. But a recent study found little evidence to support long-term therapy's effectiveness over either time-limited or minimal contact therapy (Smyrnios & Kirkby, 1993).

From a clinical perspective, I believe more useful questions to ask are the following: How does the individual therapist need to behave to form a therapeutic alliance? What is needed to affect or begin to affect the sexually abused boy's internal working model? How can I be discrepant from what the boy has internalized so that the potential for change is created? What are the cognitive and affective components that the boy has internalized, and what needs to be done to correct them?

In a very compelling paper, Shirk and Saiz (1992) examined key elements that contribute to the quality of the child's affective relationship with the therapist so that the child collaborates on therapy tasks. They state that child therapy works best if three conditions can be met. These are (a) the ability of the child to recognize his emotional and behavioral difficulties, (b) the ability of the child to make internal attributions (i.e., nonblaming) about the problems he has, and (c) the child's belief that a good outcome depends in part on his own behavior. There are developmental considerations for each of these issues. For example, it is not within a preschooler's cognitive capacity to self-evaluate in an accurate and realistic manner. The Shirk and Saiz (1992) paper as well as Shirk's (1988) earlier book are vital reading for a child therapist who desires to be both pragmatic and developmentally attuned.

However, should we foster a sexually abused child's owning his own problems and not blaming an external source for them? This is what Shirk and Saiz (1992) seem to suggest. At the very least, we need to realize that simple support of the child, even for lengthy periods, will probably not be sufficient therapy for a sexually abused child. I will attempt to suggest later on in the chapter how both play therapy and cognitive therapy can be informed by the above three conditions to be more maximally effective.

But first, let us turn our attention to the relationship. The first step is to know the attachment style of the child with whom you are working. To reiterate, children's behavior can reflect a broad range of styles and internal models, and it is very likely that you will see hybrids of insecure styles. Knowing the security of the boy's attachment to his parent(s) will allow you to know how he will generally behave and what he might expect in his interactions with you. In addition, this knowledge can inform you as to how you need to behave so as to correct the boy's experiences and to form a working, collaborative alliance. An interesting paper by Arnold Lazarus (1993) has the rather telling title, "Tailoring the Therapeutic Relationship, or Being an Authentic Chameleon." Lazarus makes the point that the therapist must adapt not only the therapeutic techniques to be used but also how the therapist presents him- or herself in the therapy. How do you do that and still maintain some sense of personal integrity?

❏ Knowing the Boy's Internal Working Model

In the previous chapter, I discussed clinical manifestations of impaired attachment. In addition to those general statements, there are individual features that each boy will exhibit. The boy's initial behavior with you may not be very illustrative of his later behavior with you. The best indicators of the boy's attachment will come from the interaction of the parent(s) with their son. (These classifications are not based on systematic, formal assessment but reflect my clinical determinations.)

SECURE ATTACHMENT AND
ITS PRESENTATION IN YOUR OFFICE

I rarely see sexually abused boys who are solidly in the securely attached end of the attachment continuum. Among maltreated children, 85% are typically described as insecurely attached (Karen, 1994). Practitioners who work with less disadvantaged families may have more opportunity to see boys with an internalized sense of parents as available, attuned, and unconditional. Parents of securely attached boys will show immediate, appropriate, and consistent concern for their son's safety. The parents make an appointment quickly after hearing of the abuse and do so of their own volition. No caseworker is forcing them to do it as part of a court protection order. Rather, this is a natural manifestation of their being a secure base.

Not only are these parents prompt in attending to their child's distress, but their thoughts, feelings, and actions about their son are congruent. If they set up an appointment, they keep it. In the few cases I have treated or supervised, these parents have been the boy's natural parents, they have not had a history of trauma, and the boy has not been in foster care, either formally or informally (with relatives). When you interview these parents about their son, they have useful, accurate information that suggests they are attuned to him. They describe him positively and in detail. Their natural distress at their son's abuse has not spilled over onto him, and they have not become another burden to the boy. This is because the parent-child hierarchy is clearly established, and role reversal is not operative. The parents may want to talk to you alone. However, this is not (a) to give you some "dirt" on their son, or (b) because they are triangulating the boy's relationship with you, or (c) out of their own neediness. Rather, they respect the boundaries of disclosure and do not want to burden their boy about their own concerns.

Because I want to know the full range of each boy's problems when he comes in to see me, I have the parent(s) complete the Child Behavior Checklist (CBC) (Achenbach & Edelbrock, 1983) along with other measures at the time of the initial appointments (see Table 2.4). The information provided on the CBC concurs with what the boy's teacher reports on the Teacher Report Form version of the CBC (Achenbach & Edelbrock, 1986). This high level of concurrence also indicates attunement and the absence of projection. The CBC has a section in which the parent can write down positive features of the child. It is labeled "Please describe the best things about your child." When that is left blank, or when it includes mixed comments, then the parents are neither balanced nor unconditional in their support of the child. For example, the father of an anxiously attached boy wrote that his son was "too sensitive." For this father, that was not a positive characteristic.

Just because a boy has a history of secure attachment with his parents, this does not mean that they are perfect people or that their parenting is superlative. Attachment security and parenting style and effectiveness are not synonymous (Rosen & Rothbaum, 1993). Many parents react to their child's sexual abuse with an acute depressive reaction. They may briefly be less available to their son. Or, the parents may develop some vague uneasiness about their own sexual desires and activities. These are normal reactions. Despite a temporary setback, the parents of the securely attached child persist with their unconditional regard as well as accurate empathy for the child's plight.

Features of the boy that suggest secure attachment include characteristics of the abuse as well as the boy's behavior with you and with his parents. It is my experience that the securely attached boy has not been as severely molested, or, if his molestation was severe, the duration is likely to have been brief. The boy may also be more able to talk to you about what occurred; his limits around what he will discuss seem to come from normal defensiveness and embarrassment rather than from denial or oppositionality.

Securely attached boys are routinely less oppositional about coming to see you. They trust their parents, and they trust adults. The reciprocity in the parent-child relationship is apparent but unspoken. It is as if the boy has an understanding that goes something like, "I told you about the bad things that were happening and you are doing something about it to make it better."

These boys do not seem to have the social skill problems or the boundary problems of anxiously attached boys. Consequently, they do not talk much out of turn, nor do they bump into you physically. They will also indicate to you in a number of ways that relationships have been positive (Crittenden, 1994). For example, they will make eye contact and learn your name. It is unlikely that they will do things that are annoying.

Because of these features, therapy can be both rewarding and relatively short-term for securely attached boys. The corrective emotional experience provided by longer term therapy will usually be less necessary, because their primary relationships with caregivers have laid a good base for future relations.

AVOIDANT ATTACHMENT AND
ITS PRESENTATION IN YOUR OFFICE

The brief descriptions that follow cannot capture the variability and complexity of anxious attachment styles and their mutations. This is true for both the parent's behavior as well as the boy's.

In my experience, sexually abused boys are about equally likely to fall into the avoidant group as into the next one to be discussed, resistant attachment. However, the avoidant boys and their parents present some very considerable challenges. Avoidance usually characterizes both the parent and the son, both of whom adhere to a philosophy of close, but not too close. In fact, Crittenden (1994) labels them as "defended." They prefer not to deal directly with people; they may inhibit desires for contact, or they may gain contact by being caregivers or hypervigilant to parental wishes (Elliott, 1994). The parents may be resistant to making appointments, or, when appointments are made, they may not show up. Parents often show passivity in their interactions with you. Because their passivity looks initially like acquiescence, their seeming compliance often is later viewed as passive-aggressive behavior.

Another striking feature of the parents of avoidantly attached boys is their inability to describe their son to you. Their long-standing posture with him is to hold him at arm's length. They are not used to thinking about him or wondering what he might be feeling. For example, one mother described her son as too "clingy," something that had "gotten worse" since "that happened." She reported this to me with a level of resentment in her voice that was surprising in its intensity. Both she and her son were sitting as far apart in my office as possible when she said this.

Another example is a boy who got too aroused by the sexual and violent content in the TV shows he watched. I was able to tell this by his comments to me during the individual portion of our sessions.

When I asked his mother what time he went to bed, she stared blankly at me, and then finally said that she did not know. I suggested she ask her son, who was sitting next to her. Without looking at him she asked, "When do you go to bed?" Clearly, she could not supervise him in the way he needed.

The implicit message such parents give their son is that he is neither interesting nor worthwhile. Often they are depressed, and I would suggest an excellent paper on the pathways to negative outcome in children of depressed parents (Downey & Coyne, 1992). These boys learn that relationships are best avoided, and that when you have to interact, you are most likely to be frustrated. This accounts for the episodic, seemingly random, aggression that is often seen in the context of social isolation and withdrawal. The boys have both defended and inhibited the feelings of anger, hurt, and jealousy that occasionally erupt (Crittenden, 1994).

The constellation of behaviors exhibited by avoidantly attached boys as preschoolers reflects an internalized model of caregivers as insensitive and frustrating. It is likely that these boys are avoidant of, and overtly indifferent to, human interaction, coupled with episodes of aggression. As these boys grow older, they may show a broader range of behaviors, but these core elements will still be operative.

Sometimes the avoidant boy will look passive, particularly in contrast to his resistant counterpart. This passivity takes the form of indifference or a seeming boredom with your efforts in the therapy office. The boy has learned to inhibit feelings and actions that are not acceptable (Crittenden, 1994). Consequently, when it comes to talking about the victimization, you will have to counter his long-standing view that adults are insensitive and unavailable. You are just another one of those grown-up people asking him to talk about painful things. Automatically, you get sorted into an unavailable adult to be avoided. This can be intensely annoying, and boys with an avoidant history can be quite frustrating in therapy.

I will remind you again that attachment style is not an intrapsychic personality disorder that the child presents to you. Rather, the behavior of insecurely attached children will elicit behavior from you that confirms their interpersonal hypotheses. You will find that you have to work hard to resist their implied invitation to ignore them, not take them seriously, or to be more actively disinterested. My trainees and

I sometimes refer to this as the enormous *power of the internal working model.*

Some of the boys that I see are in an inpatient setting. Avoidantly attached boys typically do not wait for me to show up at our regular time, nor are they even in the common area where they might see me when I come onto the unit. I have to go find them. When I do find them, I sense a distance that usually takes the form of indifference. This may drop, but only because they associate me with a walk off the unit or a chance for a Coke, not because they have let me into their relational world.

However, avoidant attachment behavior will be reflected in a broad range of behaviors with you. On one end of the continuum is the child who warms to you by the third or fourth session and appears superficially compliant. In the middle might be the boy whose behavior and comments at home indicate he is eager to see you, although you would never know it unless the parent told you. Another manifestation of avoidant attachment is caregiving (Crittenden, 1994) or excessive compliance (Crittenden & Dilalla, 1988). Superficially, he may seem compliant and concerned with you, but he is still defended against the relationship. This actually makes sense if you consider it an adaptive way to remain aloof (defended) but to still get needs met. At the other extreme is a boy whose bitter aloofness is impenetrable. This range exists for each attachment classification we will discuss.

Therapists who report no relational problems with the sexually abused boy either are working with a rare child who has a secure attachment history prior to the abuse, or the therapy is so superficial that the boy can use his social skills to behave more maturely than he actually is. In fact, Crittenden (1992) wrote that traumatic memories are activated in new situations of high arousal, that is, trauma-focused therapy. Consequently, some return of the internal working model is expected when treatment becomes more intense.

RESISTANT ATTACHMENT AND
ITS PRESENTATION IN YOUR OFFICE

Boys who have incorporated a range of ambivalent and resistant features in their internal working model are also relatively common. Unlike the defended strategies of the avoidant child, these boys are usually coercive (Crittenden, 1994). They may present with a mixture of immaturity and neediness, even helplessness. They may also appear more intense and more easy to engage, particularly for male therapists. Males recognize themselves in the interpersonal styles of these boys. We have had college friends that behave in the way they do, with a great deal of posturing, and an angry energy that infuses the relationship. They use language not to engage or communicate but as a vehicle to hold each other at arm's length.

The parent-child interaction exhibited in this group contains many of the precursors of oppositional-defiant disorder. Thus interactions are characterized by an inconsistent mixture of rejection, angry interchanges, and punitive behaviors. You may see a genuine level of concern, but this gets mixed with neglect as well as intrusiveness. The conflict between the parents' actions and their feelings toward the boy are so out of balance that the boy has a very difficult time incorporating a consistent view of the parents.

The longer you work with a boy like this, the more likely you will see a recurring duality in their relationship with you—they want you on the one hand (usually in a way that is limited), but they are also angry and do things that get you upset with them. In fact, they expect that distress is a constant in the relationship, and they seem to spend some energy in creating it. However, that may be the only feeling they know, and their anger is often a mask for high anxiety about closeness. The mix of intimacy-seeking and anger is quite striking. You may end up feeling punished in your interactions with these boys.

I do not get too worried about the anger if I see that it comes from a resistant attachment. I conceptualize this anger as energy that can be channeled for therapeutic purposes. I would rather have anger and coercion than the apparent absence of energy found in the avoidant and defended boy.

An example is useful here. This is a family of three, including a mother, an older, "perfect" sister, Michelle, and an angry 10-year-old, Charley, who was molested by a stepuncle. Charley was described by his mother as a "spoiled brat," and his teacher reported that he had bullied younger children at school. The trigger to the detection of Charley's abuse was that his usual provocative behavior took on a strong sexual tinge. His mother had long-standing issues with men and kept engaging in abusive, sexually charged relationships that spoke to her own unresolved sexual abuse. When I first met the family, I thought Michelle was favored. However, Michelle resented her mother's special relationship with Charley. I began to realize that Mom rarely spoke of Michelle, focusing only on herself and, to a lesser degree, Charley. She was clearly tied to him but in a conflicted, overly arousing manner. (I will return to the mother's role in this case when I discuss family treatment issues.)

Charley was immediately and planfully resistant and provocative with me. Because he was so pushy, I felt immediately assaulted. It took some introspection on my part, out of the office, to realize that the anxiety he had about his mother colored his relationship with me as well. He would deliberately change the subject and fail to answer my questions. The only method that began to work was when I let Charley "interview" me after I "interviewed" him. He could not wait for me to complete a series of questions. I could ask one, and he then would ask one. Not surprisingly, his questions paralleled mine with him. Some were extremely personal and aimed at my sex life and experiences. I told him that he should take advantage of this because when my questions got more boring his interviews would have to get more boring too.

The therapist will routinely see a conflicted enmeshment operating in the resistant boy's relationship with his mother or female caregiver. For example, I suggested that a mother use a basket hold with her son when he was out of control. This hold had worked well with a more avoidant boy, with the result that the two of them were brought closer together. It did not work with this pair. The boy frequently slept with his mother, an emotionally needy and intrusive parent. I had thought the structure of the constraint would be a good model for how to behave, but it activated intense resistance in the boy, resulting in the mother being deeply scratched and bruised. Only later did I realize how often each was punitive with the other, even in brief, casual exchanges. The failure of this constraint technique is not only a lesson that techniques should not be applied indiscriminately, but that they should be used only after you have assessed the relationship.

The onset of adolescence in male victims will frequently blur the attachment classification. During adolescence, you may be seeing more overt depression, anger, isolation, or dependency. The best guides to the therapist about the boy's or teenager's attachment style are how the parent(s) view him and who the boy turns to when he has emotional needs.

DISORGANIZED ATTACHMENT AND
ITS PRESENTATION IN YOUR OFFICE

Disorganized attachment is the third insecure attachment style. Very little has been written about the manifestation of disorganized/disoriented attachment in the preschool- and latency-age years (Main & Solomon, 1990). In fact, Crittenden (1994) seems to prefer viewing these children as continually caught between a defended and coercive position that is reflective of their fragmented and unpredictable style. Whatever the case, these children are born into typically chaotic and trauma-infused family systems. It is apparent that such boys have experienced at least one significant disruption in their relationships with their primary caregivers. This may take the form of foster care, either formal or informal, which may have occurred while the parent was getting treatment for personal psychiatric problems or following physical abuse or neglect. Usually I am left to get most of my intake information from the caseworker, and I work most closely with the foster parents. These are also the cases in which both parents have been abusive, neglectful, and/or sexually involved with the child.

A guiding principle in identifying children who fall into this attachment style is their unpredictability. For example, with avoidant children, you experience a narrower, more predictable range reflecting a defended stance. Over time, the disorganized boy may combine proximity-seeking with passivity, and active avoidance with stereotypical trauma-play that includes episodic anger or detachment. Your internal experience is that the child feels empty, fragmented, and not there. Never within the first few months of contact will such youngsters perceive the individual therapist as routinely soothing or as a provider of felt security. You will clearly get the sense that only part of the youngster is present in the room, and, from session to session, this part may vary. Consequently, you may not "see" the entire child until after some time has elapsed. (Both Joe and Jason, described in Chapter 12, are probable examples of this style.)

The play styles of these boys is likely to be immature and variable as well. Although it may or may not be parallel play, interactive play is likely to be rapidly shifting, immature, and stereotypic. These are also the children who can mix sudden viciousness with sexuality. This is very disconcerting to any therapist.

Most likely it will take some effort on your part to meet the parents of disorganized/disoriented children; your first meeting will often be with an alternative caregiver. When you finally meet the boy's parents, you automatically will encounter a history of trauma. You will also be faced with attempts at self-soothing by the parents, including chemical abuse, parasuicide, or other self-defeating behaviors. Parental absence or neglect is common: When you ask the parents about their own experience of being parented, they typically cannot identify any adult who was consistently positive to them while growing up. They may state superficially that their parents were adequate, but their inability to provide a balanced, detailed view of either parent is very telling.

The task of the individual therapist has to include discussing with the caseworker whether reunification is even feasible. You may need to strongly question whether termination of parental rights might not be the most appropriate outcome for the child's long-term interests.

Consider, for example, a 4-year-old boy who was molested by his biological father, a man whose rape of the mother had resulted in the boy's conception. As a child, the mother had been physically and sexually abused; she was placed permanently out of her mother's care at the age of 11. She had made numerous suicide attempts and had several assault arrests on her police record. Nurses in the neonatal nursery filed neglect reports with social services, and the boy was rehospitalized twice for failure-to-thrive in his first 13 months of life. His second hospitalization was followed by a 15-month stay in foster care. In the first three therapy sessions I had with this boy, I counted numerous times when he stared blankly, exhibited exaggerated startle to my actions, hurt himself, exposed himself, or exhibited random aggressions to me. Not once did he exhibit sustained play, not even solitary play. My internal reaction after each of these sessions was fatigue and sadness. This may seem like an extreme case example; however, the same is true for most children with this type of attachment.

❑ Therapist Issues

A central point from my explication of the different attachment styles is that you need to be a therapeutic chameleon. You need to have a stable and mature self, one that allows you to be flexible with a broad range of boys. You may realize that you work best with one type, but you need to work capably with several types.

Despite your maturity and flexibility, I need to repeat that the *power of the internal working model* is enormous. This is true for you as well as for the boys you see. Their behavior will affect you in powerful and sometimes insidious ways. How you behave when you are stressed will show up in your interactions with them. If you become strict and moralizing when you are anxious, you will become controlling, strict, and punitive with these boys. If you underfunction and get anxious when confronted, that is what your therapeutic behavior may be like. If you have an unresolved history of victimization, you may find yourself feeling revictimized in your relationships with these boys. To repeat, there is incredible and seductive power to an anxious or disorganized internal working model. You need to know who you are and how you behave in power situations or in situations where you feel anxious, and you need to respond accordingly.

For example, despite my best efforts, I found myself getting angry and controlling with a boy who had been terrorized, physically abused, and molested. The boy would start off being ingratiating and needy and then become angry and sadistic. The foster mother who worked best with him was miles ahead of me when she stated, "I know his kind. He'll be nice for another week and then he'll try to turn me into his momma. But I won't let him." Two earlier, more needy foster mothers had been driven to tears and became very fearful of this boy.

Taking care of oneself is also extremely critical. Attachment with a sexually abused boy will proceed to the degree that you feel safe to him. Your perceived safety is related to your own internal security. Working too hard in the session can translate into intrusiveness, as perceived by the boy. The opposite happens if you are tired and too passive. A defended boy's role reversal can show up when he raises concern that you are tired. If you have problems with your own interpersonal relationships, you will be less available as an attachment object. The boys need to be desirous of proximity with you; you do not need to be getting relationship needs met by proximity with them.

❏ Individual Treatment Techniques Derived From Attachment Theory

The advantage of theory is the potential for specificity in treatment goals. Abuse-specific treatment targets include boundary problems, the recapitulation of victim or victimizing behavior in relationships, and the sexualizing of relationships. More generic, attachment-related treatment problems include poor social skills, distrust of others, and impaired perspective-taking. In addition, the relationship of insecure attachment to future psychopathology emphasizes the need to repair attachment problems within the family. The contexts in which this can take place are active, focused play therapy approaches, and goal-directed, cognitive therapy in which relationships are emphasized. Both share the critical relationship element, but each is more directive and targeted than nonabuse specific therapy. See Table 3.1 for a compilation of these techniques.

Acceptance is critical to all approaches you use. Researchers have even noted that something as seemingly cut and dried as cognitive therapy works best in the context of a solid therapeutic relationship (Stark, Rouse, & Livingston, 1991).

ACCEPTANCE

The sexually abused boy must be accepted for who he is, a boy who has been victimized. To deny this history is to detract from acceptance. Pretending that talking about the victimization and its attendant feelings is optional, painless, or simply a one-step solution, reduces the likelihood of the child feeling accepted. Acceptance requires adults who neither deny the abuse nor are overwhelmed by it (Crittenden, 1992). To sympathetically accept only the victim part of the boy is to deny his larger self, the aspects of him that are not just a victim.

This position regarding acceptance may strike the reader as odd. Don't you ease the child into the relationship? Won't you "blow him

Table 3.1 Individual Techniques Designed to Correct Attachment Problems

---

1. Acceptance

   a. Tailor self to his attachment style
   b. Monitor effusiveness
   c. Therapy is rewarding
   d. Therapy is not too excitatory
   e. Develop a sense of relatedness
   f. Help him recognize the emotional and behavioral difficulties
      he has

2. Alliance formation

   a. Develop a sense of connection with the child
   b. Make treatment rewarding
   c. Create collaborative mode for problems he is facing

3. Correct the internal working model

4. Create safety to allow attachment

---

out of the water" if you're too honest? I contend that it is better to be met with acceptance in the form of congruence than acceptance in the form of denial. This is also in keeping with Shirk and Saiz's (1992) first step at developing the therapeutic relationship. The child needs to recognize the emotional and behavioral difficulties he is having. The "other-directed," (Elliott, 1994) avoidantly attached and defended boy, with a million interpersonal antennae growing out of his head in order to read any cue you might emit, needs to see that you are comfortable talking about sex and pain. If not, he will take care of your anxiety for the duration of the therapy.

Therapy with the sexually abused boy must begin with a clear statement about the purpose of the therapy. For example, I told a boy that we would be meeting together because "you're touching your privates a lot and afraid to sleep in your own bed because of what Uncle Joe did." I am not denying that for some children, the sexual abuse is relatively less an issue than abandonment by parents or something else. Those big issues need to be brought up as well.

Parents will tell you that they cannot bring up the abuse with their son, or they will ask you for advice about how to talk to him. The mental image I get is that boys in these situations are left alone and confused. The boy must wonder, "Is this a big deal or not? Am I sad or not? What does it mean that Dad doesn't look at me anymore?"

Acceptance is correctly evidenced in tangible indications that the child is prized. By tailoring yourself to his attachment style, by knowing how effusive you need to be, by making the visits with you rewarding and not too excitatory, and by fostering a sense of relationship though joint narratives or pictures, you are demonstrating acceptance and leading to alliance formation (discussed in the next section).

We need to use every strategy available to us to enhance our acceptance of the boys we see. Some therapists can do this because of their indefatigable nature and their belief in the good in everyone they see. One of my strengths is writing, including writing fiction. For one boy, who was particularly troubling to me, I enhanced my acceptance of him by first imagining and then writing out a short story about his relationship with a band teacher, a man with whom he was in constant conflict, but who, by the foster mother's report, was both a good teacher and a good person. I had a difficult time liking the boy until I finished the story, which let me construct a new story for him (see White & Epston, 1990). We do what it takes to be fully human to those entrusted to us.

ALLIANCE FORMATION

The most explicit and direct manifestation of attachment theory revolves around the formation of a therapeutic alliance. In many ways, it is part and parcel of acceptance; my distinction between the two is a bit arbitrary. Literature on treatment effectiveness routinely finds the therapeutic relationship to be of critical importance (Strupp & Binder, 1984). In fact, the quality of the therapist-client relationship may be central and more important than specific therapeutic techniques or approaches. Thus from the very beginning, it is the therapist's duty to determine how best to maximize the quality of the therapist-child attachment relationship. The acceptance described above will set the stage for the alliance.

The therapist has the greatest control over the factors that enter into forming an alliance with the child. He or she is instrumental in determining whether or not the child feels safe and has permission to discuss and work through the abuse and needs to ask the question, "How can I best use my therapeutic style to maximize the child's ability to form a secure attachment, not only with me, but so as to generalize to the current parents and caregivers?" A number of factors enter into the equation, including the sex of the therapist, the emotional and behavioral style of the therapist, the ethnic match of the child and therapist, and the therapist's maturity and current level of emotional resources. Although the child potentially influences the formation of the attachment relationship, an extensive review of the current literature indicates that the most consistent predictors of secure attachment are caregiver variables (Bretherton & Waters, 1986).

Therapeutic practices that repeat rejection must be avoided. Sexualized, aggressive, and physically unattractive children will pull for rejection from the therapist. Children can re-create their home environment, not only in foster homes, but in your office as well. The child's behavior can so exasperate the foster family that removal from the home occurs. These are times when the therapist can feel that he or she has "lost control" of the therapy process and that everyone is playing out a script from a prior relationship that the child had with a caregiver.

The child's attachment history will dictate his interactions with the therapist. For example, boundaryless children, many of them with a history of disorganized attachment, will need therapists who are clear in their own boundaries. Such therapists can tolerate and gradually alter the child's dependency, physical proximity-seeking, and variability. A resistant child, on the other hand, may expect aggression mixed with guilt and indulgence from the parent. He may therefore try to provoke this response, presenting a different challenge to the therapist, who will need to work differently than with the boundaryless child. Finally, the avoidant child may be very slow in forming an alliance, always anticipating rejection, hypersensitive to therapist's unavailability, and very well defended. Or he may take care of the therapist by being a model patient, and in doing so, still defend against a needed connection with an adult.

The sooner both the therapist and child have a sense of "weness," the better. Therapists can start by being maximally "present" in the session and being available emotionally. Small gifts to the child along with food at the sessions can be important, as can consults to the school and occasional between-session phone calls (Mufson,

Moreau, Weissman, & Klerman, 1993). Pictures of the therapist and child together create a visual symbol of connection and can be given to the child and/or brought into sessions. Therapeutic triangulation allows the therapist-child dyad to ally with each other and against a third party (e.g., a nonfamilial perpetrator), thus pushing the treatment alliance along (Friedrich, 1990). Finally, a sense of connection may be facilitated by closer attention to ethnic and gender matching of child and therapist.

It is important not to enter into individual therapy with sexually abused boys from a naive perspective. Sometimes parents withdraw even more if they feel that their child is getting some support from another person. This might be done out of relief, due to feeling overwhelmed, or even because of jealousy. Just because you are a positive force in this boy's life for a 50-minute period does not necessarily mean that you are a positive force in the boy's system or that this relationship will become generalized. Consequently, if all you do is good, supportive, attachment-based individual therapy with the individual sexually abused boy, you are still not addressing the larger system in which he operates and will continue to operate long after his relationship with you is over. Attachment-based individual therapy with sexually abused boys must have a systemic component as well, with parents receiving support and the family making some changes.

To refer back to Shirk and Saiz (1992), alliance formation requires a balance between the therapist and child about ownership of the therapy and its outcome. It is critical that the boy feels motivated to address the problems he has been helped to identify as the therapist accepts all of him, not just the victim part. Consider the following segment of an interview with Eddie, a 12-year-old who was molested at age 8 by one of his mother's boyfriends, and who then molested his 4-year-old half-sister, Heidi, just prior to coming into the hospital after a serious suicide attempt. Eddie was a challenge to me because I had to address both the victim and the victimizer in the same boy. This is from my seventh interview with him.

Eddie You just keep talking about what I did with Heidi.
Therapist You're right. There's what you did with Heidi and what Gary did to you.
Eddie I can hardly remember that.

Therapist Actually, there's what you did with Heidi, what Gary did to you, and the Eddie who could read when he was 5 years old and who makes A's in math.

Eddie I told you that? How do you remember all this stuff I tell you?

Therapist I remember because I really like you. And whenever I talk to a kid, I always look for something in them that lets me know if they can make the changes they need to make.

Eddie I'm not going to do that to Heidi anymore.

Therapist I'm glad to hear that. But the problem I need your help with now is can you keep yourself safe?

Eddie I don't know. What's the use? Who'd care?

Therapist Twelve-year-old boys don't just try to kill themselves. They do it because bad things have happened to them and make them feel like shit. Then they decide they are shit and do shitty things to themselves, like trying to hang themself.

Eddie You know all that?

Therapist I have you pegged, don't I?

Eddie I guess so.

Therapist I think I need to talk to the smart part of Eddie and get him to agree that he'll keep working with me long enough so we can get past these shitty feelings. Can I count on you to work with me on this?

Eddie Maybe.

Therapist I won't give up on you if you don't give up on me. How about it?

Eddie Okay. I guess.

The end result is that both Eddie and I are beginning an alliance. This is critical for future work. I was a bit provocative because I believed that I could connect with someone as defended as this primarily avoidant boy.

CORRECTING THE INTERNAL WORKING MODEL

Although the internal working model is powerful, it can be modified to be more flexible and adaptive. Inconsistency and lack of congruency with behaviors, thoughts, and feelings characterize the internal working models of anxiously attached children. Therapy needs to focus on these discrepancies and to assist the boy in realizing the existence of a variety of perspectives about the same situation or person. (Think about the three aspects I identified in the earlier section with Eddie: competent, victim worthy of sympathy, victimizer.) In addition, internal working models include cognitive, affective, and behavioral elements (Bretherton & Waters, 1986). The more that all three of these elements can be brought into the therapy, either through conversation, drawings, play, or a combination of these, the better. Because of a young child's developmental level, or an older child's poorly developed sense of self, he may not be able to talk about his feelings, but there are other indirect ways to promulgate the disclosure of both thoughts and feelings; these can then be corrected and reintegrated into the child's working model.

Crittenden (1992) suggests a number of different approaches that are useful for toddlers and preschoolers. With some extrapolation, they are clearly useful for other ages as well. Think, for example, of the mixed feelings a child will have about a caregiver, particularly if the caregiver has been abusive. The cognitive limitations of a child, much less the anxiety or prohibition attached to a discussion of angry feelings, will make it very difficult for the child to retain these feelings and examine them. But to do so will create opportunities for the clarification of feelings, the expression of genuine affect in the context of acceptance and validation, and the opening up of the model to become more flexible. Consider two segments of two different conversations with a 13-year-old boy named Danny, molested by his father 3 years earlier. The mother had already divorced the father prior to the last molestation, and Danny had a primarily resistant attachment to her.

Therapist So, the teacher made you feel stupid.
Danny Kids were laughing at me, even.
Therapist Everyone was making you feel stupid.
Danny I wanted to hit him.
Therapist If you could punch him, you wouldn't feel so stupid?
Danny Yeah, then he'd look stupid.
Therapist He sure would. Help me get something straight. When someone makes you feel stupid, you get mad?
Danny I guess so.
Therapist Who else makes you feel stupid?
Danny My mom. My sisters.
Therapist You want to hit them then?

Danny I do hit them (Laughing).

Therapist What would you want from them instead of them making you feel stupid?

Danny What do you mean?

Therapist What would you want from your mom? Now she just makes you feel stupid.

Danny To be nice to me. Not to call me names.

Therapist It hurts that she calls you names.

Danny Yeah.

Therapist You feel sad about her calling you names.

Danny No, I feel mad. I feel sad. Then I feel mad.

Therapist First sad, then mad. Let me draw this out. (Illustrates sad—mad on the chalkboard in the room.) Which is easier to feel?

Danny Mad. I hate sad.

Therapist You hate feeling sad. You'd do anything not to feel sad.

Danny (Crying) I hate this crying shit.

Therapist (After a pause) We learned something though. When people make you sad, when they make you feel like you don't count, don't matter, like your teacher, your mom, you fight that feeling, you push sad away and replace it with mad.

Danny You bet.

Therapist What's the saddest you ever got?

Danny I don't remember.

Therapist The saddest you ever got. Think about it. It was probably when someone made you feel like nothing, like you were nothing.

Danny I don't remember.

Therapist You can answer me if you want, or you can yell at me because I'm pushing you, but was that when you came in the ER? When you took all those pills?

Danny That was the worst.

Therapist The worst.

Danny Like I was feeling sad forever. Day after day.

Therapist Day after day feeling sad.

Danny Yeah. (Crying again)

Therapist Sad now.

Danny Let's stop this shit.

Therapist Okay, Danny. I'm sorry for pushing you. But could I say one thing?

Danny What?

Therapist Here again you got to feeling sad. Then you got mad at me. Better than getting mad at yourself and trying to hurt yourself.

Danny Yeah.
Therapist We've got to figure out what the sad is all about.

Several sessions later, Danny came in puzzled about a change in his mother's behavior that had been prompted by her own therapy.

Danny Now she's being all nice to me. But it's phony.
Therapist Your mom is being nice, but it feels fake.
Danny I hate it.
Therapist You don't want her to be nice to you?
Danny Yeah. No, I like that. But why did she wait so long?
Therapist We have to figure this out. She's mean, and you get mad. She's nice, and you get mad. I think mad means more than one thing for you. (Illustrates relationship on chalkboard, i.e., mean—mad, nice—mad.)
Danny She's confusing.
Therapist Let me add confusing. (Draws further on board.)
Danny That's it.
Therapist How about this? Tell me if I'm wrong. She's mean, and you get one kind of mad. She's nice, and you get another kind of mad.
Danny It's more confused.
Therapist One is a confused mad.
Danny Yeah. And one is a mad.
Therapist Now we're getting somewhere. Now you're making sense. You have mixed feelings about her.
Danny She drives me crazy.
Therapist She's so confusing, sometimes nice, sometimes mean, that you feel crazy.
Danny Yeah.

To summarize, the above segments can be best conceptualized as an opening up of Danny's perspective on his relationship with his mother. For the first time, he is able to articulate his confusion. He can do this because as an adolescent, he can think more abstractly. In addition, his mother was motivated to change her stance with him as well. Unlike a more avoidantly attached boy who would appear more defended against his mother, Danny and his mother were constantly referring to each other and on some levels were almost too close—thus the resistance.

If the therapist can help the child articulate his true feelings about attachment figures, then the child can begin to develop models about the parents as different individuals. The articulation of contrasting perspectives of good and bad will sound a great deal like the process outlined in Chapter 11. However, the focus here is on attachment and the internal working model. In Chapter 11, the focus is on the self, the internal representation of who the boy is. That is reflective of, but not the same as, the internal working model.

The therapist is in a curious dilemma. He or she must help the child express his feelings about caregivers. These include intense hurt and anger. But he or she must do so in a way that adds to the relationship, not detracts from it by turning the parent into a scapegoat. Blaming is counter to good therapy (Shirk & Saiz, 1992). It is also important for the therapist to create a sense of collaboration and discovery with the child, so he or she is still viewed as his ally, not simply as an agent of the parents.

The boy's relationship with the perpetrator can at times be an easier place to start in terms of opening up the child's attachment repertoire. Using a combination of drawing, play, and dialogue, the child's differing feelings about his incestuous father or brother, for example, can be identified and accurately labeled. The dichotomy between idealization and devaluing is often evident; both of these aspects need to be examined.

Consider the following from Jim, the older of two boys molested by both their father and grandfather. This 9-year-old boy's testimony had been central in sending both to prison. The father was in the county jail at the time of this session.

Therapist Your mom said you were having dreams about your dad escaping from jail.
Jim Yeah.
Therapist You know where the jail is?
Jim Yeah. We drive by there to get here.
Therapist It looks awfully big to me. Like it's hard to get out of.
Jim Not to me. I could get out.
Therapist If you could get out, he could get out. Your dad.
Jim Yeah.
Therapist Then maybe we need to make our own jail. An even bigger, stronger jail.

This strategy had been helpful in the past to ease Jim's anxiety, particularly at bedtime.

Jim I'll get the blocks.
Therapist We'll make it with double, no, triple walls.
Jim Yeah. Real strong.
Therapist So strong he'll never get out.

Over the next several minutes, the therapist and Jim build a fortress-like structure, with wooden blocks, complete with a male doll inside to represent the father.

Jim Look, he's getting out.
Therapist (Who was concentrating on safety) No, he won't. Get back in there.
Jim (Laughing) Look, he's getting out again. Grandpa is coming to rescue him.
Therapist (Still focusing on safety) Call all the cops. Call all the cops. Prisoner's trying to get out. We'll teach you to leave.
Jim (Laughing) He's not getting captured. You can't capture him. He's too strong.
Therapist You have one strong father.
Jim He even let me feel his muscles. He's strong.
Therapist (Switching focus to attachment) There's a lot of things about him you like. He's strong. He has big muscles.
Jim He wrestled.
Therapist He was a wrestler just like you are. Did he win as many trophys as you?
Jim Even more.
Therapist He's strong. He has big muscles. He's a wrestler. There are probably other nice things about him.
Jim Yeah.
Therapist It would be nice if we could let him escape every now and then and do nice things for you.
Jim Yeah. (Beginning to look close to tears)
Therapist It's okay to still like the good parts of him.
Jim Mom hates him. She threw away everything from him.
Therapist She should hate him and love him. Just like you.
Jim I don't hate him.
Therapist You don't hate him. You're what? Angry? Confused? Sad? At what he did?

Jim Confused. But I still like him.

Therapist Confused about what he did, but still liking, maybe even loving him for the good things about him.

A sign of the value of this exploration with Jim about the complexity of his feelings regarding his father is that safety issues dropped out of his subsequent play. Jim was more open in talking about the abuse, and his mother reported an upswing in positive behavior.

By actively discussing and articulating (e.g., via play) the child's varying perceptions of his attachment figures, including the perpetrator, the child is able to process discordant feelings, thoughts, and actions. It is not enough to only understand. Young children have difficulty translating thoughts and feelings into actions; Crittenden (1992) says that adults "should actively coach them on what to do to resolve interpersonal situations. . . . Games and activities can be used to accomplish this" (p. 599).

By way of contrast, an individual therapy approach, which is aimed at support of the child, completely accepts the child's diatribes about the nonoffending mother. A more difficult, but I believe more useful approach, would be to introduce the vagaries of the relationship into the therapy. Without ceasing to be the children's ally, I have been able to get resistant boys to think about what they do to push their mothers' buttons, and avoidant boys to talk about how they would be different if their mothers were more available. By doing so, old models hopefully are opened up and the potential for change is created.

CREATE SAFETY TO ALLOW ATTACHMENT

We put abused children in terrible binds. We expect them to come eagerly with us and happily incriminate their parents. Resistant boys who are chronically anxious about their mothers when apart from the mothers will not have energy for therapy. I have stated before, and continue to believe as strongly, that individual therapy with sexually abused children in foster care is of questionable utility, unless the focus is on skill building or self-regulation (Friedrich, 1990). Even then, the foster-parent/child dyad is the recommended focus, with each working together to help the child with, for example, his enuresis.

To address attachment, the child needs to have permission from his parents to work with you, to like you, and to trust you with all manner of potentially incriminating evidence. Secure attachments form when ambivalence and anxiety are kept to a minimum. Biological parents have to pass the mantle to you, so to speak. Sometimes this cannot be done; then, I think you need to create different, more circumscribed, treatment foci.

Hopefully, by this time you are getting a sense that the therapy I am describing takes a great deal of thought and skill, balancing out numerous alliances and walking a type of tightrope, all the while being unconditionally accepting and prizing of the boy. You need to work hard as well, always looking for opportunities to get the issues on the table. These children deserve no less than that.

4

Attachment: Group Therapy

When people leave, they always seem to scoop themselves out of you.
—Smiley, 1989, p. 40

I have long been interested in the influence of a person's background on the personality theories he develops. Lonely, socially isolated, sexually awkward, and misunderstood Harry S. Sullivan, who reportedly did not have a friend as a child, developed a remarkable interpersonal theory that emphasized the importance of friends. His term *personification* reflected his belief that our self-perspective is derived from our interpretation of the perspectives of the people around us, the people with whom we interact (Sullivan, 1953).

Even during infancy, a child is becoming oriented toward his peers. Consequently, his relationship with peers will be a critical aspect of his development, regardless of his sexual abuse history. Although the temptation might be to avoid the use of group therapy given the dysregulation problems that are present in sexually abused boys (Friedrich et al., 1988), that temptation needs to be avoided wherever possible. Group therapy carries within its very nature a number of powerfully corrective emotional experiences that are directly or indirectly related to relationship formation and hence to attachment theory (Yalom, 1975).

For example, groups provide an opportunity to develop a sense of universality, or a perception that the child is not alone in terms of his distress and that there are other boys who have experienced similar traumatic events. Trauma tends to be secretive, and the group is an immediate correction to that secretiveness. Even in groups I lead that are quite structured and focused, the simple validation that comes from one geeky boy sharing something with another geeky boy and seeing some understanding is probably as powerfully therapeutic as any of the feelings- or self-control exercises I introduce.

There are a number of other interpersonal aspects to groups that are also relevant. However, specifically for sexually abused boys, the opportunities for perspective-taking and role play are critical. As mentioned in Chapter 2, attachment is more than simply a cognitive process; it has affective, cognitive, and behavioral domains. The type of therapy that most often is done individually does not lend itself very readily to role playing or to accessing the cognitive/affective/behavioral aspects of attachment. Thus a corrective emotional experience that can alter the boy's internal working model is more likely to be available in group therapy.

Think about helping a boy address his relationship with his father— his mixture of yearning, anger, and rejection/avoidance that have resulted from the incest. In individual therapy, you can talk about it, draw out the feelings, and address it indirectly with play. You may also be able to comment that the boy gets mad at you (transference) the way he would like to get mad at his dad. I have found that anything other than that is too overwhelming and may leave the affective and behavioral components untouched.

Group work allows the boy to add an experiential component that is less threatening to enact, because the transference in the group is more muted. The boys can demonstrate to each other the conflicting urges they have regarding their perpetrators (e.g., to hit them, to go to the ball park with them). The boys can script and role-play dialogues with the perpetrators. They can get vulnerable in front of each other as they act out and describe their hurts. Now we are talking about multimodal therapy, which addresses all levels of connection—cognitive, affective, and behavioral. This is far more possible in group work than with individual work.

The success of a group will depend on how cohesive the group can become. Rejection and revictimization are to be avoided, and this requires careful screening. Putting a socially awkward boy, who invites rejection, into a group is likely to be based on good intentions but may not be very successful.

There is evidence that insecurely attached children have difficulty negotiating the emotional demands of group functioning (e.g., status, role apportionment, and conflict resolution). For example, 76% of securely attached 11-year-olds made friends, compared with only 45% of those who have been anxiously attached (Elicker, Englund, & Sroufe, 1992). Peer group formation (consisting of three to five children) most naturally occurs among securely attached children. Typically, only one anxiously attached child gets included in natural peer groupings (Karen, 1994). These facts alone point to how difficult group formation might be, especially if the group has significant process and/or interactive components. Not surprisingly, most groups of sexually abused children do not emphasize group process.

❑ Techniques

GROUP COHESION DEVELOPMENT

The ideal situation is for boys in any group to feel connected with at least one other boy and to have a sense of connection to the unified and cohesive larger group. Although this ideal may not be commonly attained, some approximation to it is possible, particularly within well-screened groups of reasonably similar children.

Resistantly attached children are more likely to be intrusive with other children in peer and group settings. Allowing a pattern of intrusiveness, even victimization, to develop within a group is countertherapeutic and destroys group cohesion. Cohesion can be enhanced by creating a sense of acceptance and continued modeling of acceptance by the therapist or cotherapist. In addition, expectations can be

Table 4.1 Techniques

---

1. Group cohesion development
2. Boundary development and maintenance
3. Creating group safety (e.g., safety friends)
4. Correcting internal working models in a peer context
5. Empathy development

---

established for supportive behavior among peers, including the modeling of support and encouragement by cotherapists as well as by more socialized group members. The use of a point system that encourages appropriate social behavior can also enhance a group that appears more cohesive, particularly if a group prize is the reward. The group prize should be in addition to any group snack, the group snack itself being another key to building cohesion. Please refer to Table 4.1 for a listing of techniques.

The boys' identification with the group can also be promulgated by treating them as an entity or an entire group. Sometimes this can be done by providing labels, including group or team names. Boys can generate lists of attributes that characterize their team, and their enthusiasm and exaggeration in creating the list is perfectly acceptable.

Cotherapists also need to frequently refer to the work of the group as a whole, or to the common struggle that each boy has. Identifications between the boys, including common victimization history, is recommended, with each boy given special notice because of his expertise about victimization.

Using group activities is also recommended, including group projects. Some therapists have described the use of a group collage in which group members work individually and collaboratively on the formation of a larger project. Other excellent activities are described in "Welcome to Your Group" and "Making Friends," the first two modules of a larger, structured protocol (Mandell & Damon, 1989).

BOUNDARY DEVELOPMENT AND MAINTENANCE

Both intrusive and avoidant caregiving are likely to create boundary problems in children. (This is also discussed from a dysregulation perspective in Chapter 8.) These problems are exacerbated by sexual abuse, particularly abuse that is frequent and long-standing. Boys may also exhibit these problems because of intrusive or psychologically unavailable parenting. Within most groups, even with good screening, there will be at least one or two boys who exhibit clear difficulties with boundaries. These are evidenced by overly frequent physical contact; bringing private, sexualized play and comments into the group setting; interrupting other people; and making overly personal statements. Group members need to learn individually about boundaries and practice respecting them as a group. Rarely do boys and/or victims think about boundaries. However, activities that are designed to bring boundaries into emphasis and focus are strongly recommended.

These activities tend to promote cohesion and connection through the use of a common language. For example, the boys can generate ways in which they can treat each other with respect. It is even useful to bring up scenarios of intrusive and rejecting parenting or interactions with caregivers. Reenacting the interactions and discussing the feelings at each stage can help solidify a sense of personal space and integrity.

One boy was able to talk about his frequently dashed hopes of positive interactions with his (divorced) father. This boy was also quite intrusive with the therapists, and our subjective experience was to avoid him. However, he was able to recount a poignant time where he felt "dissed" by his father. This was a word that the boy brought to the group and that we could then use with each other. By referring back to his "contribution" of the word and praising him when it came up, he became calmer and less intrusive.

The information and education about boundaries can open some of these boys' eyes to being more observant about their interpersonal behavior. They can then combine this information with their feelings of intrusion. These are initial steps in the formation of more appropriate boundaries and in opening up a discussion of some of the feelings that come with having been violated.

CREATING GROUP SAFETY

Preventing victimization among group members is certainly part of both correcting attachment and enhancing the establishment of trust and confidentiality. These goals require respect of the other and commitment to the group process as a whole. Both of these are characteristics of secure attachment, and their emphasis and maintenance during the course of the group can have effects on peer relationships, both currently and into the future.

It is very important that the boys learn to check in with each other about their behaviors and whether or not the other boys feel threatened. This has to be modeled and prompted by the therapists. Group members may need to contract with group leaders and with each other to not behave in a threatening manner. This can include both overt behavior as well as sexualized comments and innuendos. Group safety can also be enhanced by the establishment of some self-soothing techniques (discussed in greater detail in Chapter 8).

Jinich and Salkas (1994) describe using "security friends" in groups with latency-aged male victims. Security or safety friends are stuffed animals given to each boy; the boy has the option of holding the animal throughout the session. Each boy is told that sometimes the group can be scary, and the purpose of the security friend is to help the boy to feel safe. That bond can also be fostered with other similar statements that function as a security blanket or transitional object (Winnicott, 1965). These appear to be very well received, even by oppositional boys.

In a paper on boys' play groups that are not attachment based, Schwartz, Dodge, & Coie (1993) discuss the emergence of chronic peer victimization. The boys who were victimized entered the group with a prior history of submissive social behavior, including nonassertiveness, lower rates of initiating social conversation, and fewer attempts at persuasion. Attachment-based researchers would suggest that these boys are more likely to be classified as avoidant (Egeland & Erickson, 1983; Egeland, Sroufe, & Erickson, 1983). These findings have obvious clinical utility in enhancing the safety among boys. We need to teach these boys how to initiate interactions, start conversations, and exhibit appropriate persuasiveness and assertiveness. Very useful group techniques that both develop assertiveness and improve communication are spelled out in great detail by Wexler (1991).

Whether or not the teaching of simple skills in a peer context will generalize to other situations is unclear. However, in the context of acceptance, it is likely that the boy now has more options for future social situations.

INTERNAL WORKING MODELS AND PEER RELATIONSHIPS

Insecure attachment with the parent is often manifested quite similarly in relationships with other caregivers and with peers (Bretherton & Waters, 1986). In the same manner that individual therapy has an attachment basis, group therapy does as well. A key feature in correcting one's internal working model is to experience relating to someone who is clearly more committed, affirming, and respectful.

However, simply having an unarticulated experience is not enough. Boys must learn a language for feelings and develop the capacity to accurately identify feelings. This is hard work for boys from families that eschew feelings. However, they can write letters to various family members about their conflicting feelings toward them. Drawings of family members exhibiting various feelings are also useful and move beyond the purely cognitive-verbal level.

The group also provides an opportunity to re-create the child's family. Within the group setting, the boys can practice addressing their parents about their feelings toward the parents. The boys can be encouraged to discuss with their peers the complex and often diverse and conflicting feelings they have about their parents. This creates the context for change. Role playing can allow the boys to learn how to think about and how to address their parents in a different manner. Videotaping these role plays (so that the boys can reprocess their feelings) creates the type of multimodal impact needed for change. A parallel group for parents also geometrically increases the likelihood of parents and children making true changes.

EMPATHY DEVELOPMENT

Group members need to learn how to provide each other with accurate, empathic feedback about their feelings regarding each other. This has to be modeled numerous times by the cotherapists, both with each other and in a number of practice sessions around imaginary or role-played interactions.

I feel uncomfortable talking about the development of empathy, particularly when I know that the typical duration of a boys' group ranges from 8 to 12 weeks. Even the longer groups (up to 24 weeks' duration) are still not long enough and cannot generate the numerous opportunities that are required for the complex skill of empathy to be learned and applied in a variety of situations. Empathy occurs throughout numerous and frequent interactions with an attuned and responsive caregiver. However, in the interest of preventing further victimization (either sexual or otherwise aggressive) by the boys in the group, it is important to have some focus on understanding the perspectives of others.

What comes to mind is the accurate perception of another child's feelings. Strayer (1980) reported that, in children, sadness is actually related less to empathic behaviors than are the more positive or happy emotions. This same author noted that empathy has cognitive, affective, and motivational components. Serious, trauma-based group sessions are not likely to be situations in which empathic behavior can be expected. Rather, situations that are experimentally manipulated so that peers are feeling more positive and upbeat are more optimal opportunities in which empathy can be manifested and discussed.

A peer group can generally begin to address some of the cognitive and, to a lesser degree, motivational components of empathy. Boys can describe situations in which they feel empathic toward others and the frequency with which they observe these types of feelings. They can be encouraged to discuss as well the conflicting feelings they have in response to another person's distress. They can be asked to recount empathic behaviors directed at them or not directed at them (a perfect example is the experience of being sexually abused). They can also imitate modeled empathic behavior displayed by the therapists.

A consistently used mechanism to study empathy empirically has been to measure how individuals respond to the distress of others. This can be re-created as clinical exercises for the group. Real-life situations in which the boys were treated unempathically, or scenarios depicting insensitivity, can be processed verbally or motorically. The boys can also be given instructions to observe instances during the next week(s) when they made decisions to behave more sensitively.

It is important to remember that the generalizability of these empathy exercises outside the group room is untested (Damon, 1988). In part, the activities may have the effect of providing a perspective on the behavior that must then be bolstered via other interactions. Too often I have met young offenders with the "knowledge" but not the actions needed to keep them from further victimization, either sexual or otherwise.

5

Attachment: Family Therapy

The more a thing is torn, the more places it can connect.

—Stricker, 1990, p. 273

I'll admit to a secret wish. I would like to take the psychopharmacologists and medical geneticists, all the new reductionists, the people who are convinced that biology is everything, and have them watch the subtle, but profound, and potentially pernicious environmental influences on children. My hope is that their perspective would become more balanced, and we could work together better, each of us respecting the role of the other. One needs a special set of "lenses" to see the interactions that seasoned clinicians witness in families. A slight, fleeting sneer on the father's face as his son is beginning to cry. The smoothing of the skirt when the boy is beginning to open up. The older brother interrupting to ask an unrelated question after you have just said something about the family's pain. Each of these behaviors is an almost hypnotic, overlearned cue to "shut up" and that "your feelings don't count." It is not surprising that sexually abused children report more often than other children the feeling of "not being real," an item from the Trauma Symptom Checklist–Children (Friedrich, Jaworski, Huxsahl, & Bengston, in press).

A cardinal rule of insecure attachment is the formation of conflicting, incongruent constructions and expectations about relationships, so that feelings do not go with thoughts, and each diverges from the actuality of the event (Crittenden, 1992). Anxious attachment is best exhibited in family relationships; similarly, that is where there are the best opportunities to positively influence it.

This chapter focuses on family therapy approaches that are aimed at addressing the attachment failure evident in the child's relationships with caregivers. Goals of attachment-based family therapy are to facilitate safety against further abuse, help the parent commit or recommit themselves to the child, reduce the rejection that is evident in the son-parent relationship, and, as much as possible, help the parents become more attuned to their child and develop greater reciprocity in how they interact with their son.

Because we are talking about boys—whose behavior problems are often aggression related—it makes sense to refer to literature on families of aggressive children. The best comes from social-learning researchers and practitioners at the Oregon Social Learning Center (Patterson, Reid, Jones, & Conger, 1975). An enormous body of literature from this center can guide much of the clinical work we need to do in families of sexually abused boys. Patterson (1993) has documented the role of two variables, *inept monitoring* and *ineffective discipline*, in the emergence and persistence of aggressive behavior. The relevance of these variables to families of sexually abused boys is obvious.

Inept monitoring may have contributed to the initial victimization as well as to creating a context for the boy to begin acting out sexually. It is also implicated in the failure to protect the victim or to realize his distress and respond accordingly. Inept monitoring also reflects reduced commitment as well as a lack of attunement to the child, both of which are attachment features.

Ineffective discipline may predate the abuse. In addition, it is likely to be aggravated by the sexual abuse experience. Parents may suddenly become less sure of how to respond to a boy's distress, rendering them even less effective. A brief spurt of sexual acting out following the abuse may be ignored, tolerated, or not even seen by parents who are already overwhelmed by parenting circumstances.

Both of these variables are pertinent, not only to sexual abuse, but also to attachment. Disciplinary conflicts between parents and young children reflect not only the social learning components of the interactions, but also the operation of the attachment system, including the attachment history of all parties (Greenberg, Speltz, & DeKleyen, 1993). Maltreatment of any sort has a profound effect on behavior, escalating aggressive behavior even in very young children (Main & George, 1985).

Attachment cannot be taught. Superficial interventions, such as parent education, do not address impaired attachment (Crittenden, 1992). I agree with Crittenden that it cannot be corrected via strategies that involve parent education alone. I do believe that attachment can be corrected by approximations, although I do not believe that it can be corrected through the use of coercion or rage reduction techniques with the child. Even more benign forms of coercion (i.e., parent management) are not helpful unless attention is also paid to improving the quality of the parent-child relationship (Speltz, 1990).

For example, Speltz (1990) describes in detail attachment-based therapy with an oppositional preschool boy. Even at the end of a lengthy, intense intervention, including laboriously teaching the mother to tolerate child-directed play, Speltz ended by stating that although the mother was now more committed and responsive to the boy, attunement had been relatively unaffected by the intervention.

Attachment is an interpersonal process that occurs over time, and the correcting of attachment must be thought of in the same manner. Sending parents to parent training because they hate their child will not aid them in liking him more or having more compassion for him and his hurts. They may learn some new strategies, but unless they are committed and attuned to their son, they are likely to use these new strategies coercively with him (Friedrich, 1990).

The same is true of all the techniques listed in Table 5.1. Each of them is unlikely to correct attachment unless it is part of an often lengthy process in which all parties are doing some changing. In addition, the primary commitment to change has to come from the most powerful parties, the parents.

Table 5.1 Techniques

---

1. Positively connote everything
2. Identify similarities among family members
3. Create small, rapid treatment gains that make child more likable or parents more energetic
4. Family-of-origin work
5. Externalize the problem
6. Home visits
7. Child-directed play
8. Goal setting

There are many issues that impede a positive mother-son relationship. The mother may not want the son to be soft and, consequently, will pull back emotionally to prevent "contaminating" him with her softness or femininity. Sometimes this withdrawal is so abrupt it is experienced by the boy as abandonment (Silverstein & Rashbaum, 1994). Imagine how sexual abuse makes this issue even more complex. Some parents may feel the need to "pull back" even more because they perceive that the boy has been "contaminated" by the abuse. Or they may perceive his heightened emotionality as a weakness, and the only strategy they have learned to use is to behave in a tough, rejecting manner. They may also feel less capable of trusting their instincts to be supportive, particularly if their own trauma has been reactivated.

If there is an underlying theme to any of the strategies suggested here, it is this: You are trying to help the parents to see the child in a new way. In the language of the narrative family therapists, you help to create a new story for the family in which they accept and value their son (White, 1989; White & Epston, 1990).

❏ Useful Perspectives

The writings of White (1989) and his colleagues at the Dulwich Center (Durrant & White, 1990) have been remarkably freeing for me. When I am empathic to the family, I can get bogged down in the pain and alienation that permeates their every interaction. Sometimes I will end up feeling stuck, trapped, or drowning halfway through the session. A narrative approach based in a contextual, interpersonal perspective pays attention to the various interactional contexts wherein a person's difficulties emerge. These contexts have resulted in a range of oppressive stories "authored" by the various "perpetrators" in the parent's life (Kamsler, 1990). Dominant stories keep the parent from accessing their own responses because their strengths have been edited out of their life stories.

This approach allows you to sincerely believe that almost all parents want a better life for their child. Your task is to enlist the parents in creating a more positive story about their parenting efficacy and their love for their son. You can help them look for exceptions to the rule about their son being a "dirt bag loser." And you can help them be more compassionate of him if they see him in a new way, not as evil incarnate, but as someone who is struggling to overcome this enormous problem that keeps trying to sneak up on him.

Also central to understanding family therapy with sexually abused boys, particularly with single mothers, are the chapters and detailed case examples describing mother-son relationships in *The Invisible Web* (Walters, Carter, Papp, & Silverstein, 1988). This book distills the wisdom of four female family therapists who eloquently and compassionately describe the dilemmas present in the mother-son relationship. One of the authors, Olga Silverstein, writes, "The dynamics of the mother-son relationship still lies at the very foundation of our contemporary social structure, yet paradoxically is seen as the source of all dysfunction in the sons" (Walters et al., 1988, p. 158).

Bentovim (1992) has written about the combination of attachment theory and family therapy. He has also been influenced by a narrative approach to therapy. He describes families in which abuse has occurred as "trauma-organized systems." These families are essentially "action systems." The essential actors in the system are the victimizer (who traumatizes) and the victim (who is traumatized). By definition, there is either an absence of a protector, or the potential protectors have been neutralized. The cause of the abuse gets attributed to the victim. In fact, behavior problems in the victim as a result of abuse, or to avoid further abuse, are often seen by the family as justifying its negative behavior toward the child or as validating any further victimization he may experience. For example, I have heard parents completely ignore the boy's trauma and describe him as a pervert, "forgetting" his earlier victimization. His "perverted" behavior now makes him so unacceptable that the parents can no longer rear him; he is further rejected by being placed out of the home. Potentially protective figures continue to be neutralized by the system, which minimizes the victimizing behavior as well as the traumatic effects of the victimization. Bentovim states that the motto of those involved in the trauma-organized system is "first—see no evil, second—hear no evil, third—speak no evil, and fourth—think no evil" (Bentovim, 1992, p. xxi). Events in the lives of individuals create stories by which they live their lives, make relationships, and initiate and respond to actions. Traumatic events create powerful, self-perpetuating stories; in turn, these create trauma-organized systems in which abusive acts get reenacted and reinforced.

Bentovim's (1992) discussion about action-oriented systems and systems that act but do not think fits in extremely well not only with dissociation, but also with the development of insecure attachment styles. Dissociation (discussed in Chapter 6) represents a break between action and thinking, something that characterizes trauma-organized systems. Insecure attachment emerges when different modes of processing (e.g., cognitive, behavioral, affective) are not congruent. The boy hears the father say that he loves him, but the father's actions (ignoring his son's distress) and the feelings (muted, withdrawn) attached to that statement are discordant with the statement.

It is for these reasons that a focus on creating a new story (in some ways a highly cognitive task) is extremely useful to the family. The story that they create with the therapist has to be integrated with the action that they are now trying to exhibit. This creates the opportunity for greater congruence between action and thinking.

❏ Creating a New Appreciation of the Child

REFRAME THE CHILD'S ACTIONS

Most readers will be familiar with the concepts of reframing and positive connotation. *Positive connotation* is a term used by strategic therapists (Selvini-Palazzolli, Boscolo, Cechin, & Prata, 1978). It is an integral part of a constructivistic approach to family therapy and directs the therapist to help the family construct a new reality, or a new story about the child, the family, and the meaning of their interactions together. An excellent, case-oriented guide to this approach is a book edited by Michael Durrant and Cheryl White (1990) titled *Ideas for Therapy With Sexual Abuse.*

The rule of thumb for this strategy is that everything is positively connoted. An example can help illustrate this. Many of you have had the experience of realizing, in the first few seconds of a family therapy session, that the parents have seized control and that their mission seems to be to let you know how bad the boy has been in the last week. They seem bent on rejection, which not only will further solidify the boy's internal working model of them as bad and inadequate, but will inevitably result in the boy acting out in some way that affirms the parent's negative beliefs. He's being a loyal son, in other words.

When a therapy situation such as the above arises, you need to let the parents know that you hear their concerns, and you must behave in a manner that indicates support of their distress. However, the tirade against the son amounts to "more of the same" criticism that you have already heard about the boy. You are rapidly backpedaling and hoping to figure out a way to interrupt this "more of the same" that is keeping the family stuck. How do you do it?

Here is an example from my work with a mother and her two children, Larry (age 13) and Darla (age 15). Both youngsters were victimized by their father. They came in for a family session, and the mother announced that Larry was stealing underwear from Darla and herself. This announcement was delivered with what I perceived to be a smug look on her face. My heart began to sink because the last thing I wanted to hear on that day, that hour, was that Larry was developing a sexual fetish or solidifying a paraphilia. Darla chimed in to suggest that her brother was sick. The mother rattled off a list of lingerie that was missing, and Darla made sure that no items were missed. From somewhere, almost preconsciously, my reply came to me, and it went something like, "He seems to be telling us that he needs something soft."

The response from both the mother and Darla was silence. Even Larry, who was previously an avoidant boy, looked at me for the first time that session. More to interrupt any retort that either of the two of them had for me than anything else, I went on and said, "Probably all of you need some softness at this time. He certainly isn't going about it in the best way, but it does tell us something about what he needs."

I was not trying to minimize the boy's behavior. In fact, I typically get a feeling of dread when I hear about paraphilic-like behavior in sexually abused boys because this can add another lengthy treatment component. Rather, my aim was to help the family think more positively about the connections among them, and to refocus the mother on the need for support that was clearly being exhibited by her son. I also do not think that a single reframing is going to turn a family around. In the case of the family described above, they needed to be brought back over and over again to their commonalities. A stance of positive connotation is one that you adopt with all families. Comments about aggression or sexually reactive behavior need to be met both seriously and in a way that begins to alter and add to the cognitions that family members have about each other. For example, descriptions of aggression can be reframed, depending on the circumstances, in a variety of ways. A brief list of possibilities would include the following:

1. Misplaced enthusiasm
2. Misguided assertiveness
3. Doing what comes naturally because of his maltreatment
4. At least he has not given up trying to get our attention
5. Spunkiness
6. What would you do if you had learned that the world was deaf?
7. You are the only one he trusts with all those feelings

IDENTIFY SIMILARITIES AMONG FAMILY MEMBERS

Below is a transcript of a segment of therapy with the mother of two boys (ages 9 and 7), both molested by their father. In addition, the older boy, Bobby, had been molested by his paternal grandfather. The mother had been sexually abused by an uncle and by her older brother. She was hospitalized after discovering her son's molestation, and personality testing with the Millon Clinical Multiaxial Inventory–II (Millon, 1992) indicated a mixed personality disorder with dependent and avoidant traits. She also viewed her own mother as a continually frustrating person, although she saw her regularly. If we think about her profile from an attachment-based perspective, we see that the mom would be well defended around intimacy (Crittenden, 1994). She would desire intimacy but become fearful and avoidant of it at the same time.

In my first interactions with this mother and her sons, I noticed that she was partial to the older boy (Bobby) but rejecting of the younger boy (Kerry). She believed that Kerry looked and acted like the boy's father (Jerry). This created a relatively constant battle between Kerry and his mother, and Kerry's resistant attachment style was evidenced in the fact that he had problems sleeping by himself. Sometimes he tried to sleep in his mother's bed. Other times he would grab her buttocks, call her fat, and yell and hit her. The mom generally held me at arm's length during the session, but she enjoyed being provocative as well. The following excerpt captures my style with the mother.

Therapist How are the wild boys of Rochester?

Mom Kerry's been getting up on the wrong side of the bed all week. Everything I say he's contrary to.

Therapist He sure wants to give us a run for our money.

Mom That's the truth. You'll be tired of us by the time this is over.

Therapist I doubt it. Has he done something this morning?

Mom He didn't want to get out of bed to get ready for school. So I told him he couldn't walk with Stacy, his girlfriend from across the street.

Therapist What happened?

Mom (Laughing) He got up.

Therapist Good for you. You knew what he had to hear to cooperate with you.

Mom I was ready to wring his neck though. He's been doing this thing lately, just like Jerry. Moving his plate and silverware around and around until it's just so. He picked at a fork last night and told me it wasn't clean. He's so much like Jerry I could scream.

Therapist I told you last week I would fight you on that one. Kerry being Jerry and all.

Mom (Laughing) I knew you wouldn't want me to say that. But he is. He looks like him. He pulls his socks off just so. He has to tuck his shirt in. Now Bobby, he's casual, like me, not like Mr. Perfect.

Therapist Kerry's Mr. Perfect?

Mom Little Mr. Perfect.

Therapist But I thought you told me that you were too perfectionistic as a housekeeper. Maybe Kerry got it from you.

Mom Yeah, but what else are you going to do if you're not allowed to leave the house? I don't have anything else to do but clean the house.

Therapist I think he got it from you, his perfectionism and stuff.

Mom He's so mistrustful. He says, "Where are you going?" "Why are you doing that?"

Therapist Look where trusting got you. You trusted your uncle, and he took advantage of you.

Mom Yeah, I guess I'm kind of like that.

Therapist There's a similarity to you. Both of you know how you always have to be on your guard.

Mom But he looks just like him. He don't look like me.

Therapist Too bad I'm not a plastic surgeon. Make him look like your side of the family, and then I could get you to stop thinking Kerry is Jerry.

Mom (Laughing) I wish.

Therapist I am going to keep harping on you about this.

Mom I bet you will. (Laughing)

Therapist What will I keep saying?

Mom Kerry's more like me than I thought.

Therapist If you can keep that in your mind this next week, you'll see that what I said is true.

An example of the constructionist approach is to create new realities and cognitions about the child, the parent, and their relationship. Parents who have never thought of themselves as an expert at anything are now expert in their boy's victimization because of their own history of abuse. The therapist can turn to the parent for input on such matters as how the boy is feeling, what would be helpful to him, and what the parents would like to do differently than their own parents did when they were molested. Rarely do I find parents who, at one time or the another, have not thought about how they would behave differently from their own parents. The story of their life has been one of being misunderstood and rejected. With support and working together the story can be rewritten.

IDENTIFY RESILIENCIES AND POSITIVES

Both the work of Walters et al. (1988) and White (1989) speak to the need to help the family look for exceptions to the rule. Trauma-organized systems, as discussed by Bentovim (1992), are closed systems and need a therapist to provide corrective input. One of the strategies to adopt when families discuss a boy's misbehavior during the previous week is to help them look at times during the week when he was not exhibiting that behavior. Those are usually possible to find. The advantage of this strategy is that you can often identify some resiliencies on the part of the parents as well. For example, a single mother who felt overwhelmed by her son's verbal aggression, when asked to discuss situations in which he behaved more appropriately, was able to identify the fact that every time the boy's grandmother attempted to intervene, he would misbehave most vehemently. This created an opportunity to talk about her son's loyalty to her, and lack of loyalty to her mother, with whom she had a great deal of problems. This appealed to the mother and helped her see her son more positively, with the two of them working together toward a common goal.

There are almost always instances in which the son has behaved. Parents of coercive boys are inept monitors (Patterson, 1993). If you can help them to monitor more closely, they can start paying attention to some of the positives that naturally occur.

STRUCTURE POSITIVE INTERACTIONS

In a related vein, not only are many of the parents that I work with poor monitors of their child's behavior, but they also tend to be avoidant and/or resistant in their interactions with their son. Prolonged periods of positive interaction are quite unusual and the repertoire of these families is actually quite circumscribed. I know from my own experience with my son, for example, that even a short bike ride prior to bedtime made him more compliant with my requests to brush his teeth and get to bed. This fact speaks to the emotional economy that exists between parents and children. Far too often, parents are overdrawn in their emotional bank account and in the red with their child. Shared activities, particularly if the parent concentrates on reducing ambivalent interactions with their son, can help the family generate a more positive feeling about each other and can put emotional money in the bank.

That a parent can behave positively cannot be taken for granted, however. I have had the opportunity to watch parents in settings with their child (e.g., during visits on an inpatient unit where I have been working with the son). For months prior to the boy's hospitalization, I was assuming that the family was having some positive time together, something to which we had agreed early on in the family sessions. However, watching the interactions led me to realize that the parent was acting toward the child, even when playing a friendly game together, as if the child was contaminated, dangerous, and/or a perpetrator. Sometimes it is benign neglect: Fathers sit passively and avoidantly rather than capitalize on free time to shoot some baskets with their son. It is as if these fathers never thought of the possibility.

Parents who are becoming aware of their own victimization and are hypersensitive to boundary violations can become physically uncomfortable and even rejecting of their child's physical presence. Just because we give parents a technique does not mean that (a) it gets put into place, or (b) it is used with the type of attunement and acceptance of the child that we hope for. Very careful follow-up and role play in the office can help to ensure that the family's emotional economy begins to move into the black. Establishing specific goals that include more positive interactions can clarify the task for a parent who has never thought in this way before.

The use of time-out with these children can be very appropriate, but again, as mentioned above, if time-out is not done correctly, it can add to the aversive interaction that occurs between a parent and a child. In fact, it re-creates the frequent experience of separateness that is so much a part of the boy's life (White, 1989). It takes a fair amount of attunement to the child to know when and how to use time-out and to use it as it is supposed to be used, not in a punitive manner or accompanied by excessive verbal criticism. Behavioral strategies will be discussed more in Chapter 9.

CREATE SMALL, QUICK TREATMENT GAINS

Parents are pragmatic consumers. They usually stick with something that works. Most are unfamiliar with therapy and have no idea that it can be helpful. Graduate students in psychology or social work have automatically positive expectations about therapy as something that can enhance growth. Parents think about it as personal snooping, painful prying, and another opportunity for a disappointing relationship.

In order to hook families into therapy, it is important to make therapy pragmatic. We need to help them see that therapy can be helpful. Included in quick treatment gains would be helping a child with a psychiatric medication (such as Ritalin for ADHD-like symptoms; Clonidine for angry outbursts; and a range of newer medications for anxiety, sleep problems, and depression). There are no good treatment efficacy studies with children for any of these medications other than Ritalin, however. Rejecting parents might view a lack of medication response as further proof of the child's inherent badness.

Ritalin is not likely to be helpful if there is a significant component of anxiety (Caron & Rutter, 1991). In addition, in several cases, I have seen iatrogenic effects in which the boy now attended to his victimization for the first time but experienced an increase in depression and self-injurious behavior.

Enuresis is another symptom that can be rapidly treated (Schroeder & Gordon, 1991). If the parent can be consistent and nonblaming and the boy has a history of reasonable cooperation, they can use a bell-and-pad system for enuresis in a positive way. The technology of the process can appeal to a boy and lend a powerful placebo effect. If the boy can then reduce his frequency of bed-wetting with this method, the parents can see him as being attuned to their own need of having fewer sheets to wash. Hypnotically assisted treatment of enuresis and/or encopresis can also be useful at this juncture (Friedrich, 1990). Regrettably, medical management of enuresis is not as effective as behavioral approaches, because anxiously attached parents seem to prefer interventions that require less interaction with their son.

It is also important to pay attention to the parents' symptomatology. Some parents can certainly benefit from the use of an antidepressant, particularly the more recently developed ones on the market (e.g., Prozac, Zoloft). Although more typically marketed for depression, these medications can address a broad range of symptoms, including agitation, dysthymia, and other symptoms of atypical depression. They entail your having a physician to whom you can make referrals.

Again, in spite of the enormous popularity of these medications, their efficacy has been established only with inert placebos, which is a weak test (Fischer & Greenberg, 1989). But we are in an age of reductionism and would rather attribute our problems to biochemical and neuroendocrine dysfunctions. I believe that the key therapeutic ingredient is that the drug name has a "Z" or an "X" in it. Something about that fact makes them work!

FAMILY-OF-ORIGIN WORK

If you facilitate parents to see the similarities they have with their child, you open up an entire arena for therapeutic work, (i.e., family-of-origin of the parents). This is not an automatic positive, however, and the therapist needs to be judicious in how much of this is made a focus. Some parents are going to be overwhelmed by working on their own victimization. Consequently, this work must remain for a later date, or maybe not at all. If a parent is having difficulty getting his or her son to therapy or seems to always be out of emotional energy, helping him or her to examine what was learned in the family-of-origin and how that is now reflected in his or her parenting behavior is most likely not going to be helpful. Remember that insight can sometimes be counterproductive and, by itself, does not lead to behavioral change.

At the very least, having parents know more clearly the ways in which their own experience of being parented shows up in their current parenting can integrate cognition and behavior in a way that was unlikely prior to therapy. Education in these areas can help parents become more committed to a child, even if the timing of their behaviors with their son or the attunement of their interactions is off. Increased commitment is a big accomplishment.

It is important as well to reframe the parents' current behavior as an active effort at being different from how they were parented. Not only do you positively connote their son's behavior, you do that as well with them. Parents of resistant and/or avoidant children are going to be mirroring their own attachment styles with their child. However, the fact that they are in therapy is room enough to suggest that there are differences from their own parents. The connections are made to the family-of-origin, both for the purposes of understanding their own behavior and for differentiating from their family-of-origin.

I believe it is important for the therapist to be an active constructor of reality. It does not work to ask the parents how they want to be different. You must state that they are. For example, "You are here to-day because there is a part of you that always knew you would be different from your folks; that if you ever had a child who had been hurt, you would surprise them, maybe even yourself, in rising to the occasion."

Consider if the parents have a week in which they report even a minuscule but positive step with their son. Put yourself in these parents' shoes and be attuned to their anticipation that you will be critical (because their internal working model is that they never get it right with authority figures). Then you can experience how positively "jarring" the following is: "It looks like you stared your Mom in the face and said to her, 'I'm going to try something different. I am going to succeed.' You took a first, critical step. I think you surprised yourself and her."

Knowledge of family-of-origin may also make you aware of how little a parent has to build on. It is very important that you do not lose sight of the fact that some families are untreatable (Jones, 1987), or the likelihood that true change comes only with years of hard work and acknowledging serious problems. Do not be afraid to call the case-worker and set up a conference in which long-term planning, including termination, is put on the table.

EXTERNALIZE THE PROBLEM

This strategy is actually one of the most helpful techniques I have recently learned to use. Again, it comes from the narrative-constructionist approach and reflects White's (1989) belief that if we are defined by our external context, problems do not lie in us but are external to us. Because of its broad-based appeal and utility, we could discuss this either here or in Chapter 13. Because one of the benefits of externalization is that parents can view their child in a more kindly way and can behave in a more accepting manner, I have included it here. Externalization is seen as a language-based separation of the problem from the personal identity of the patient (Durrant & White, 1990). Externalization captures only one step in the process of changing the parents' relationships with their child. It is important to (a) determine the relative influence of the problem, (b) help the parents identify a new story about their reaction to the child, and (c) inquire about unique and unexpected outcomes (Kamsler, 1990).

An example can illustrate its use. Mark was an 8-year-old boy whose masturbatory behavior incensed his mother. Several times she stated to me that, "If I see him do that one more time, I'll cut it off for him." This threat was delivered in front of Mark. It helped that we looked for times when he was not masturbating (relative influence) for she realized that he rarely touched himself when he was active and involved. Masturbation was an issue only when he was left by himself (e.g., sitting in front of the TV for long periods of time). In addition, I gently suggested that her threats did not sound like herself talking, especially because I saw her primarily as quite loving. Rather, they sounded like a "ghost from the past." She was able to see that was true and agreed to separate herself from the influence of her past (create a new story). In fact, she could tell me of at least one time (unique outcome) when she thought first that Mark was responding to his sexual abuse and secondly that he was "out to get her."

But I believe that what helped even more was for us to frame the masturbatory problem as a problem that "snuck up" and "caught Mark unaware." This helped Mark to start thinking about behavior in a different way. Masturbation was now something Mark could have some control over; the urge to masturbate existed outside of Mark, and masturbation did not make him bad. This strategy also helped the mother view Mark in a more positive way. Her perspective of Mark changed even more when I started externalizing the problem that she had with gambling, a problem that upset her caseworker as much as anything. I told the mother that she was not a "bad woman" but that the "damn urge to gamble" is sneaky and crept up on her when she was least expecting it.

Externalizing the problem works with a broad range of behavioral difficulties. These include PTSD symptomatology, dissociative behavior, aggressive outbursts, and bowel and bladder control. In fact, White (1989) has written a remarkable paper on treating encopresis using the narrative approach.

HOME VISITS

Programs such as HOMEBUILDERS (Kinney, Haapala, & Booth, 1991) are based on a belief in the utility of in-home services. These programs have also added to the emphasis on family preservation, usually a worthwhile and doable goal. These programs emphasize how useful actual visits to the family's home can be. Interestingly, in a recent review of intensive family preservation services, Bath and Haapala (1993) found that this type of approach was less useful with neglectful families than with abusive families; families that had multiple types of maltreatment (e.g., neglect and sexual abuse) were the hardest to treat and had the highest risk for the child being placed out of the home. These findings parallel my own experience; furthermore, there is evidence that neglectful parents are more pathological than physically abusive parents (Friedrich, Tyler, & Clark, 1985).

There are several advantages to home visits. Not only do they give you an opportunity to observe the parent and child interacting in a more naturalistic environment, but you can also observe the quality of interactions in their entirety, and you can tailor interventions that more closely fit the family and their house or apartment.

In addition, visiting the home underscores your acceptance of the family. You are putting "money" in the emotional bank account you have with this family. This will also let you do the type of problem solving that cannot be done in your office. For example, in the home you can see where the child is timed-out (and you can role-play the process while you are there); you can also view the sleeping arrangements of the children and make some determinations about relative safety. For example, only through a home visit did I gain an appreciation of one family's sleeping arrangements that made my patient vulnerable to abusing a younger sibling. In addition, your sociable gesture allows the mother and father to feel prized by you.

CHILD-DIRECTED PLAY

Speltz (1990) used child-directed play as a key ingredient in transforming the quality of interaction between a mother and her resistantly attached and oppositional preschooler. The mother in this case had a remarkably unattuned and intrusive style with her son. In an effort to let the boy feel more supported by and willing to engage with the mother, Speltz taught her to allow the boy to dictate the parameters of play. She was simply supposed to follow his lead and try to remain more involved and less controlling in her interactions with him. This strategy has the added advantage of structuring positive interaction between a parent and the child. You and the parents can set goals that include regular opportunities for child-directed play.

GOAL SETTING

I believe therapy with families of sexually abused boys needs to be quite focused and clear to the parents. I also believe that nondirective approaches that are not well defined are viewed with suspicion and are less helpful. Thus I believe in the importance of establishing goals with each parent.

Goals not only keep the therapy clear, focused, and accountable, they can create a sense that they can be accomplished. In this sense, they instill hope and create a sense of possible solutions, rather than simply a focus on problems. Goals can be set up in the three treatment areas discussed in this book: attachment, dysregulation, and issues of self. From one to three goals are decided on for each of these three categories, with five to seven goals agreed on overall. I will discuss goal setting in this chapter and will make suggestions of goals at the end of Chapters 9 and 13.

Goal setting should be done in the first several sessions with the nonoffending parents. It is done best when it is presented as a strategy that keeps therapy focused and accountable. This is even more important if social services is involved. The parents are elevated to a role where they can be in a position to prove to their caseworker that they have made the agreed-on changes. This is an example of therapeutic triangulation. Meeting these goals can even be linked to removal of the protective services petition if one has been given by the court.

Using the form provided in Appendix B and following the example in Table 5.2, the therapist comes up with two to three goals in the attachment area. These could include the following:

1. Spending more time together
2. Increasing the amount of positive statements made to the child
3. Increasing the amount of positive physical contact with the child

Table 5.2 Goal Setting: Attachment

	Goal 1	Goal 2
Optimal level of change (+2)	Positive interaction (talking, complimenting, reading out loud) with Ned 5 to 6 times per week	Ned chooses a joint activity and I cooperate 4 to 5 times per week; doesn't end in a fight
Acceptable level of change (0)	Positive interaction (talking, complimenting) with Ned 3 to 4 times per week	Ned chooses a joint activity and I cooperate 2 to 3 times per week; ends in a fight less than 1 time per week
Current level of behavior (–2)	Avoid getting involved with Ned: No regular, positive interaction	Ned rarely asks to do things; when he does, I'm too busy

Operationalize the parents' current behavior along two or three of these goals. For example, if they are having almost no periods of positive interaction with their child during the week, that behavior would be inserted at the lowest level (e.g., –2). You and the parents then work together to come up with two more levels of change—acceptable and optimal levels of change (e.g., level 0 and level +2 respectively). Operationalize these levels with the parents' input, including their own words for their goals. Ideally, goal attainment scaling is done with five levels, ranging from –2 through +2, with different gradations of unacceptable and acceptable levels of change being included (Kiresuk & Sherman, 1968).

For example, Joyce was the single mother of a 10-year-old boy, Ned, with whom she had a rather coercive relationship that was accelerated by the sexual abuse he experienced from his stepfather, her first husband. Ned was the product of an unwanted sexual relationship Joyce had with an older friend of her parents. Joyce had never told them who Ned's father was and continued to see him several times a year at family gatherings. In addition, he remained sexually coercive with her. Joyce supported Ned after his disclosure because "he's really all I have." In addition, she had long been disturbed by her husband's behavior toward her and Ned. After several sessions with Joyce and Ned, it was clear that they were estranged, that he was quite reactive to the trauma, that he continued to be very fearful of his stepfather, and that Joyce's feelings about her adequacy as a person and parent had sunk to a new low. In addition, Ned increasingly looked like his biological father and this detracted from Ned's relationship with Joyce. Ned was absent during this portion of the interview.

Therapist I like to help parents figure out things they want to change, write them down, and keep track of how we both do in accomplishing them. Does that make sense to you?

Mom I guess.

Therapist Correct me if you think I'm wrong, but one thing you mentioned to me was that you don't think you and Ned get along that well.

Mom I'm ashamed about that.

Therapist I'd rather you be ashamed than not. I know you'll do something to change it then.

Mom Really? I never thought about it that way.

Therapist Yeah, criminals don't have shame. Good moms always think they can do better.

Mom I'm hardly a good mom.

Therapist That's why we're here in this office to work on some things that will make you a better mom and help Ned not drive you crazy.

Mom You can say that again.

Therapist One of the things I've heard you say several times is that you think the two of you should do more things together.

Mom Sometimes I do. Most times, I guess. But sometimes we just get on each other's nerves. Then it's not good.

Therapist Too much togetherness. Too much of a good thing.

Mom You got that.

Therapist You also said that you go in spurts. Lots of time together, followed by some kind of falling out, then you avoid each other.

Mom It's even more like that lately, since the thing with his father happened.

Therapist So you know how to be together. We need to help you do it in a way where both of you get some benefit.

This dialogue then led to the development of two goals that are outlined in Table 5.2. These were then discussed with Ned and both Ned and Joyce agreed to focus on them. I outlined my role as a facilitator and consultant and reminded them I would check on progress regularly. Other goals for dysregulation and self-issues were also agreed on with Joyce; these are listed in Chapters 9 and 13, respectively.

After goals have been established, it is useful to give the parent a written copy, to keep a copy available for weekly review, and, if necessary, send a copy to the caseworker. Some parents have even kept the goals on their refrigerator and, in this way, incorporate you as a transitional object (Winnicott, 1965).

The version I am describing here is abbreviated but still enables you to use it clinically as well as empirically (i.e., measuring overall level of change for the families you and your colleagues see). Goal setting is also useful in both individual and group therapy approaches, particularly with boys who are at least latency-aged.

PART II

Dysregulation

6

Dysregulation: An Overview

Afterwards when he is finished . . . lots of mouthwash helps.
—Bridges, 1990, p. 193

Any compilation of the behavioral sequelae of sexual abuse will include numerous examples that reflect the phenomenon of dysregulation. Several theories have been suggested to explain the impact of sexual abuse, including the traumagenic model of Finkelhor and Browne (1985), the posttraumatic stress disorder (PTSD) perspective (American Psychiatric Association, 1994) and the information-processing model (Hartman & Burgess, 1993). Each of these theories contain at least one feature that could be included in dysregulation. For example, the primary dysregulatory features of the traumagenic model, as identified in Chapter 1, are two elements: traumatic sexualization (or the traumatic and precocious introduction of the child to sexual behavior) and powerlessness (or the experience of being out of control).

PTSD is one of the few diagnostic categories in *DSM-IV* that includes among its diagnostic criteria an etiological feature (i.e., a traumatic event). The diagnosis describes a number of related responses, including intrusive thoughts, hyperarousal, numbing, and avoidance. The information-processing model was also developed to specifically explain the victimization experience from a neuropsychosocial framework (Hartman & Burgess, 1993).

There is a connection as well between dysregulation and attachment. Over time, patterns of parent-infant interaction become a self-regulating feature of the child's personality (Bowlby, 1973; Sroufe, 1989). Although the attachment may be insecure, it is predictable, and in that way the child "knows" what to expect. Predictability adds to the child's steady-state.

In a recent, extremely thorough and well-written compilation of the effects of trauma, Herman (1992) writes that "traumatic events overwhelm the ordinary systems of care that give people a sense of control, connection, and meaning" (p. 33). When the usual means of dealing with experience are not useful, the person becomes overwhelmed and disorganized. The resulting, dysregulating impact of trauma occurs along a range of effects, including neurophysiological, behavioral, and cognitive. The remainder of this chapter reviews each of these in turn.

❑ Neurophysiological Effects

There is an expanding literature that discusses the neurophysiology of trauma (Perry, 1993a, 1993b). Traumatic life experiences can have an impact on the development of the brain, specifically on those portions of the brain involved in mediating the stress response. During acute stress, the physiological response of the body is usually rapid and reversible. When stress is prolonged (as would be the case with recurrent abuse, a chaotic home environment, or frequent disruption) there is an increasing chance that a more abnormal and persisting pattern results, particularly if prolonged stress occurs during critical and sensitive periods of development. Perry (1993a) states that "a child who is reared in an unpredictable, abusive or neglectful environment . . . will result in a poorly organized, dysregulated CNS catecholamine system" (p. 17). The catecholamine system is involved in the regulation of a large number of processes. These include affect, anxiety, arousal/concentration, impulse control, sleep, startle, autonomic nervous system regulation, memory, and cognition. Clearly, dysregulation cuts across numerous dimensions of functioning and, consequently, many psychiatric categories. These processes are reflected in all of the behaviors that will be discussed in this chapter.

In addition to a dysregulated catecholamine system, some writers in this area suggest that after prolonged stress, neurotransmitter depletion can become a conditioned response, leading to excessive responsiveness (overarousal) with subsequent, even minor stressors (van der Kolk, 1988). For example, there is evidence that early maltreatment is associated with serotonin depletion (Perry, 1993a). These findings certainly bring to my mind several clinical instances of anger in sexually abused boys who usually were viewed as passive loners. This pattern of isolated, angry outbursts is also characteristic of the avoidantly attached child (Karen, 1994).

Although there are no similarly comprehensive, longitudinal studies with sexually abused boys, Putnam and his colleagues (Putnam, 1991) studied a cohort of sexually abused girls who were matched with a similar, nonabused comparison group, many with disrupted and chaotic rearing experiences. Tentative findings suggested that sexual abuse is associated with precocious puberty; this is in keeping with other research suggesting that the production of sexual hormones is affected by prolonged stress. The fact that male sex hormones are associated with anger is particularly relevant to this book (Jensen, Pease, ten Bensel, & Garfinkel, 1991). Appreciating this additional biochemical component can aid our understanding of another contributor to the behavioral reactions that we have to help treat.

❑ Behavioral Effects

Although the neurophysiological responses to trauma that were outlined are impossible for the average therapist to measure or quantify, behavior is eminently observable and quantifiable. In this section, I will present several types of behavior that can have a trauma-genic component. These include sleep disorders, posttraumatic stress disorder, ADHD (attention deficit-hyperactivity disorder), affective lability (including panic attacks), suicidality, compulsive behaviors,

Table 6.1 Behavioral Effects of Dysregulation

1. Sleep disorders

2. Posttraumatic stress disorder with its attendant features of intrusive thoughts, avoidance, numbing, and hyperarousal

3. Attentional problems, including ADHD

4. Anxiety disorders, including increased lability, generalized anxiety, panic, specific phobias, and compulsions

5. Suicidality/Self-harm

6. Compulsive behaviors

7. Explosive outbursts

8. Dissociative disorders

9. Sexually reactive behavior

explosive outbursts, dissociation, and sexual behavior problems. These are briefly summarized in Table 6.1.

SLEEP DISORDERS

Perry (1993a) has implicated the role of the neurophysiological system in regulating sleep. Other researchers have noted that children with behavioral and academic problems have far more sleep problems than children of similar ages who do not have problems (Morgan, 1990). There is also a developing empirical literature on sexually abused children that identifies sleep disorders as a fairly consistent reaction, particularly in very young children (Hewitt & Friedrich, 1991).

There are a number of potential contributors to sleep problems, including a depressive reaction to trauma. An alternative explanation is that the traumatic experience may have caused an upset in the child's usual ability to self-regulate. The developing child gradually acquires the progressive mastery of a number of different bodily functions, including toileting and falling asleep. This requires self-control. A child who has been traumatized can regress behaviorally, disrupting previous areas in which self-control was achieved.

Another contributor is the fact that molestation may have occurred around bedtime, in the bedroom, or in the bathroom while getting ready for bedtime. The child is more prone to pair the sleep state with the trauma, and this anxious arousal is counter to an adaptive sleep response (van der Kolk, 1988).

POSTTRAUMATIC STRESS DISORDER

PTSD does not characterize every child who has been sexually abused, although it is more likely to occur when the child has experienced more significant abuse by a closer relative (McLeer et al., 1988). This suggests that greater trauma and reduced support are both related to the emergence of PTSD symptoms. David Wolfe and his colleagues (Wolfe, Sas, & Wekerle, 1994) found significant predictors of a PTSD response in sexual abuse victims. These included the nature and severity of the abuse, as well as the child's self-report of guilt feelings. This was true even after language, age, and sex were controlled. This finding of a guilt-PTSD relationship underscores the cognitive components of PTSD.

Herman (1992) suggests that the many symptoms of PTSD fall into three main categories—hyperarousal, intrusion, and constriction. Hyperarousal reflects the persistent expectation of danger and includes such behaviors as hypervigilance, an exaggerated startle response, sleep difficulties, irritability, and anxiety, even panic. *DSM-IV* (American Psychiatric Association, 1994) reflects an increasingly sophisticated understanding of PTSD by the mental health professionals. For example, several researchers in this area have suggested that PTSD symptoms exist along a continuum, and the chronic experience of sexual abuse is not the same as single, overwhelming experiences. Terr (1991) has suggested a Type I and a Type II trauma. The former is a simple, traumatic experience, whereas the latter reflects prolonged, repeated trauma. Type II trauma includes denial, psychic numbing, self-hypnosis and dissociation, and alterations between extreme passivity and rage. Mention is now made of acute, chronic, and delayed-onset PTSD. In addition, associated behavior problems have been better researched and include survivor guilt, increasingly narrow social interaction, a heightened sense of ineffectiveness, and problems with impaired affect regulation.

Because trauma often shears the connection between the language of the event and the experience of the event, memories are often encoded in the form of sensory fragments (Crittenden, 1994). In fact, van der Kolk (1988) has suggested that in states of high arousal, the linguistic encoding of memory is inactivated, and the central nervous system reverts to earlier forms of memory (e.g., sensory). This would make the trauma more difficult to process verbally. Intrusion captures the person's reliving of the event(s) and includes flashbacks, nightmares, and visual hallucinations. The person's life becomes arrested because the trauma is repetitively intruding into his awareness. It is likely that intrusions are fragmentary recollections of the traumatic event. Although most of us hear from the boys that we treat about intrusive thoughts or recollections of fragments of the trauma, these are not simply visual or mental intrusions. In fact, van der Kolk (1994) suggested that, in children, the intrusions are likely to be tactile, olfactory, or auditory as well. They may occur randomly or with some precipitating event (e.g., some reminder of the perpetrator). A teenage patient spoke about occasional sensations of choking and strangling that were related to forced oral intercourse, but only with my help did he link that to his compulsive throat clearing. Then as he thought of the trauma, he became anxious all over again, and we needed to back away from the topic. Empirical evidence for tactile intrusions comes from a study of over 800 women who were examined for the occurrence of a number of body symptoms of sexual penetration. Although a relatively infrequent phenomenon (usually occurring in less than 5% of women), it was significantly more common in women with a sexual abuse history (Froderberg, Friedrich, Suman, & Houston, in preparation).

Constriction is the third general component of PTSD and includes such symptoms as numbing, detachment, and a foreshortened sense of the future. Other symptoms include the numbing response of surrender, as well as avoidance of situations that are reminders of the event. Although it is easier to see how symptoms from the first two clusters are related to dysregulation, numbing and avoidance are also related. An undercontrolled or overcontrolled and avoidant boy is going to have problems with self-soothing and maintaining some internal homeostasis. A boy who uses overcontrol is still using a less adaptive strategy to re-regulate himself and to create some distance from the experience. The more distance, the harder it is to resolve. In some ways, the symptoms of constriction parallel the demeanor of the avoidantly attached boy who is also characterized, for example, by his well-defined posture.

I think here of a boy who demonstrated numbing and constriction by difficulty with eye contact and disjointed discourse that was devoid of feeling. However, during the session, the muscles in his cheeks were clenching and unclenching. He was a tightly wound, avoidant boy whose only problem, according to his mother, was that he had bruxism (or grinding his teeth) while sleeping. He was referred for brutally and excessively beating a boy who had playfully tilted his cap. The moral is that too much of any one response (e.g., suppression) makes you vulnerable to its flip side (e.g., explosion).

The sense of a foreshortened future also drives some of the hopelessness mixed with atypical depression seen in the sexually abused boy. Adolescence brings with it, for the first time, the capacity to think ahead, see the future, and envision who you might be. This capacity gets stolen by trauma. You can now understand the comment, "What's the use?" which often comes from your adolescent patients.

ATTENTION DEFICIT-HYPERACTIVITY DISORDER (ADHD)

ADHD is commonly thought to be biological in its nature and origins, thus warranting its treatment with stimulant medication. It has the features of overactivity, inattentiveness, and impulsivity (Anastopoulos & Barkley, 1992). In addition, it is more common in males, making it even more appropriate for this chapter. However, there are several varieties and pathways to ADHD or ADHD-like behavior. In fact, very few children who receive this diagnosis are simply reflecting a biological predisposition. There are many pathways to problems with arousal regulation, and the majority of them are environmental. This is quite relevant to the maltreatment area.

For example, there is some very compelling research that indicates that experiences in a young child's life are important and significant correlates of ADHD-like behavior in young children (Jacobvitz & Sroufe, 1987). With a longitudinal sample of children followed from the prenatal period, these researchers found that maternal interference and overstimulating care were more related to a diagnosis of ADHD by the age of 6 than prenatal, postnatal, or other medical or physiological variables. Whether or not the overstimulating care was related to changes in the arousal area of the brain implicated in ADHD was not studied. However, the child's disruptive environment was implicated in the emergence of this disorder, a relatively common presentation in sexually abused boys.

Field (1985) has also suggested that mothers are mediators of both soothing and arousal in children. (This should certainly bring to mind the notion of an internal working model, discussed in Chapter 2.) If the mother and child are not synchronous, as in the case of the intrusiveness or overexcitatory behavior mentioned in the Jacobvitz and Sroufe (1987) study, this may lead to physiological disorganization. This, in turn, can be reflected in extremes of under- and overarousal, which can get labeled ADHD.

Although sexual abuse was not examined specifically in the Jacobvitz and Sroufe (1987) study, a related phenomenon of maternal boundary dissolution was studied with this same sample of children (Sroufe et al., 1985). This phenomenon is characterized by sexually stimulating behavior between the mother and child, usually the son. This includes rubbing inside the clothing and sexualized kissing and talk. A follow-up of those children for whom this seemed to be a pattern revealed enormous behavior problems, including features of inattentiveness, oppositionality, and sexual provocativeness.

The studies by Sroufe and colleagues were prototypal studies of the behavior of incestuous parents and caregivers. Seductive parents are interfering and overstimulating. Even if the sexually abused boy appears to be more modulated on a stimulant medication (e.g., Ritalin), that does not mean that the origins of his behavior are separate from the abuse. In fact, most children, regardless of diagnosis, will look more attentive on Ritalin (McGuiness, 1989). Although the family may now think that the boy's problems are over, I believe that an abuse focus to therapy is still needed. Use the time bought by the Ritalin to help the family learn new ways of relating and continue any remaining abuse-focused therapy with the boy.

Finally, the type of attentional problems that are noted in traumatized children often occur with other agitations, including anxiety. Donovon and McIntyre (1990) describe difficulties with self-regulation in traumatized children diagnosed as ADHD to be, in actuality, anxiety-driven hypervigilance. An argument for a treatment approach that is not solely pharmacologic comes from an examination of the concept of comorbidity by Caron and Rutter (1991). They reviewed studies indicating that inattentive children who are also anxious do not improve on stimulants. Conduct-disordered children with ADHD as a secondary diagnosis also typically do not show long-term improvement with Ritalin alone. Not only do these data support a more comprehensive form of treatment, they also remind us of the need for careful assessment.

EMOTIONAL LABILITY/PANIC

Acute anxiety is a relatively common response to sexual abuse (Lipovsky, Saunders, & Murphy, 1989). Sometimes you will get a phone call describing a boy who is now crying atypically with little provocation or who is experiencing signs of panic. Sudden tearfulness and bouts of panic along with significant mood swings are characteristic of a child who is having difficulty with self-regulation. Affective lability in a boy may also bring further rejection from family members, who want the boy to be more malelike and who are irritated by his "sissy" behavior.

Although panic is usually described as an adult phenomenon, a recent review has suggested that "panic attacks are common among adolescents, while both panic attacks and Panic Disorder appear to be present, but less frequent, in children" (Ollendick, Mattis, & King, 1994, p. 131). I have worked with a number of sexually abused boys who developed panic attacks after victimization. Panic is a basic emotion of fear that is a manifestation of an alarm reaction. Alarms can be either rational or irrational and thus the cognitive component of affective lability is critical for its understanding. Variability in how a boy displays affect suggests an internalizing behavior problem. Although such problems are more likely to characterize sexually abused female children, they are certainly evident in male victims as well (Friedrich, Urquiza, & Beilke, 1986).

SUICIDALITY/SELF-HARM

Self-injurious behaviors have an affective component, and they are often very unpredictable and impulsive in this age range. Depression is not the primary motivator for self-destructive behavior in sexually abused boys (Holub, Bauer, & Friedrich, in press). When I listen to these boys tell me why they want to die, they usually do not report much sadness. Rather, it is an identification with a self-image foisted on them that they are not worthwhile, that they exist to be used, and that their loneliness has no end in sight. These facts—in combination with a need to escape from an untenable situation, to escape recurrent intrusive thoughts and fantasies, or in response to feelings of numbness, along with the impulsivity often seen in males—create a potential for either overt or covert self-destructive behavior.

There is evidence as well that abuse is related to suicidal behavior (Briere, 1992). I believe it is primarily an indicator of our field's persistent blindness to abuse that the numerous studies of suicidality in children and adolescents routinely fail to measure abuse variables. For example, the book *The Suicidal Child* (Pfeffer, 1986) mentions sexual abuse only once and then in passing.

Published clinical examples of self-destructiveness and self-mutilation are usually about women, not men. Think of the boys you have seen who rip off hangnails or pick at an open scab that is runny and bloody. I asked a sexually abused 14-year-old boy if that didn't hurt, and he said, "I like it, I like to make myself hurt."

The first sexually abused boy I ever met "knowingly" was one of three boys being molested by their father. Their mother was also involved. This was a baptism by fire. I had to realize boys were molested as well as girls and that nonpsychotic mothers could also be perpetrators. This boy was trying to impale himself with heavy scissors by running under them after he threw them up in the air. His agitated kindergarten teacher triggered the referral. Since that beginning, I have encountered numerous examples of self-injurious behavior in boys, aimed at hands, genitals, rectum, chest, and mouth. Other instances have included deliberate and not so deliberate walking in front of vehicles. I worked with one boy who would lie down behind a car with his head wedged under the rear wheel. When he was discovered and ridiculed, he then did it under a bus. I have also heard from boys who

said they wanted to die after sodomy or oral rape. When you see suicidal behavior in boys age 15 and under, sexual abuse should be an
automatic consideration.

COMPULSIVE BEHAVIORS

Compulsive behaviors are another form of internalizing behavior
related to dysregulation. Their presence does not necessarily indicate
an anxiety state, although the behaviors may be used to reduce anxiety,
even when the boy has almost never articulated the connection. It is
useful to think about compulsions as compensatory, with the boy using these acts to bind their anxiety via the routinized behaviors.

Terr (1981, 1990) describes the repetitive play of traumatized children. This play does not have a spontaneous quality but is grim and
monotonous. The same acts are repeated over and over again and,
frequently, are a literal reenactment of the trauma. I can recall at least
three boys who routinely rammed fingers and objects into the mouths
of anatomical dolls. When one cloth mouth gave out, they moved to
another. Unless this play is interrupted, the child could repeat the same
sequence over and over, never working through the underlying
trauma. Stereotypical, trauma-play again reflects dissociation or the
rift between memory and identity.

Although obsessive-compulsive disorders in children are quite unusual (although more common than is usually thought) and there is
no empirical link between traumatic events and the emergence of compulsive behavior, I have seen a number of traumatized children who
have, for brief periods of time, engaged in such compulsive behaviors
as checking, washing, and counting. In fact, an item from the Trauma
Symptom Checklist–Children (Briere, 1989b) that reads "Washing myself because I feel dirty inside" is endorsed more frequently by sexually
abused children of both sexes than either nonabused children or psychiatric controls (Friedrich, 1991c).

Crittenden and DiLalla (1988) have described "compulsive compliance" as a manifestation of physical abuse. The child exhibiting this
behavior is showing increased inhibition of disagreeable internal
states or behavior. This would suggest overcontrol, an indicator of
dysregulation. It most likely occurs in children who are avoidantly

attached, and I believe harkens back to the "false self" concept of Winnicott (1965).

EXPLOSIVE OUTBURSTS

A book focused on boys must include aggressive and oppositional behaviors. However, neither of these behavioral patterns are monolithic, and boys other than the more archetypal conduct-disordered boy (e.g., angry, insensitive, rule-violating) are also oppositional, at least with family members. In fact, resistantly attached children frequently assume more and more coercive features to their interactions with others.

Consider, for example, a boy who has explosive outbursts and who is also very depressed, even suicidal. His outbursts are sandwiched between periods of appropriate, albeit overcontrolled, behavior. This can also reflect a boy who is feeling dysregulated and who has experienced traumatic events (Perry, 1993b). In fact, Perry (1993b) states that children who have been traumatized often use an "alarm" reaction characterized by freezing, or extreme passivity that can be labeled as oppositional-defiant behavior, albeit of the more passive-aggressive variety.

"My son's a slug," the parent says to you, and, in fact, the boy seems unmotivated and overinhibited. This does not mean we should not look for anger, however. We should not attribute every behavior of the sexually abused boy to his victimization. But in some cases of sexual trauma, the boy will become anxious after being provoked by a sensitized stimulus. He may then feel out of control, be less able to comply with requests, and act out. A parent who already views the boy critically may label this behavior as defiant and interact with the boy accordingly. Over time, this can set up a coercive pattern of interaction, in which oppositionality becomes more entrenched (Patterson et al., 1975).

DISSOCIATION

Dissociation is a phenomenon that has been linked with trauma since the end of the 19th century (Herman, 1992) and is conceptually linked to PTSD. In fact, Perry (1993b) has stated that the most common childhood equivalent of "running away" from a threatening situation is dissociation. The dissociative response is also at the center of the information-processing model of trauma response (Hartman & Burgess, 1993). The authors state that an overwhelmed system shifts into a survival response of numbing or dissociation.

It is amazing to me that two phenomena that I now deal with all the time, childhood sexual abuse and dissociation, were clinical issues that I never studied formally in graduate school. I "knowingly" encountered them only rarely prior to 1978. I did not know what they were, so I was not prepared for them when I saw them.

Definitions of dissociation usually include several features, including amnesia for an event and feelings of unreality or depersonalization (Putnam, 1993). Not surprisingly, behavioral manifestations of dissociation can include daydreaming, a seeming absence of involvement, and disengagement from the social milieu. Dissociation is a skill like any other—the more the child has used it in the past, the more likely he will use it in future situations that are distressing.

Braun (1988) defines dissociation as a disruption of memory and identity. In an integrated child, memory is an essential part of identity: "I am so and so because of the things I remember doing." When memory for an event is taken away, you are less sure of who you are and have less ability to learn from what has happened. Dissociation has a number of protective functions (Putnam, 1993). These include making certain behaviors automatic, resolving irreconcilable conflicts, escaping reality, isolating catastrophic experiences from awareness, discharging certain feelings, protecting oneself from physical pain, and altering one's sense of self. These functions ensure that one does not experience the traumatic events.

Many theorists, including Anna Freud (1963), have described people as having developmental strands or lines. Braun's (1988) model of dissociation, the BASK model, appears to borrow from this concept. Braun states that people operate along at least four continua; he uses the acronym, BASK, to label these lines—B (Behavior), A (Affect), S (Sensations), and K (Knowledge). The integrated person is consistent across these lines, with his thoughts, for example, being congruent with his feelings, and his behavior reflecting his knowledge. The person who has been traumatized has had his integrated experience shattered and fragmented. That is why you have people with no memory of the trauma (disruption in knowledge), or individuals who claim to be blind when there is no medical evidence (incongruent sensations), and people whose outward behavior does not reveal the inner sadness and emptiness they would reveal, given time and support (incongruent behavior). Dissociation does not imply a single entity. Rather, it is a group of syndromes that range along a continuum of pathology and chronicity. For example, *DSM-IV* includes dissociative amnesia and dissociative identity disorder and adds a few new subcategories (i.e., acute stress disorder and trance and possession disorder) (Kihlstrom, Glisky, & Angiulo, 1994).

Because behavior is the child's way of communicating to the parent, we should also think about the behavioral reactions outlined as being part of a dyadic process, in this case, attachment. A distressed child in a secure relationship will seek to reduce his distress. For example, a fearful child, at bedtime, will seek parental attention and hopefully be soothed by it. Insecurely attached children will also act in ways to reduce their distress, but these responses will be exaggerated and inappropriate. For example, at bedtime, seeking parental support may not be an option given an avoidant working model; thus behavior problems more likely will persist beyond those of a securely attached child. That may also be why the angry outbursts seen in the anxiously attached child will be exaggerated. This child is literally screaming for attention and support, and he is also acting in a way consistent with his internal working model. These children expect to be frustrated and coerced in any supportive interactions coming from a caregiver. Consequently, they behave in frustrating and coercive ways. To briefly summarize, the ability to reduce the stress of a situation will be related to whether or not the child learns to rely on a dissociative response.

SEXUAL BEHAVIOR PROBLEMS

Sexual behavior problems in sexually abused boys are the final manifestation of behavior dysregulation discussed here. Kendall-Tackett et al. (1993) indicated that sexual behavior problems are the most reliably identified sequelae of sexual abuse. However, child behavior is quite variable, and sexual behavior is no exception. Gil and Johnson (1993) have suggested a typology of sexual behavior in children that includes behavior clearly reactive to the abuse. The four categories they developed include (ordered in increasing severity) (a) normal sexual exploration, (b) sexually reactive, (c) extensive mutual sexual behaviors, and (d) children who molest. This continuum is a welcome improvement in the field.

The degree to which the behavior is cognitively mediated (i.e., planful) will vary from child to child. Most sexually abused children who exhibit sexual behavior are not thinking about their next action nor are they linking it to the abuse they experienced. There are clear developmental differences between sexually reactive children and sexually aggressive adolescents and adults. I can think of almost no time when it is useful to either conceptualize sexually reactive children as, or call them, perpetrators. One needs only to read of the enormous rejection and modeling of violence in the homes of sexually abused boys who go on to molest other children to see it clearly as a problem of both attachment and dysregulation (Burgess, Hartman, & McCormack, 1987).

One potentially useful way to conceptualize sexually reactive behavior is to consider it as one of the forbidden games or the stereotypic trauma-play described by Terr (1990). At times, there is an automatic quality to it, sometimes seen in reports of automatic, compulsive masturbation at very predictable times by the boy.

Other children are able to inhibit their sexually reactive behavior except in contexts that are excitatory or even reminiscent of victimization. Sexually abused children seem to find each other, and precautions around their safety together are clearly needed. This also underscores the need for the boy's therapist to assess the sexual environment in the boy's home. In initial research with the Child Sexual Behavior Inventory (CSBI) (Friedrich, Grambsch, et al., 1992), we found that family-related stress, along with family sexual practices, were related to overall sexual behavior in the sexually abused child.

❏ Cognitive Effects

In addition to neurophysiological and behavioral effects, dysregulation also occurs on a cognitive level. The interrelationship of guilt and PTSD (Wolfe et al., 1994) reflects how cognitive features (e.g., guilt) and behavioral reactions (e.g., PTSD) go hand in hand. The authors state "how the individual comes to view his or her victimization experience in terms of personal blame or perceived threat are strong theoretical mechanisms linking trauma and PTSD reactions in victims" (Wolfe et al., 1994, p. 46). Attributional and appraisal reactions regarding the trauma are activated in the child, and his interpretation influences his coping responses.

Trauma can affect how a boy thinks about himself. Maltreatment interferes with the child's development of a success-based orientation, including the degree of control he perceives regarding his actions (Cicchetti, Toth, & Bush, 1988). The interplay of cognition and dysregulated feelings is likely to be reciprocal. Intense arousal and feeling overwhelmed trigger and reinforce cognitions that the trauma is impossible to manage.

Persistent, intrusive thoughts can also be dysregulating to the traumatized boy; he will tell you that he thinks he's "crazy" or his mind is "racing." Because some cognitive mechanisms are used as coping strategies, helping a boy to think more accurately about the trauma can also be helpful in reducing the overwhelming feelings (Taylor, 1983).

How a boy interprets an abuse experience will vary depending on his age, both at the time of the abuse and currently. Very young children are likely to automatically blame themselves for negative events (reflecting their egocentricity). This will occur and can persist in spite of a therapist's arguments to the contrary.

Jones and Barlow (1990) have proposed a model for the etiology of PTSD that includes perceptions of cognitive control. The development of anxious apprehension (usually correlated with the distorted processing of information paired with strongly negative affect) accounts for the downward spiral of symptomatology associated with PTSD. The individual believes that these events are unpredictable and uncontrollable.

Other cognitive effects of trauma are the problems seen in memory and school performance. Van der Kolk (1994), in a study of complicated PTSD, found incest victims to have less overall autobiographical memory as adults. The information-processing of trauma model of Hartman and Burgess (1993), as well as Crittenden's (1994) linking of memory systems to the degree of maltreatment and the quality of attachment, point to problems with memory in at least some sexual abuse victims. This underscores the need for the clinician to be very sensitive to the literature on how well children recall traumatic events (Ceci & Brunk, 1993; Goodman & Clarke-Stewart, 1991). I will attempt to provide some guidance on this in Chapter 7.

School problems are another issue and harken back to both the language problems mentioned in Chapter 1 and the attentional problems discussed earlier in this chapter. Although boys are usually not studied as a group, school problems are more common in sexually abused children, even when variables such as SES and maternal education are considered (Egeland, 1994; Einbender & Friedrich, 1989; Trickett, McBride-Chang, & Putnam, 1994). Sameroff and his colleagues found a direct relationship between cumulative environmental and family risk factors and a drop in IQ by the age of 4 in a prospective study (Sameroff, Seifer, Barocas, Zax, & Greenspan, 1987).

❏ Assessment of Dysregulation

In a manner similar to the assessment of problems with attachment, the thorough assessment of dysregulation would include the parents and child and use a variety of measures. Support for the assessment of both parents and children in this domain comes from research with mothers of severely maltreated children (Famularo, Fenton, Kinscherff, Ayoub, & Barnum, 1994). These authors found, in a sample of 109 cases, that 15.6% of the mothers currently had PTSD and 36.7% had a past history of PTSD. Posttraumatic stress disorder was also significantly overrepresented in the children of mothers diagnosed with PTSD. Another study, which had the added advantage of repeated measures, found that mothers appeared to be traumatized by the abuse of their children (Newberger et al., 1993). These empirical findings suggest how the dysregulation experience of the child not only reverberates through the family but, in so doing, reduces parental support availability and potential for soothing (i.e., being a secure base) (Everson, Hunter, Runyon, Edelsohn, & Coulter, 1989).

Briefly, parents can be assessed with the Trauma Symptom Checklist–40 (Briere & Runtz, 1989) or the Trauma Symptom Inventory (Briere, 1994). These are trauma-specific measures that assess a number of dysregulation-pertinent domains, including dissociation and PTSD. If you have clear concerns about dissociation in the parent, the Dissociative Experiences Schedule (DES) (Bernstein & Putnam, 1986) appears to be valid (Kihlstrom et al., 1994). Information about life stress in the family can also add to understanding the overall stress in the child's life prior to the abuse. Careful screening of abuse history is relevant as well and overlaps with the assessment specific to attachment.

Assessment of PTSD, dissociation, and sexual concerns can be done with the Trauma Symptom Checklist–Children (Briere, 1989b), a self-report measure we have found useful for ages 7 to 18. With younger children (ages 7 to 10), it can be used as a structured interview. Parental input on sexual behavior and dissociation can be obtained via the Child Sexual Behavior Inventory (CSBI) (Friedrich, Grambsch, et al., 1992) and the Child Dissociation Checklist (Putnam, Helmers, & Trickett, 1993). An adolescent self-report measure of dissociation is the Adolescent–Dissociative Experiences Schedule (A–DES) (Armstrong, Putnam, & Carlson, 1993). A more specific PTSD measure is the Children's Impact of Traumatic Events Scale–Revised (CITES–R) (Wolfe et al., 1991), which we have also found to be clinically useful in monitoring therapy progress and in keeping the therapy abuse-specific.

Because of the broad range of behaviors in the dysregulation domain, a general measure of child behavior problems is useful. The Child Behavior Checklist (CBC) (Achenbach & Edelbrock, 1983), and the accompanying Teacher Report Form (Achenbach & Edelbrock, 1986) have been used most frequently (compared with other measures) to study sexually abused children. Using both the parent and teacher measures allows the clinician to be aware of how generalized the boy's problems are (e.g., at home and at school; behavior, academic, and social relations problems). If the boy is doing better in school than at home, this may say something about the need for structure and support at home. (See Table 6.2 for suggested measures in this domain.)

Table 6.2 Dysregulation-Relevant Assessment Measures

I. Parent-Completed Measures

    A. Generic
        1. Life stress

    B. Abuse-specific
        1. Trauma Symptom Checklist–40 (Briere & Runtz, 1989) or Trauma Symptom Inventory (Briere, 1994)
        2. Dissociative Experiences Schedule (Bernstein & Putnam, 1986)
        3. Lifetime Victimization History

    C. Completed on child
        1. Child Sexual Behavior Inventory (Friedrich, Grambsch, et al., 1992)
        2. Child Dissociation Checklist (Putnam et al., 1993)
        3. Child Behavior Checklist (Achenbach & Edelbrock, 1983)
            a. Sleep problems
            b. Anxiety
            c. Attention problems
            d. Somatic complaints

II. Teacher-Completed Measures

    A. Teacher Report Form (Achenbach & Edelbrock, 1986)

III. Child-Completed Measures

    A. Generic
        1. Child Depression Inventory (Kovacs, 1991)
        2. Trauma Symptom Checklist–Children (Briere, 1989b)
            a. Anxiety
            b. Depression
            c. Anger

    B. Abuse-specific
        1. Trauma Symptom Checklist–Children (Briere, 1989b)
            a. Posttraumatic symptoms
            b. Dissociation
            c. Sexual concerns
        2. Children's Impact of Traumatic Events Schedule–Revised (CITES–R) (Wolfe et al., 1991)
        3. Adolescent–Dissociative Experiences Schedule (Armstrong et al., 1993)

7

Dysregulation: Individual Therapy

The reason for despair was not . . . suffering, but the impossibility of communicating . . . suffering to another person.

—Miller, 1983, p. 255

One of the mental images that comes to mind when I think about some of the sexually abused boys I have seen is of thin-skinned containers, ready to burst. Sometimes I do not get to them until fragments are flying all over the room. This image probably coalesced in my mind after hearing one adolescent tell me that he had tried to die because "I couldn't live in my skin anymore. My skin wasn't big enough." His incredible eloquence gave words to an internal awareness of an exploding self. This is a core aspect of dysregulation.

Another equally valid image is of a walled-off, overcontrolled, highly defended, and unavailable boy. His distress may not be as obvious, but one can bet that he is expending a great deal of energy he does not have in order to maintain these brittle barriers.

The degree to which the boy has problems with dyscontrol will vary with a number of factors, one being the nature of the abuse. Dyscontrol is more likely in cases of frequent, severe abuse of early onset and long duration that carries with it painful aspects (Cicchetti, Ganiban, &

116

Barnett, 1991; Kendall-Tackett et al., 1993). Less severe abuse, or abuse that is part of the child's environment or that has an erotic or loving aspect, seems to create similar levels of confusion but not as much fragmentation and resulting dyscontrol.

The best "holding environment" (Winnicott, 1965) for these thin-skinned, reactive boys is the family. A compassionate, structured response by parents to a boy's distress is tremendously therapeutic, especially if the boy is given the opportunity to verbalize his distress. Not only does it leave him feeling more in control, but his parents' behavior reinforces his belief in the support of those around him.

Individual therapy also has the potential to be helpful, particularly with somewhat older boys who appreciate how they are having problems getting along or when the prospect of family support is lacking. In some ways, individual therapy with sexually abused boys carries with it the potential to either better or worsen the boys' self-regulatory capacities. Self-control strategies often need to be tailor-made, something that is appropriate for individual therapy. Although peer relations may be impaired, group participation can be more disruptive than soothing. Crittenden (1994) even states that for maltreated children, language may either function to increase opportunities for change and self-correction or to reduce the possibility of change. More specific to therapy, these comments suggest that because language and affect go together, too much talk about affect or feelings may not be positive for some children. Again this argues for knowing your patients very well.

Sexually abused children may not automatically associate distress with support. A more common association may be that support brings pain because it is never enough or it is not the right type. Consequently, the therapist must remember that the child does not assume that just because he discloses painful aspects of the abuse, he will then be supported by the therapist and learn to feel more in control. I also believe that for many young children, articulation of abuse and attendant feelings can be developmentally inappropriate. The key issue in these cases is again the provision of benign, attuned support in the context of play (Donovan & McIntyre, 1990).

However, you only have to read some of Gottman's (1994) writings on emotionality and conflict in husbands to realize that individual therapy mimics the high emotional intensity relationship of which males are often avoidant. As a group, feelings are confusing and incite flight-or-fight reactions in boys.

Reactivity is a common phenomenon as well. A brittle, overcontrolled boy who flies off the handle at the slightest provocation or is reduced to tears by a small challenge is very reactive. This aspect of dysregulation pushes the therapist or parent away from the child because they never know what to expect from him. However, their withdrawal only adds to his reactivity. Adding language about feelings to this boy's therapy may be less successful than adding language about self-control.

This underscores the need for structure and predictability in the therapy process. When structure is provided, regression or decompensation can be prevented. Structure can help to titrate the intensity of the individual therapy relationship. Unless structure and predictability are present, the therapist may be equated with distress and consequently viewed as negative and abusive.

❑ Techniques

I appreciate that good therapy is never a collection of techniques. Listed below are processes and broad strategies that should be extensions of a working alliance that is respectful of the child's developmental level. See Table 7.1 for a summary.

EXPLAIN THE TREATMENT PROCESS

Sometimes we do not realize that children are naive to the therapy process and are not familiar with it in the way that we are. They do not know what is expected of them, and a fair amount of anxiety can be generated simply because of this ambiguity. Preparing the child for therapy and explaining to him his role as a client and your role as a therapist can be an important first step in providing the structure necessary to the treatment process. Therapy preparation has a long history in being very useful to increasing the amount of self-disclosure (Day & Reznikoff, 1980). The more rapidly the boy can understand what is expected of him, the more he can collaborate with you.

Table 7.1 Techniques

1. Explain the process of therapy in order to reduce a child's anxiety

2. Establish specific goals so that structure is inherent in the therapy process

3. Modulate the intensity of treatment by taking steps to concretely structure the session or indicate safety

4. Teach the child self-soothing techniques, including relaxation and self-hypnosis

5. Use imagery and hypnotherapeutic strategies to manage problems of dysregulation

6. Use psychoeducational approaches, including written exercises or role plays, to provide words to the child for his or her distress so that the vague feelings can become labeled and integrated

7. Employ "as if" treatment

8. Use cognitive-behavioral strategies to assist the child in reducing anxiety

9. Attend to sexual behaviors, thoughts, and feelings

Part of most therapy will be disclosure of trauma. The boy should be informed that the disclosure can be something that is measured and scheduled. A child can be allowed to formally schedule when and how he wants to talk about his victimization experiences. The therapist and the child may also develop a word or phrase for the abuse that makes it easier to discuss. This can reduce anxiety and give the boy an even greater sense of accomplishment once he has completed that process. The boy may also be given a number of options he can use in order to disclose in treatment, including play, drawing, talking, and movement. Issues of confidentiality and who will hear the disclosures, as well as your role with the disclosures, are very important. This may also be when you discuss with the child issues of safety, aggression, and physical contact in therapy sessions. Written agreements about disclosures, safety, and touch can be very comforting to the child, who will need repeated exposure to incorporate all that is expected of him in the treatment room.

Because of increasing concerns regarding the effects of repeated questioning about the traumatic events, therapists should be judicious (Ceci & Brunk, 1993). You want to put the issue on the table and, if affect can be related back to the trauma, a partial disclosure may be sufficient.

ESTABLISH SPECIFIC GOALS

Goal setting is useful both in family and individual therapy. For latency-aged children, goal setting does not have to be as formal as the goal attainment scaling discussed in Chapter 5. In addition, I almost never establish goals with preschoolers. However, the establishment of certain goals, particularly goals pertinent to self-regulation, can also be a way to keep the child focused on the therapy. Goals also provide the necessary structure and predictability that add to a sense of calmness in the boy. These are goals that can be brought out in each session. With some regularity, they may be shared with the parent, so that a partnership is fostered. This is best done with parents who can be counted on to assist the boy in focusing on the goals. Achieving different goals also provides the child with an opportunity for a sense of mastery.

Examples of dysregulation goals that I have set with boys include the following: using soothing strategies at bedtime; exercising self-control in difficult situations; using relaxation when they sense anxiety during the day; writing down confusing thoughts and feelings; self-monitoring; reducing the frequency of masturbation; and choosing more carefully when to talk about personal topics.

MODULATE TREATMENT INTENSITY

The therapist's intuition comes into play here as you determine when the child is becoming overwhelmed and curtail his rising distress. Children can be taught how to signal the therapist that they are becoming distressed, although that is a strategy that has selective utility.

I believe that increasing distress arises when affective or behavioral arousal is divorced from words that can be soothing or moderating. As the therapist notices the boy's increasing agitation or activity, adding language to the feelings or the distress can be a way to help the boys link the stress with words; this then fosters integration as opposed to further fragmentation. Again, this needs to be done with some judiciousness. Simply announcing to the boy that he appears distressed is not likely to be helpful. Resistant or avoidantly attached boys are likely to view that as punitive. Usually it is important to begin with third-person types of interpretations (Brady & Friedrich, 1982). For example, the boy may be asked to help you learn what boys do to let people know they are upset. If this can be tolerated, you can talk about previous times when he was upset and how he communicated it at that time. Words may not be the key for some boys, but simple visual language (drawing) of the behavior or the stress they are feeling can serve to moderate it. Drawing the boy's feelings or discussing his urge to run away from the room at the time of the distress can be other useful strategies.

The trauma interview I described (Friedrich, 1990) that uses drawings extensively can be incorporated at this point. It is borrowed from Eth & Pynoos (1985) and has three stages: establishing a framework for the child to draw what happened; promoting a full description (in words) of the experience; and helping the child to gain some closure on the event (e.g., compliment the child, help him realize positives he has learned about himself).

With highly reactive boys, it is also possible for the therapist to predictably partition the session into working portions and a play portion. This reflects the "rule of thirds" mentioned by Herman (1992). The child is provided with an agreed-on amount of time to first touch base, then work on issues, and finally to be less threatened and more in control. By a "work portion," I do not necessarily mean that you and the boy are exclusively trying to do more traditional, verbal psychotherapy. For a young boy, playing with figures in a dollhouse and communicating to you what goes on there is clearly work. For him, a clean break from that might be needed if he is becoming overwhelmed. A part of the "play portion" can be placed at the end of the session to give the child a chance to reorganize.

If the boy regularly engages in some of the stereotypic, routinized play sometimes seen with severe trauma, it is not helpful for him to continue to repeat this, session after session. Even if he reenacts it with lots of force and action, it still is not therapeutic. It reflects an encapsulated experience that is unaltered and needs to be altered in some way for it to be useful to him.

One 6-year-old boy, Frank, would routinely (two to three times per session) re-create a scene in which his mother was battered. Furniture would be carefully put into place, then predictably turned over, complete with grunts and other sound effects. My biggest concern was that this boy was also directing his anger at his mother at home, wearing her down further. My efforts to interrupt and alter his play were helpful only when I worked to make it less automatic by both predicting what would come next, complete with drawings and steps written on the blackboard, and when I paralleled him, with similar furniture, at my desk next to the dollhouse. Then he could talk about his terror and his stupid mom, decide he was also angry at his dad, and decide whether he would be Frank, Sr. or Frank, Jr. in his behavior with his mother.

TEACH SELF-CONTROL STRATEGIES

Relaxation training and learning self-hypnosis are often underused or simply dropped into the treatment mix in the therapy of sexually abused children. For these techniques to be useful, the child needs to know how to use them and have some opportunity to practice them with a supportive adult. This also facilitates the boy generalizing the use of these self-control and self-soothing techniques to other settings in addition to the treatment room. This is where goal setting can be useful. Once the boy has learned some self-control techniques, helping him to identify situations in which he can use these strategies and then having him agree to use them at a certain frequency is a very appropriate treatment goal. An excellent resource for anxiety-management techniques with children is available (Morris & Kractochwill, 1983).

USE IMAGERY AND HYPNOTHERAPEUTIC STRATEGIES

Rather than the progressive muscle relaxation that is most often taught to adults, some combination of imagery and rapid tightening and releasing of different extremities can help the boy calm himself. Imagery that is used for relaxation can be incorporated into hypnotic strategies as well. Hypnotherapy is one of the most important skills a therapist can learn. Not only does it model a style of attuned relating, it is ideal for problems with dysregulation.

The attuned-relating component is manifested in several features of hypnotherapy. The therapist must learn the language of the client.

The use of mirroring and pacing during the trance is part of good parenting (Friedrich, 1990). In order to be maximally effective, the therapist must be a very good observer of subtle shifts in posture, breathing, and muscle movement. Finally, hypnotic states mimic a naturally occurring dissociative state, this time one the boy is learning how to do voluntarily, not involuntarily.

Hypnotherapy is also helpful with a broad range of problems of dysregulation. Hypnotherapy, as well as relaxation or imagery (which I view as only minimally distinguishable from hypnotherapy), can greatly assist in the anxiety-driven hypervigilance that makes it difficult for boys to go to sleep and pay attention in class. Elsewhere, I have described strategies for hypnotherapeutic management of secondary enuresis and encopresis (Friedrich, 1990). More unusual sequelae, including compulsions, panic, phobias, and conversion disorders can be managed either hypnotherapeutically or via hypnosis-assisted cognitive behavior therapy.

In addition, I have used hypnosis to modulate the intensity of different aspects of PTSD. Although the management of intrusive thoughts might be readily apparent to the reader (e.g., hypnosis-created early warning systems), hypnosis can assist in managing both numbing/constriction as well as avoidance. Even the descriptive word, "intrusive," adds to our sense that flashbacks are traumatic, in and of themselves. However, there are clinicians who think about flashbacks in a more positive way (Briere, 1989a, 1992). Each flashback can be constructed as an opportunity for the boys to learn more about the trauma or to identify positive features in themselves as they coped with the trauma.

Initially, my approach to flashbacks was to help the boy create barriers or layers of protection. This is a type of externalizing process (White, 1989). Another technique that helps reduce the intensity of the thought is the use of an imaginary dimmer switch or a rheostat, through which the boy can learn how to "turn down" the intensity and frequency. Adults in the boy's life can be coached to encourage him to use the strategy at those times.

Barriers and protection can be helpful, but you are modeling reactivity rather than behaving in a proactive manner. Now, I find it more useful to mix a combination of protective images with suggestions regarding new learning from the flashbacks.

An example can be useful in describing this strategy. This is with Garth, a 10-year-old boy whose very appearance was of a boy being constantly bombarded by intrusions. He winced involuntarily, compulsively wiped his hand across his mouth, and had an exaggerated startle response that made him an increasing target for ridicule by classmates. His mother said that before the abuse (which was two forced instances of oral copulation with a same-aged peer and the teenage perpetrator, Harlan) he had gotten along well with friends and had none of the hyperarousal now evident. Garth also loved to draw, suggesting some visual potential that could be tapped in the hypnosis. He was in a trance during this following segment, and the induction had Garth recalling a pleasant visit to his grandparents' farm.

Therapist One of the things that happens when bad things are done to kids, and you know what I'm talking about, is that we don't want to remember the bad. But it keeps exploding (Garth's word) in our minds, and we wince, and our muscles get tight, and we try to wipe away the feelings, and we hope another one isn't coming too soon. Isn't that right?

Garth Uh huh.

Therapist We spend so much time trying to protect ourself from these explosions we don't see how brave you were during all this. How even though Harlan was trying to trick you, you were still able to trick him. Isn't that right?

Garth Uh huh.

Therapist The easiest one is that he thought he had tricked you into not telling, but you tricked him, didn't you?

Garth Uh huh. (Smiling)

Therapist That's right. You told your mom. Boy was he tricked. I want Garth to hold on to that picture of you tricking Harlan for a bit. How good it felt to know your mom was going to help and it didn't feel so lonely. Isn't that right?

Garth Uh huh.

Therapist We can find other ways you tricked him too, can't we?

Garth Uh huh.

Therapist To do so, we need to get just a piece of one of those explosions, not the whole one, but just a piece. A piece of it that shows you tricking Harlan. Can you let a tiny glimpse come to your mind?

Garth   Uh huh.

Therapist   Hold a piece that shows you tricking him. How you didn't swallow it all like he wanted you to.

Garth   I didn't.

Therapist   Exactly. You tricked him. And how you didn't like it, even though he said you would.

Garth   I didn't.

Therapist   Exactly. More tricking. You are one tricky dude. See what you can learn from watching the explosion carefully? That's what's nice about relaxing like this. The explosions aren't as bad because you can see how much you tricked Harlan.

Garth   (Nodding his head).

Therapist   In fact, wouldn't it be cool if we could watch each explosion, pick out the good parts about you being tricky, and then getting rid of the rest?

Garth   Uh huh.

Therapist   This next week, I think you will find it easier and easier to stare those explosions in the face, see only the new stuff you need to know, and then you'll have to wipe away the feelings less and less. That sounds like something that could work, doesn't it?

Garth   Uh huh.

Through continued use of imagery and self-monitoring, Garth and his mother reported a complete stop in mouth-wiping 10 days later, and only rare intrusions 3 weeks later. I'm sure as well that the presence of a supportive mother aided the entire process immensely.

For younger children, or for children who are quite depleted, the provision of a tape recording that contains a hypnotic induction as well as some soothing messages can be very helpful. Not only does it give the child a specific model to follow, but your voice and the tape recordings become transitional objects (Winnicott, 1965). As such, they add to the child's sense of connection to you and support by you.

PSYCHOEDUCATIONAL APPROACHES

Therapy can sometimes be psychoeducational and involve the use of didactic information about safety and sexual education. Psychoeducational techniques tend to be less dysregulating and may be more useful with extremely reactive children. A variety of these techniques, useful for both genders, are described by Mandel and Damon (1989). For example, a child can learn about abuse dynamics, how to talk about a wide range of feelings and how to recognize them, and about some of the ways that feelings get distorted or displayed through the use of written exercises or role plays that occur in the sessions. One component of their utility is to give the child a language to use with you and his parents, particularly if the parents are simultaneously involved in parallel group treatment as suggested by Mandell and Damon (1989).

"AS IF" TREATMENT

Other therapists have talked about "as if" approaches to therapy (Johnson, 1991). The child may never directly acknowledge having been molested, in spite of evidence to the contrary. In this case, he is encouraged to talk to the therapist as if he had been molested or to give the therapist advice for working with a same-aged child who had a similar abuse experience. In some ways this is similar to the use of third-person interventions discussed earlier (Brady & Friedrich, 1982). This particular technique underscores the need for the child to be given some element of control in the therapy.

COGNITIVE-BEHAVIORAL INTERVENTIONS

There are a number of excellent books that have been written regarding cognitive-behavioral approaches and self-control strategies (Kendall & Braswell, 1985). Cognitive-behavioral therapy is the area of therapy that provides some of the best validated treatment techniques available generally (Meichenbaum, 1977) and for sexually abused children (Deblinger et al., 1990; Mannarino & Cohen, 1994). These include anxiety reduction techniques, such as relaxation training and self-hypnosis instruction. In addition, children can be assisted in developing a repertoire of strategies (ranging from thought stopping to anxiety management) that are useful in a variety of settings.

Take, for example, panic. The boy has learned to associate intrusive thoughts and the emergence of increased anxiety. The first strategy, monitoring, would be to help him identify that these intense, overwhelming feelings are not occurring all the time, but rather occur at logical times and during predictable situations. The fact that they occur at bedtime can be linked to this being the time when he was victimized. Learn how to enhance his observing self with these thoughts. You might ask him whether or not the intrusions mean that he is being revictimized. He is allowed to check again that he is safe, and he can provide himself with some reassurances.

The boy can also be taught some thought-stopping techniques that interfere with the panic or the intrusive thoughts. He can learn to use distraction, talking to a parent, or other strategies that could be helpful in interrupting the panic or PTSD cycle.

Lipovsky (1992) wrote an excellent synopsis of cognitive-behavioral approaches for child survivors of sexual assault. Abuse-focused therapy provides an excellent context for the use of cognitive therapeutic interventions. Cognitive therapy can be designed to provide boys with additional coping techniques to deal with distress, correct their irrational thinking, and clarify the basis of beliefs they have regarding the meaning of abuse and their role in the victimization. The primary techniques used include thought stopping, guided self-dialogue, and cognitive restructuring. Thought stopping is specifically designed to correct ruminative and intrusive thinking. The therapist practices with the child so that he learns how to stop his persistent thinking in the session.

It is helpful for therapists to have a number of stock questions about intrusive thoughts and avoidance. This will enable them to aid the boys to open up about these aspects of PTSD and, in turn, give the boys the sense that the therapists "know what they are talking about." Examples of questions can be derived from the CITES–R (Wolfe et al., 1991) and the TSC–C (Briere, 1989b). Some stock questions relevant to avoidance include, "Do you try to stay away from things that remind you of what happened?" and "Do you sometimes have trouble remembering what happened during the sexual abuse?" Suggested questions relevant to intrusion are "Do you ever have trouble falling asleep because pictures or thoughts of what happened keep popping into your head?" "Do you have dreams or nightmares about what happened?" and "Do you ever think about what happened, even when you don't want to?"

For example, the following dialogue with John, who is 9 years old, captures some initial questioning around intrusive thoughts.

Therapist Are you ever just sitting there, minding your own business, and scary pictures pop into your head?

Boy (Begins to shake his head "No" and then says) Yes.

Therapist Those scary pictures are hard to talk about (picking up on the boy's initial reluctance).

Boy Yes.

Therapist Can you tell me what they look like? The scary pictures?

Boy (Pause) No.

Therapist You don't even want to think about them long enough to tell me what they look like?

Boy I don't even want to think about them.

Therapist What do you think would happen if you drove by your father's house? To the pictures?

Boy Sometimes I drive in the car with my mom and I keep looking at my shoes so I don't see him.

Therapist So you have tried all kinds of ways to keep those pictures from popping into your mind or being reminded of your dad?

Boy I don't even want to think about it.

Therapist Well, you've already told me a lot by telling me that bad thoughts about your dad pop into your mind and you work hard at keeping them out. I want to thank you for that. It gives me an idea about what you have to deal with.

Boy They're not only about my dad.

Therapist Some are about your dad, and some are probably about other scary things.

Boy Sometimes I remember my dad hitting my mom.

Therapist That's a scary thought that you can talk about. One that keeps popping into your mind.

Boy One time he hit her so hard that he made her bleed. Her mouth. Her tooth was loose.

Therapist (Noting the boy's looking away from him) You can even see that picture right now.

Boy (Nodding his head, "Yes.")

Therapist It would help me if we could work together to figure out all the different kinds of pictures that pop in your mind. Could we do that?

Boy (Nodding his head, "Yes.")

Therapist One of the pictures is your dad hitting your mom, is that right?

Boy Yes.

Therapist Another picture is of your dad.

Boy (Nodding his head, "Yes.")
Therapist Can you tell me what he is doing in the picture?
Boy No.
Therapist How about if I ask you a question and you say yes or no
if I am right or wrong?
Boy Okay.
Therapist You get pictures sometimes of your dad touching your bottom.
Boy: More than touching my bottom.
Therapist Even worse than touching your bottom.

This dialogue continued until John was able to identify that he has intrusive thoughts in four different domains, including his father hitting his mother, being sodomized, thinking about his teacher yelling at him, and thinking about the big dog that lived in his neighborhood. In fact, careful interviewing around PTSD issues frequently will reveal a range of intrusive elements. It is as if the boy is made more vulnerable to intrusive thoughts and avoidant behavior by having more than one trauma.

The remainder of the session with John focused on helping him identify his needs regarding the intrusive thoughts. With some children, I try to prevent any thoughts from coming in, to give them some respite and to ease their sleeping difficulties. With other children, I do not want to take the thoughts away, nor will the child let me. What I do want to do is to make the image more dim, farther away or less frequent, and occurring only at times that the boy chooses.

Guided self-dialogue helps the therapist learn about the child's self-talk, which can be negative, anxiety arousing, and can even foster avoidant behavior. Negative thoughts about the boy's inability to manage abuse-related feelings can be challenged within the session, and the boy can be given an opportunity to practice outside the session with support by caregivers. Cognitive restructuring will be described in more detail in Chapter 11.

SEXUAL BEHAVIOR PROBLEMS

These symptoms are another reflection of dyscontrol. They, along with PTSD, constitute the two most commonly identified sexual abuse sequelae in preadolescent victims of sexual abuse (Kendall-Tackett et al., 1993). Sexual behavior problems are preferably dealt with in the family context (described in Chapter 9). However, that is not always feasible, and, in addition, there are links between thoughts, feelings, and actions that can be solidified in individual therapy.

It is very important to have information about the boy's sexual behavior. A neglectful, embarrassed, or nonobservant parent may tell you that there are no problems in this area, but, on the CSBI (Friedrich et al., 1992), the parent may endorse a number of items when they are spelled out in more precision. (The latest version of the CSBI is available in Appendix A.)

The most reliable index of sexual problems would be the boy's sexual behavior, usually self-stimulating behavior. Rarely will you get far unless some specific behaviors are evident. However, if you have an opening with the boy, do not be afraid to ask about sexual thoughts, fantasies, where and when he gets erections, and who he has thought about peeping on. I try to matter-of-factly educate the boy on how being sexually abused affects his thinking and feelings in a number of areas and to use that as a basis for a thorough interview.

If sexual behaviors or thoughts and arousal are described, a cognitive-behavioral approach is the most useful. You begin by helping the boy identify when it happens and his attendant feelings. Usually such feelings fall into one or more of three categories: violence, sexuality, and loneliness. In the case of persistent sexual thoughts and behaviors, helping the boy to interrupt these sequences is quite important. Response-prevention is also useful and may require some external contingencies. Most boys feel validated and normalized by this process. By talking frankly to them, they realize you know them and can help them.

With severely abused boys who have persisting sexual behavior problems, external controls are absolutely necessary, as is an examination of deviant arousal patterns. I have worked with several boys (ages 10 years and under) who were regularly penetrating themselves anally, masturbating to violent fantasies, injuring their genitals, and behaving sexually with other children and animals, and all this was occurring without awareness by caregivers. For some boys, it will be very critical for you to help them monitor sexual urges on a weekly basis, to help them learn how those thoughts and urges emerged and how they will continue to come around if they are reinforced, and then to help them to extinguish these thoughts. This again requires changes in the contexts (e.g., monitoring TV shows, removing pornography, eliminating parental nudity and cosleeping) (Johnson & Berry, 1989).

❏ Conclusions

It is important that the therapy become a reliable, predictable, and safe process for the child. This can prevent "spillover" from the therapy to the home and school situations. Emotional contagion results in the child being ostracized by peers or rejected further by parents. Other elements of the therapy process that can be difficult for the child to manage include the gender of the therapist (particularly when the therapist is the same sex as the child's perpetrator). However, at this time, there is nothing in the literature that would support any particular therapist-child gender match.

8

Dysregulation: Group Therapy

I knew how to make myself invisible.

—Rhodes, 1990, p. 160

A paper I coauthored with three good friends—Lucy Berliner, Anthony Urquiza, and Robert Beilke—on short-term group treatment of boys has generated as many comments and letters from colleagues as anything else I have written (Friedrich, Berliner, Urquiza, & Beilke, 1988). The reason seems to be that we were very frank about several brief, boys groups that we co-led. The boys were active, intense, sexualized, and easily provoked. We witnessed outbursts of acting out (i.e., aggression) and acting in (i.e., suicidality). We were over-whelmed, highly reactive, and drained by the end of each group. The boys' parents and foster parents were often upset with us because we failed to calm down the boys sufficiently and the aftereffects of the group session would linger for another day or so.

I was profoundly affected by those early experiences. I had not pre-dicted the outcome, even though I had worked with many boy victims and adolescent perpetrators. I was groped, grabbed, poked, and clung to in ways that seemed incredible. I know that boys groups can work, and another friend, Carolyn Cunningham, has told me several times she enjoys the boys groups she leads (Cunningham & MacFarlane, 1990) as much as any of her other clinical activities. I have also led boys groups that have seemed to be powerfully effective. But I know that my use of pair therapy (described in Chapter 12) would not have occurred as soon if I had not seen the dyscontrol generated by a group.

The focus of this chapter is how to therapeutically use the energy, anxiety, and even panic and fear that can be generated in a boys group. I am not in favor of strictures or simply tightening the reins. I prefer to planfully approach each group as unique, prepared for all eventualities but flexible enough to allow the energy to emerge and drive the therapy along.

The approaches and techniques I will describe flow from my belief that language is a powerful moderator of overwhelming thoughts and feelings, that structure can be a very important source of safety and comfort, that the therapist must be several steps ahead of the process, and that careful screening and group preparation are critical to the success of any group. Given the focus on language and feelings identification, along with the child being capable of observing himself, it is difficult to recommend group approaches for children younger than early school-age. The necessary capabilities are simply not available to these youngsters, even if they were not maltreated (Donovan & McIntyre, 1990).

My initial comments have emphasized precautions about the dysregulating effects of group therapy for boys. However, there are reasons why individual therapy is also dysregulating (Porter, 1986). These include the fact that individual therapy involves one-on-one discussions of sexuality with an adult who keeps the material a secret and a possible, implicit expectation regarding sexual favors even if therapy guidelines have been stated and restated.

Because we are talking about dysregulation, it is crucial also to think about the boy's "holding environment" (Winnicott, 1965) during the course of the group. It is essential that a caregiving system be in place for each group member (Pescosolido, 1993). Parent figures who are not capable of understanding their son's distress, or who misinterpret the boy's heightened reactivity in a negative way, essentially eliminate the largest potential of the group. Even a capable foster parent of a boy whose natural parents are continuing to deny the abuse is likely to be put through the wringer while the boy is in group.

Attention must also be paid to group membership. There are as many boys inappropriate for group as are appropriate. Easily ostracized, highly reactive boys, in situations without a cotherapist, will not benefit. Even with cotherapists, boys who are significantly deviant from the others in terms of victimization experience and life circumstances should be carefully screened. Remember, universality is a key group ingredient that is not activated with too much heterogeneity.

In addition, do not expect that a victim-focused group will be sufficient for boys who have also been sexually aggressive. Just because we are putting boys together and having them talk about feelings and learn some canned phrases does not mean therapeutic change is occurring. Group work is powerful, but it takes some work to pull off.

❏ Techniques

A rather elegant format for considering the targets of group therapy is one by Pescosolido (1993). He outlines two broad areas of impact: victimization dynamics and posttraumatic stress. A total of 10 impact-specific dynamics are identified for these two areas of impact, and 8 of these are relevant to the concept of dysregulation. These include: victim/victimizer identity struggle; accelerated sexual arousal; body conflict; psychophysiological dysregulation; postsexual abuse reenactment potential; postsexual abuse triggers; intrusion; and numbing. The victim/victimizer identity struggle and the postsexual abuse reenactment potential are virtually the same. Pescosolido has outlined techniques and strategies for each of these areas. His model certainly warrants an independent reading, although some of his strategies will be incorporated into this chapter. Another excellent paper is one by Scott (1992). His three-part model for issues of dyscontrol also subsumes many of the issues identified by Pescosolido. A summary of suggested techniques is included in Table 8.1.

Table 8.1 Techniques

---

1. Create safety

2. Reduce arousal/agitation

3. Practice boundary work

4. Interrupt victim/victimizer dynamics

CREATION OF SAFETY

It is to be expected that safety issues will be important in any group with sexually abused boys. Therapists who work with boy victims should accept that as a given. It is important for the therapist not to become overly agitated or alarmed about boys who are behaving in less mature and overly aroused ways. A therapist who understands that this is a given with boys groups will be a calmer therapist; this, in turn, will help to reduce the overall anxiety in the group.

A strategy that is often used to reduce the overall agitation is to resort to a period of physical activity. Some therapists start off the group with intense, sports-related activities. Although we can say that the physical activity is designed to develop cooperation and sharing in the boys, a more realistic and pragmatic interpretation is that if they are tired out, we will see less agitation.

Although I eschew the establishment of rules in my individual work with boys, it is paramount that the group have clearly established rules from the very beginning. These include rules regarding confidentiality, safety, aggression, and physical contact. Not only should these be announced in the first several group sessions, they should be written on a blackboard so that they are constantly evident in the room.

In addition to establishing rules, the early implementation of a point system, particularly for the age range of 6 to 12 years, is very critical to the success of the group. A point system will affect the ease of managing the group and making it more therapeutic. Generally, point systems work best when points are given out liberally, no fines are given, and the group is encouraged to work together for a group prize (e.g., a snack at the end of group or having pizza delivered). A suggestion about point systems would be to list every boy's name on another sheet of blackboard with a space behind each name for handing out points using a rubber stamp or stickers. Early on in the group, in order to shape group cohesiveness and adherence to rules, the boys should earn points for listening, sitting still, sharing, picking up after themselves, and so on.

Because we are working with sexually abused boys, each boy should have the opportunity to tell his story. One of the cotherapists can serve as a recorder, and the boys can use designated times to share their story. Props may be imported into the room for ease of storytelling. Precautions should be made so that each boy's story does not contaminate another boy's story. The group should also be helped to discuss ahead of time how each boy wants the other boys to respond to him as they are talking about painful and embarrassing situations. You can help the group arrive at a consensus about socially appropriate responding to the stories. This consensus should be listed for the boys to have in front of them during the telling of the stories.

REDUCING AROUSAL/AGITATION

There are an increasing number of psychoeducational materials that are useful in group work with children (Mandel & Damon, 1989). I do not believe that a purely psychoeducational group is very useful to severely abused children, but I do believe that it provides an inherent structure that makes the group more familiar to the boy.

Relaxation strategies, including deep breathing and progressive relaxation, can be taught in a group therapy context. I do believe that they are most useful and generalizable if they are taught to older boys and adolescents. Precautions should be taken so that training in relaxation and deep breathing do not become threatening to the boys. However, if this happens, the therapist should be aware that it is not an atypical occurrence (Friedrich, Berliner, et al., 1988). In addition to more structured training in relaxation, the group can also generate lists of self-soothing activities. Older children can set goals with each other and with the group therapist to use some of the relaxation strategies outside of the group.

Two of the symptoms of PTSD, intrusiveness and numbing, are also appropriate group issues. Each of them lend themselves to the use of drawings as well as to role play and psychodrama. Intrusive thoughts are difficult to talk about, and the use of drawings can be a way for the boys to share with the remaining group members what the thoughts look/feel like and other features about them. Boys should be encouraged to draw pictures of how they feel at the time of the intrusive thought and where they might be when these thoughts are most likely to come into their minds.

With regard to numbing, I admit that I was initially surprised by the number of boys who described feelings of being numb or detached from their body and feelings of unreality. Through guided group discussion, these boys can talk about times when they feel more or less numb. Pescosolido (1993) describes techniques, including playing statutes and pretending to be an ice cube melting, as psychomotor strategies for helping the boys to articulate these feelings.

Arousal and agitation in a boy usually reflects some quality of feeling cut off from awareness or articulation. This would suggest how important it is for the boy to "bring his body into the group session." These strategies are also useful with regard to boundary making. As a way to help the boys talk about anxiety and agitation, they can be instructed to draw a picture of themselves and to indicate, using different colors, what parts of them are worried, sad, angry, and numb.

PRACTICING BOUNDARY WORK

Boundary work is another key element in group work with boys and is, in actuality, one of the most pressing rationales for group work with sexual abuse victims. It is ill-advised to practice boundary work within the context of individual therapy given issues of transference and countertransference. However, a group of similarly aged peers is ideal. Whether or not boundary activities become generalizable to the home setting is another question and clearly one in need of empirical validation.

Too often in these groups, particularly given the emphasis on safety, there may need to be exercises that cover the broad range of boundary issues. For example, it can be useful, in small doses, to create situations in the room in which boys are being intrusive with each other and then having to back off. These situations can take the form of interrupting while another person is talking, standing too close, standing too far away, and so on. You create more room for change if the full panoply of behaviors is out in the open.

A number of individuals who write about group work with boys describe strategies by which boundaries are constructed. Sometimes this can be through the use of masking tape (where areas on the floor are marked off). Other times boundaries are literally constructed through the use of cardboard, paper, cloth, and so on. Once these boundaries are constructed, the boys can be encouraged to talk about the boundaries, their roles and functions in their life, the times when boundaries were violated, and the resultant feelings.

One strategy that also involves boundary maintenance is a "soap bubble" technique. Boys have the opportunity early on in the session to make soap bubbles. They then borrow from that play to act as if they were soap bubbles, working hard to maintain an appropriate distance so that no one gets "popped."

It is also important, and this goes along with safety, that boundaries be available within the room. Boys should have permission to sit under their chair if the content of the group becomes too difficult or threatening. You may need to create a safe place within the room to which a boy can retreat. Sometimes, in fact, it is useful to allow boys to keep their coats on during the group. This strategy actually arose because of a boy who would never take his coat off in a group. As a way to reframe his behavior, I suggested that he was feeling the need to stay safe in the room, and this then gave permission to other boys to use the same strategy.

INTERRUPTING VICTIM/VICTIMIZER DYNAMICS

Larson and Maddock (1986) discuss an important dynamic that should be considered in all group work with sexually abused boys. That is the notion of a victim/victimizer potential. Essentially, both of these aspects are contained within the same individual. Boys will vary in terms of the degree to which their upbringing and abuse renders them more of a potential victim or victimizer. This should be a given in each group and certainly a topic of conversation in group discussion.

To further the discussion of this victim/victimizer dynamic, boys can be encouraged to draw and then discuss different feelings. These would include feelings of big, little, scared, strong, weak, being mean to others, and being mean to self. In addition to discussion, through the use of role play and psychodrama these feelings could then be demonstrated along with their consequences.

Guided group discussion of the boys' behaviors when they feel mean or when they feel scared can also elicit these dynamics. The group can be encouraged to come up with a listing of how each boy behaves when he feels weak and how he behaves when he feels strong. Role playing the feelings can add to the learning.

Although this will be discussed in more detail in chapters pertaining to issues of self and the internalized parts model (Schwartz, 1987) it can be used here quite effectively. Using the cotherapists as models, each can discuss different aspects of themselves, including strong, weak, scared, competent, less competent, and so on. To make it more pertinent to the group, they can then talk about times when they feel vindicative and times when they feel as though other people are intruding on them. This can then be translated so that the group members identify different parts of themselves that are helpful and harmful. Through the use of different vignettes that are presented by the cotherapists, the boys can react either in a victimizing or victim manner.

The four broad areas that are subsumed under the techniques described earlier are specifically designed to address issues of dysregulation. To begin to master some of these issues, it is easy to see that brief, primarily psychoeducational groups are not as comprehensive as need be. However, when implemented successfully, the strategies carry with them a tremendous amount of potential for change.

9

Dysregulation: Family Therapy

The boy has no boundaries . . . no skin.

—Caddy, 1989, p. 110

Given what I have already mentioned regarding internal working models and how they emerge as a function of parent-child attachment, the family is certainly a critical arena in which the sexually abused boy has learned dysregulation. Hopefully, the family can learn how to provide some self-regulation. How are those changes made? My basic premise is that if the parents feel anxious by the therapy process, are dealing with their own unresolved abuse, or continue to be upsetting to the boy at home, the boy will continue to experience greater and greater problems with self-control.

Parents can continue to upset or dysregulate their son in a variety of ways. The obvious ones are the intrusive and coercive strategies that create distress in most people: Yelling, hitting, and threatening the child with rejection or punishment are clear examples of this variety. Behaving inconsistently is also a key feature.

However, distress can also be generated by the avoidant, aloof, and dismissive behaviors exhibited by some parents. There may be no internal difference between two boys: one whose thoughts are racing because his father just slapped his mother, and another who lies awake, fearful of intrusive thoughts once he falls asleep, but is unable to ask for the comforting presence of a parent. It is almost impossible to feel out of control in the supportive "container" of a family or the "holding environment" (Winnicott, 1965).

Broadly speaking, family-based treatment must have as a goal the reduction of a range of distress and anxiety in the home. Anxiety reduction happens to be a basic premise to the family therapy approach promulgated by Murray Bowen (Bowen, 1978). He discussed the transfer of anxiety among family members, a phenomenon I see in families of sexually abused children, and described this anxiety transfer process as mobile, fluid, and pervasive. It is activated when a parent becomes anxious and then focuses on a problem in the child. Bowen described a literal transfer in which the parents' anxiety would then be reduced, whereas the child's anxiety would increase. In fact, he stated "there was a quality about this that suggested almost a quantitative transfer of anxiety" (Bowen, 1978, p. 7). In his book on psychosomatic families, Minuchin and his colleagues described the rise in anxiety in the child with brittle diabetes as his parents began to argue (Minuchin, Rosman, & Baker, 1978). In enmeshed families, the parents' anxiety went down while the child's went up. These theorists seem to be saying that the greater the differentiation of self in the various family members, the less likely it is that they would be influenced by the anxiety in the other person.

In many cases, we are speaking of more than just simple anxiety. The physiological and cognitive arousal that is associated with posttraumatic stress disorder can leave parents and children feeling constantly activated and can thus result in increased hypervigilance. Chronic states of arousal may lead to oversensitivity and even suspiciousness. Given these circumstances, how can a child learn to be self-soothing, be able to fall asleep at night, or focus on his school work? Individual efforts at helping the child learn self-control absolutely need a significant, family component.

Table 9.1 Techniques

1. Create safety

2. Reduce overstimulation and sexualized behavior

3. Psychoeducational/behavioral family therapy

4. Use of family rituals

5. Family members as PTSD triggers

6. Goal setting

❏ Techniques

In this next section, I will discuss a number of generalized processes that can be useful in reducing the dysregulatory experience in families of sexually abused boys. These broad strategies are not meant to be exhaustive but rather present a range of options that can guide your family-based treatment. These options are briefly summarized in Table 9.1.

CREATING SAFETY

Creating a sense of self-control in a child will be directly related to creating safety in the family. Safety from further victimization has to be a starting point in working with sexually abusive families (Trepper & Barrett, 1989). The boy will perceive his family to be unsafe for a number of reasons. They include:

1. Lack of permission to disclose abuse
2. Threat of recrimination for disclosure
3. Threat of subsequent abuse
4. Family behavior reminiscent of the child's victimization

Trauma-organized systems are action-systems (Bentovim, 1992). The families of sexually abused children do not give much credence either to words or to the accuracy of words. Consequently, the family therapists working with sexually abused children and their families find themselves supplying words for previously unprocessed actions. Included in these actions are covert and more overt signals that indicate the absence of permission for the child to talk about his victimization. To the boy in this system, it will feel as if the abuse is ongoing. It cannot be talked about, so it has not stopped.

Examples of this include chronically psychologically unavailable parents; parents who withdraw their earlier, albeit limited, support; or parents who continue to emphasize the perpetrator's needs over those of the child. For example, a mother would regularly visit her parents with her two children, although the older boy was a victim of his youngest maternal uncle. The grandmother would not give this boy treats, although she made a point of doing so with his younger sibling. I never would have known this was occurring without specifically asking the questions, "Who in the family is the most upset that you told?" and "How does that person still show it?" Just because a family comes to therapy does not mean the child feels supported. You cannot take support for granted in any instance of betrayal.

Providing words to action systems goes beyond the creation of safety discussed in Chapter 5. Dysregulation arises in part because the link between feelings and words is absent (Zimbardo et al., 1993). The family must give the child permission to talk about the abuse. They must make efforts so that the child does not feel threatened by recrimination due to his disclosure. Finally, the boy will not feel safe if the family cannot restructure itself in order to prevent sexual abuse from recurring. The inept monitoring in aggressive families has to be countered (Patterson, 1993). In this way, the activated system becomes a "languaged" system, and the arousal and internal distress can begin to subside. Careful interviewing and an ongoing assessment of the relative safety of the boy in his system is absolutely essential.

Reunification is another confusing issue that contributes as much to dysregulation as does any other phenomenon in the course of family therapy. If you are conscious of how dysregulating this is and how premature moves can effectively stall any future movement, then you can mobilize yourself even more to state forcibly that the perpetrator has to have done the most important work of his therapy before even the first reunification step is taken. Trepper and Barrett's (1989) guidelines in this regard are the best I have seen.

REDUCE OVERSTIMULATION AND
SEXUALIZED BEHAVIOR IN THE FAMILY

Many parents do not realize how overstimulating they can be to their sexually abused child. One example of overstimulation is aggression (e.g., battering, physical punishment, terroristic disciplining). Another example is the overstimulation that results from open displays of sexual behavior or the tolerance of sexual behavior among siblings or between siblings and parents. When I am working with families, it is helpful to keep in mind the numerous ways families send confusing sexual messages (Bolton et al., 1989).

These findings illuminate the need for the family therapist to address both the physically punitive behaviors in the family and the modeling of sexualized relationships. You have to find out who is hitting whom and who is walking around naked. This cannot simply be done by asking parents whether or not they behave in an aggressive or sexualized manner and then asking them not to do so. Many families do not "know" that they interact in an aggressive or sexual manner. Families stuck in action systems do not have words for what they do (Bentovim, 1992). The therapist needs to look for direct examples of anger or sexuality in the therapy session so that the behaviors can be addressed in a clear but nonrejecting manner.

Sexual behavior in a young boy will persist longest in those families who are not good observers of sexual behavior (Friedrich & Luecke, 1988). Poor observers also seem more likely to blur sexual boundaries. For example, the boy who is involved in the role of confidant with a depressed, single parent may also be getting subtly sexualized. When you see this type of relationship occurring, it is very important to make some determination about the boundaries of that relationship.

Sibling incest has been reported to occur in families that fall on either end of the continuum of sexual repression (De Jong, 1989). Overly repressed families create a context in which sexuality seems to have no outlet. In addition, emotional closeness is usually not present between parents and children. Siblings seek each other out for support, and this can become sexualized. Other families in which sibling incest occurs are much more titillating and sexually excitatory (Larson & Maddock, 1986). The family can set some limits on sexual behavior between siblings. They do this by installing a lock, providing closer observations, or simply capitalizing on the fact that the sibling inhibits his or her behavior for fear of future punishment. However, just because sexual behavior is no longer occurring does not mean that siblings are not punching and hitting each other, with the punching and hitting directed at the crotch or buttocks. With an undifferentiated boy, sexualized punching may have the same effect as more overt, classically sexual behaviors.

This is also the arena in which families can learn how to behave more positively with each other in a physical manner. Sexually repressed families in which incest or extrafamilial abuse occurs may be very limited in their ability to provide physical nurturing to their children. This is often multigenerational. Parents need to be helped to know what their child needs in the way of physical contact and touch. Not only do guidelines need to be established, but families need to be instructed and encouraged to behave in more nurturing ways with each other.

Sexually reactive behavior in boys is a not uncommon phenomenon (Kendall-Tackett et al., 1993). Not only may parents be unable to see this as a problem, but the sexual behavior may also magnify their ineffectual parenting because of their own histories of abuse. The longer that sexually reactive behavior continues, the more likely it will be to take on an oppositional or coercive quality. In addition, the beginnings of a paraphilia may be in the making (Gil & Johnson, 1993). All of these factors argue for a direct approach to sexually reactive behaviors, including masturbation and other self-stimulating behaviors, exhibitionism and sexual posturing, sexual behavior with peers, and other boundary violations.

I have suggested elsewhere that sexual behaviors can be managed with a largely behavioral approach (Friedrich, 1990). These steps include:

1. Assess parental attitudes and behavior related to the sexual behaviors in question
2. Monitor the frequency of the behavior
3. Positively reinforce the child's nonsexual time

4. Create a time and place to exhibit the behavior
5. Normalize the sexual behavior as related to the abuse
6. Revisit the child's abuse experience if needed to link behavior with abuse experience

You will meet with frustration if you impose this on a family in which the parents are clearly inept and overwhelmed. Commitment to the child, energy, and reasonably good monitoring are needed. The parents must also be familiar with, and committed to, several parenting strategies, including distraction, positive reinforcement, and logical consequences. The symptom prescription in the fourth part of this plan can backfire if the parent's history with the boy is primarily coercive. I try to model an approach to facilitating compliance and then ask parents to practice it with me before they try it out at home. For example, in the case of a boy who was compulsively masturbating, I suggested to the father that he say the following:

Mom and I appreciate your letting us know that what Uncle Rick did to you is still bothering you. So we know you still need to keep rubbing your penis. But you can't do it out where we are. Because you seem to need to do this, we want you to rub yourself for 10 minutes a day until you no longer need to do so. But you'll have to do it in your room and it will have to be when I'm home so I can remind you. We'll make it between 6:00 and 6:10.

This message was first given to the 8-year-old boy in my office, reiterated by the dad, and then said again on an as-needed basis. The linking of the abuse by his uncle to his masturbating was important in verbalizing the action system (Bentovim, 1992). Obviously, this approach must be tailored to each family and may need to be kept very simple. When applied appropriately, this strategy is quite successful; it greatly reduces the sexually reactive behaviors, and it quiets the family's reactivity to the boy.

PSYCHOEDUCATIONAL/BEHAVIORAL FAMILY THERAPY

A psychoeducational, problem-solving, and primarily behavioral approach with families of sexually abused children has considerable utility in modifying out-of-control behavior. I was an early convert to structural and strategic family therapy, and I loved the grand artistry these approaches sometimes involved. Using an educational and/or behavioral approach with families of sexually abused children did not appeal to me in the same way. In fact, it seemed boring and trite. Hence, it did not seem either appropriate or very effective to me.

My thinking has changed considerably. Educational and symptom-specific approaches that are clearly understandable to the parents can do several things: (a) help them feel accepted rather than rejected, (b) give them some concrete strategies can result in their feeling empowered, and (c) make therapy understandable. Teaching a parent how to effectively and nonpunitively respond to a child is an enormous accomplishment.

Psychoeducational approaches are in keeping with adding language to the action system (Bentovim, 1992). Families need to understand how victimization occurs, the effect of victimization on children, and the boy's need for support and soothing. More than one naive parent has been turned off by my efforts at strategic approaches. They are avoidant enough around therapists as it is. However, this certainly does not preclude the use of reframing, which has its origins in strategic therapy.

In addition, the most rapid way to eliminate aggressive and out-of-control behavior in boys is with behavioral strategies. I admit to a great deal of concern about using behavioral strategies with families who are punitive with their sons. However, if you identify families that can be consistent and nonpunitive, and you instruct them carefully, point systems and simple reinforcement protocols can be used to reduce crotch grabbing, swearing, or sexual posturing. They work as well to eliminate, to a large extent, other types of aggressive or disruptive behaviors in the home (Barkley, 1987; Patterson et al., 1975).

FAMILY RITUALS

Steinglass and his colleagues have studied the multigenerational transmission of alcoholism and have identified the presence of several buffering variables, including family rituals (Steinglass, Bennett, Wolin, & Reiss, 1987). They found that children of alcoholics who could identify certain family rituals were less likely to become alcoholics themselves. These included rituals such as regular church attendance, observance of birthdays, certain meals, and so on. Helping a family that you see for only a few months to develop certain rituals may not be feasible. However, this concept is quite useful as a guide toward therapy aimed at preventing dysregulation. Members of families profit if they interact with each other in reliable and predictable ways. To the degree that you can enhance that, possibly around bedtime, meals, or schoolwork, you can go a long way toward helping the child feel as if his environment is at least predictable.

FAMILY MEMBERS AS PTSD TRIGGERS

I encounter situations in which nonoffending parents and siblings, who either were or were not privy to the sexual abuse, serve as reminders of the victimization. Often this is not classic PTSD reactivation but is related more to the child's perception that the parent has been unsupportive or his shame because of what siblings may or may not know. Again, a key issue is the ability of the child to alter the unmodulated experience of arousal or anxiety. The best way to do this would be to give voice to it either verbally or by other expressions. The pairing of arousal with language can be immediately integrating and hence calming to the child. In addition, by talking about it, the family stops avoiding an opportunity for support. This also gives you opportunities to reframe the child's behavior as a natural consequence of sexual abuse and not as a reflection of his oppositionality. A boy who becomes oppositional when mom begins to date can be reframed not as being mean and insensitive (as other men have been in her life) but acting as a natural and important barometer of the feelings of safety and comfort in the family.

The perception that the nonabusive parent has somehow been allied with the perpetrator is quite pervasive. In some situations, it may be based on actual or partial truth. There are also developmental reasons for this, and these are related to young and immature children not being able to discriminate their parents.

The lack of protection by a parent is an issue that parents do not wish to think about or accept. Children are afraid to give voice to it as well. However, betrayal must be discussed and some type of reparation system may need to be developed so that the child can feel as if he is being heard and validated. This also gives the parent-child relationship a new opportunity to reestablish itself on a better footing.

A lingering fear for many children is the threat of the return of the perpetrator. An 11-year-old boy, whose father still had 3 years on his sentence, would repeatedly ask his mother, "Will I be forced to visit him if he wants me to?" This question reflected several levels of feelings, including a hope for safety and a hope for contact. In addition, it was the spoken fear of his mother, Tammy, and illustrated how Troy was the spokesman for her anxiety. By reminding her of her fear, the net effect was that she became angry with him, rejecting him further. It was very important that we identified her own anxiety and, in a cognitive approach, sorted out how she tried to push both the anxiety and, consequently, Troy away. When she could sort this out, she could respond more appropriately and Troy's questioning dropped off.

The literature on PTSD in Vietnam veterans is applicable here. Herndon and Law (1986) describe the conundrum in which the PTSD victim wants to talk, but the partner is shocked and needs to avoid the upsetting topic. They state that the family system has the potential for both maintaining and eliminating the disorder. To do the latter requires a rationale that explains the situation and how it affects the relationship. Herndon and Law describe an analogy in which a person is warm on the outside but with the inner core of an insulated ice cube. Parents will describe the feeling that they are carrying the weight of the relationship and that the stress of this is leading to a breakdown. This is where it becomes critical that the parents receive their own support so that they, in turn, can provide the type of support that their son needs.

In summary, the traumatized child lives in a family "holding environment" that is very often oscillating at a high rate of speed and not very effective at calming the child. Parents are not aware of how they trigger their child's behavior or how their anxiety infuses the system. Family-based therapy that focuses on the establishment of safety, removes triggers from the home, and is easily understandable to the parent because of its directness and its goal setting, will go a long way toward addressing the dysregulating experience of child sexual abuse.

GOAL SETTING

Goal setting can also be used with dysregulation issues. The therapist and family members can think of ways in which the boy gets overly aroused, in which the parents lack calming or soothing skills, and so on. For example, for many boys bedtime is very difficult, not only because it creates a demand for the somewhat inept parent to get the boy to comply, but also because it may be the time of the day when the victimization occurred. In addition, it represents another separation from the parent. Some parents avoid dealing with bedtime until the last minute. This can aggravate feelings of being out-of-control and overwhelmed. Families can set goals for behaving differently around bedtime. With one mother we actually planned how the last hour of the evening would go, and how much time she would spend reading to or playing with her son. It was not until she heard clearly why that time was difficult for him was she able to think about him in ways other than him being disrespectful of her wishes.

Using the format outlined earlier in Table 5.2, therapist and parent arrive at a number of positively worded goals (i.e., to increase the frequency of positive behaviors). Germane to dysregulation are goals that pertain to the following:

1. Better monitoring of the child's behavior
2. More consistent discipline
3. Increased use of positive parenting strategies, including praise and distraction
4. Observable strategies for enhancing the child's sense of safety
5. Predictable rituals
6. Practice of self-soothing strategies

To return to the case of Ned and his mother, Joyce (first described in Chapter 5), Joyce and I were able to arrive at three goals related to Ned's problems with self-control. My earlier interviewing of the two of them led me to the realization that Ned was not getting to bed very regularly. He also would hit Joyce, and she had resorted to hitting back. The third issue came up only because I try to routinely inquire about nudity and other sexual behavior in the home. Joyce admitted, in an

Table 9.2 Goal Setting: Dysregulation

	Goal 1	*Goal 2*	*Goal 3*
Optimal level of change (+2)	Ned cooperates on the preset bedtime 6 to 7 times per week	Ned no longer hits Joyce but states his feelings to her. Joyce uses listening skills.	
Acceptable level of change (0)	Ned and Joyce agree to a regular bedtime and Joe cooperates on 4 out of 5 school nights; Joyce uses logical consequences when necessary	Ned hits Joyce less than 1 time per week and Joyce uses a logical consequence	Joyce practices complete privacy in Ned's presence
Current level of behavior (−2)	Ned gets his own bedtime	Ned hits Joyce 6 to 8 times per week and Joyce hits back each time	Joyce is nude or partially clothed 2 to 3 times per week in Ned's presence

embarrassed tone, that she could be more private about dressing and undressing in her bedroom. Only two levels were established for this last goal. See Table 9.2 for goals established in three areas.

PART III

Self-Theory

10

Self-Theory: An Overview

What does this boy feel? He scarcely knows himself.

—Mura, 1985, p. 48

The third dimension of the integrated treatment model pertains to issues of the self. Although the self is traditionally viewed as an individual formulation, a boy does not exist in isolation. Consequently, I am talking about self-other (Nakkula & Selman, 1991). The development of the self and how the boy comes to view himself in relation to others is an important construct, one that enables us to understand many of the psychopathological outcomes of sexual abuse. In addition, the self is an active, cognitive construction, continually undergoing developmental change (Harter, 1983b).

The word *self* brings to mind a number of broad concepts that are not part of this chapter. These are such constructs as self-esteem and personality, which are either too vague or too broad. In part, what is meant here is a stable identity, a person who can ask himself such questions as, "Who am I?" "What will I do with my life?" and "How will I be different from my father?" These are more complex and sophisticated questions than, "Who cares about me?" "Who can I depend on?"

"Where can I find safety and security?" The latter are questions that get asked earlier in the process of self-identity formation.

The broad range of long-term problems related to sexual abuse includes problems with a person's ability to define and integrate different aspects of the self (Cole & Putnam, 1992). The boy may develop disturbances in his physical and phenomenological sense of self. An example of a physical self-disturbance is evidence that sexually abused boys have increased disturbances in their body image relative to nonabused boys with psychiatric problems (Hussey, Strom, & Singer, 1992). Other self-related issues include identity confusion and dissociation of aspects of self (Westen, 1994), which could include loss of memory about self or a sense of separate or fragmented selves (Cole & Putnam, 1992). Very little research has focused on the above self-issues in the sexually abused child. Self-esteem has been studied but with mixed results. In fact, in a recent review of the impact of sexual abuse on children, the authors found that self-esteem was the variable with the most equivocal findings (Kendall-Tackett et al., 1993). I believe this is a result of poor measures being used with children who cannot accurately report who they are.

Research on the effects of sexual abuse has almost exclusively focused on overt, behavioral reactions (Kendall-Tackett et al., 1993). Approximately one third of sexually abused children do not exhibit overt distress. That does not mean, however, that they are not affected. In fact, Cole and Putnam (1992) state that "all incest victims suffer in their self- and social functioning" (p. 180). These authors believe that the severity of outcome depends on which developmental tasks were disrupted by the abuse.

If we appreciate that the self includes both overt behavior and internal, less observable processes, then overt behavior may be different from how the child actually views himself. An asymptomatic boy may not have a sense of his own physical or emotional integrity. Cole and Putnam (1992) suggest that outcome measures should extend beyond symptom checklists or simple, generic measures of self-esteem. They suggest the use of measures that evaluate the person's ability to understand and integrate multiple elements of self. An example is the victim, who despite being competent in one or more areas of his life, behaves incompetently or dangerously in the sexual and self-care domains. The internal working model (first discussed in Chapter 2) is also a concept pertaining to self-formation (Sroufe & Fleeson, 1986). Internal working models are a series of road maps that are predictably related to notions of self in relation to the other.

The study of the self is not just intrapersonal, however. Humans are interpersonal organisms, and, in the case of the child, who is embedded in a social matrix, this is an even more important consideration (Kegan, 1982). Self is a social construct and emerges out of the transactions between the individual and others. Thus self and social development are closely related (Cole & Putnam, 1992).

Because this is an integrated model, the principles of attachment and dysregulation are closely interrelated with the development of the self. For example, as discussed in Chapter 6, a central task of the child is to learn how to inhibit action (Maccoby, 1980). The child's capacity to inhibit action leads to the development and maintenance of a sense of self. This is true because emotional consistency and predictability, across time and situations, are essential in the formation of self (Linehan, 1993). The self emerges as we observe ourselves and integrate the responses of others to our actions and behaviors. The chronically dysregulated child cannot observe himself or remain in place emotionally long enough to register and incorporate the responses of others.

The home environments of many sexually abused children can also add to problems in self-formation (Benedict & Zantra, 1993; Levang, 1989). If the responses of others tend to be critical, inconsistent, and even irrational, the boy is invalidated. More important, regular, consistent, and contingent feedback between actions and outcomes is critical to self-development (Harter, 1983b). Many families do not teach the boy how to interpret his internal environment (i.e., his feelings). This also detracts from self-knowledge, an important component of self-development.

Consider this example. Long before the sexual abuse, the boy is at a gathering of relatives. He is being teased and provoked, and his frustration level is increasing because of insensitive behavior by cousins and adults. He is seconds before tears and is feeling angry, lonely, and rejected.

"Look, the little wimp is going to cry," says an uncle. This is a powerfully discounting statement. The boy tightens up and lashes out.

"Quite a guy. A real chip off the old block," is how another uncle replies to the boy's burst of aggression. This uncle's statement is also discounting because the boy now has no accurate words for all the confusion that he has shoved out of his awareness by lashing out. Learning how to shove feelings away is part of being male (Tannen, 1990), but it creates the risk of feelings of emptiness. Emptiness is as much about the rejection of feelings as the absence of them (Linehan, 1993).

Five years later you are sitting across from this boy. He has told you about being placed on detention in school because of punching someone in the hallway. "How do you feel about that?" you ask, being the kindly therapist. "I don't know," he says.

Although "I don't know" seems to be a universal response to therapists' questions, the contributors to it are complex. The boy may have replied in this way out of oppositionality, lack of permission to talk, or because he truly did not know his feelings. Is it any wonder that he cannot talk to you about his feelings?

Consider another example. The young boy either states (or acts as if) "I feel proud." His behavior is met with "Shut up, you little shit." Not only is this clear rejection, but it sets up an incongruity between the boy and his external world. It should not be a surprise that the incongruity between the boy and the external world not only cannot get internalized, but it also leaves the boy externally focused, unable to develop an internalized sense of who he is. Consequently, he will be extremely vulnerable to the actions of other people, and his behavior will be described as unstable, reactive, and defensive.

There can be numerous manifestations of this failure to internalize a coherent sense of self. For example, Kohlberg (1984) describes stages of moral development. The boy runs the risk of remaining at the most basic level because he cannot internalize a consistent, core set of values. We see this in reduced empathy, a frequent consequence of victimization.

This chapter will review several topics, including the need for a developmental perspective on the self, the presentation of several conceptualizations that are particularly relevant to how the self is altered in the context of trauma, and a consideration of psychological issues that are most directly tied to disruptions in self-development.

❏ The Development of the Self

Any understanding of how an organism develops needs to take into consideration several processes. How does the organism change and yet maintain integrity? How do individuals deal with the increasing complexity brought about by development? Werner's (1948) organismic developmental theory describes two ongoing processes: differentiation and integration. Differentiation captures the increasing complexity of the child's self-perceptions and behavior, whereas integration is the process whereby the boy's disparate features become unified into a coherent whole.

The boy's understanding of himself and his ability to perceive his attributes and emotions accurately follows a developmental course and contains both cognitive and affective processes (Harter, 1983a) (see Table 10.1 for a summary). The developmental course includes a number of shifts as the child becomes more sophisticated, or differentiated, in his self-understanding. One of the shifts that occurs refers to broader and more complex self-descriptions. For example, the child's sense of self usually begins with a sense of one's physical self. This transitions to the physical self in motion, then to the social self, and then to the psychological self. This latter self contains one's emotions and cognitions. Recent research has found increased somatic symptoms in sexually abused children. These symptoms appear to reflect a heightened focus on the physical self in the young abused child (Friedrich & Schafer, in press; Hussey et al., 1992; Westen, 1994).

The concept of *self-integrity* can also be applied across a number of developmental transitions (Cole & Putnam, 1992). A consolidated sense of self begins to emerge in infancy and forms the foundation for the development of a sense of autonomy and agency. The self-referential pronoun "me" comes into play at this age. Preschoolers build on this foundation and may overuse denial and dissociation as ways to deal with sexual abuse. These are two coping strategies that increase markedly during the preschool years. However, both of these strategies interfere with the child articulating a sense of who he is, his responsibilities, and what he can and cannot do.

I had a striking sense of the abused child's reduced autonomy in a study I did of severely physically abused preschoolers (Friedrich et al.,

Table 10.1 Normal Developmental Outcomes at Different Ages

Infant/Toddler	Consolidated sense of self Recognizes self Uses self-referent pronouns Autonomy and agency emerge
Preschool	Sense of self is based on concrete, observable attributes Uses denial and dissociation to cope
Childhood	Psychological sense of self emerges Self has positive and negative features Self-reflection Cooperates sensitively with peers Incorporates perspectives of the other into his or her sense of self and self-other transactions Inference, reflection, and reasoning increase denial and decrease dissociation
Adolescence	Sexual aspects of self must now be incorporated into self-image Introspection about self and other aspects of self are integrated into a whole Acute self-consciousness

1983). Almost all of the subjects were boys. In contrast to their matched, nonabused counterparts, they had decreased language capabilities (less articulatory capacity). Furthermore, when asked to draw a picture of themselves, not only was the developmental quality lower, but a number of the abused children oriented their drawings to the examiner and not to themselves. Essentially, they were drawing themselves upside down and for the examiner's ease of viewing. Rather than the joyful egocentricity of this age, these preschoolers were already other-directed. They were oppositional but still seeking to please.

The self continues to develop in childhood and adolescence (Cole & Putnam, 1992). It is at this age that a psychological sense of self emerges, and such phenomena as pride and shame both emerge and can be described. This is also the age at which the child can consider positive and negative qualities simultaneously. As their cognitive abilities increase, healthy children will use less denial and dissociation and be able to appraise themselves realistically, as well as to integrate both positive and negative features. The fact that sexually abused children use more dissociation interferes with these normative tasks.

Imagine how difficult it would be for a 10-year-old boy to think that he is both a good athlete and a sexual deviate. These two features simply do not go together. The inherent conflict in these disparate self-perceptions interferes with a boy's psychological complexity; he tries to cope by ignoring, denying, or dissociating the disagreeable aspect of self. Is it any wonder the following interchange gets played out, over and over, in numerous therapy offices?

Therapist Let's start today by making a list of everything good about you. What do you like about yourself?
Boy I don't know.
Therapist What do you do well?
Boy I don't know.
Therapist Ah, come on. Surely there is something you like about yourself.
Boy (Silence).
Therapist Well, what do you want to change about yourself?
Boy I don't know.

Although we could interpret this as oppositional behavior by the boy and get upset and rejecting, we could also think of these answers as being a function of his having no language for feelings, a massive developmental failure in the ability to identify aspects of self, and a fear that "if I even think about myself I will have to think about the sexual abuse."

It is in adolescence that the boy begins to integrate disparate self-related features into a unified and continuous sense of self. His view of himself meshes with his self-perception, as well as that of others (Cole & Putnam, 1992). He is increasingly able to use instrumental coping strategies of reflection, reasoning, and planning. If development is disrupted via sexual abuse, the continued overuse of immature coping strategies will continue, and acting impulsively or avoidantly becomes more likely.

Adolescence is also the age when sexuality is clearly salient. The sexually abused adolescent male is poorly equipped to (a) think about sexuality, (b) think about his sexual abuse and its implications for his sexuality, and (c) accept/respect any gender-identity confusion he may have, either preceding or secondary to his sexual abuse. What might have been a hidden issue, not observable in childhood, is now more likely to be overt. In other words, the asymptomatic 10-year-old boy is now symptomatic regarding the sexually inappropriate behavior he is exhibiting. The notion of delayed onset is another reminder about the need for a long-term, developmental perspective on sexual abuse outcome.

Hopefully, this brief developmental synopsis illustrates different issues at different time periods. I hope it also underscores how complex the developmental process is and the potential enormity of the task of getting this process back on track.

I believe that the most integrated and well-laid out theory of self comes from Robert Kegan (1982). His theory combines Piagetian development with Ericksonian notions of ego development. Over the course of a person's life, he or she moves through different phases that are sometimes more intraindividual and other times more interindividual in nature. A principle feature of Kegan's theory has to do with the organism as a "meaning-making" individual. We are constantly working to understand who we are vis-à-vis another person. The emphasis that I place on understanding the abuse experience and its effect on the child is derived in part from Kegan's theory that children are going to be actively working on understanding their victimization. Children will do this regardless of whether we think it is necessary or not or whether we believe that the child is focused on that issue or not. Kegan would state that it is a given that the child is grappling with the meaning of the victimization except, presumably, in those cases in which the child is unable to fully bring all of his cognitive powers to the victimization (e.g., dissociation).

❑ Conceptualizations About Self and Sexual Abuse

Perspectives on self and sexual abuse begin simply and become more complex. The traumagenic factors of stigmatization and powerlessness are pertinent to issues of self (Finkelhor & Browne, 1986). Both of these speak to problems pertaining to a resulting sense of inadequacy and reduced self-efficacy. Their behavioral manifestations can include avoidance or lack of initiative. These two variables are also reflected in how the boy thinks about himself.

Another framework for this chapter is empirically derived and reflects the sexual-abuse-specific attributions developed in research on the CITES–R (Wolfe et al., 1991). The 78-item CITES–R has four factors. One is titled "Abuse Attributions." This factor includes items pertaining to self-blame and guilt, empowerment, vulnerability, and the world as a dangerous place.

Attributional theory is cognitively based and states that the individual develops beliefs about different aspects of his life, including why an event has occurred (Rosenhan & Seligman, 1984). Attributions vary along the domains of internal-external, stable-unstable, and global-specific. A teenage boy who blames himself for having been sexually abused and who believes there is little he can ever do about it or anything else in his life has attributions that are internal, stable, and global. There is also some overlap between the CITES–R Abuse Attribution factor and the Children's Attributions and Perceptions Scale (CAPS) (Mannarino, Cohen, & Berman, 1994). This is an 18-item, abuse-specific measure that has four subscales: Feeling Different From Peers, Interpersonal Trust, Perceived Vulnerability, and Self-Blame. All but Interpersonal Trust would be directly relevant to issues of self.

Briere and Runtz (1993) have described six main effects of sexual abuse that have been derived from their research with adult victims. The two most directly relevant to self are cognitive distortions and impaired self-reference. By cognitive distortions, the authors mean the assumptions and self-perceptions of the victim that result in the victim's view of the world as dangerous and of himself as less capable and incompetent. Impaired self-reference includes the absence of an internal base or model for behavior; for example, the victim's relative inability to be aware of his internal personal processes and existence.

As further evidence of the overlap between attachment theory and self-issues, we can consider the parallels between the internal working model derived from attachment theory and the internalized object derived from object relations theory (Guntrip, 1969). Object relations is an intrapsychic model describing how the developing child incorporates aspects of people (objects) into his memory and eventually his self. An internalized "bad object" could be, for example, a child having incorporated into his sense of who he is the features of a cruel and rejecting parent figure. Bad objects are internalized under prolonged adverse circumstances when the child is in a heightened state of arousal. Object relations theorists state that these are some of the most difficult internalizations to correct (Guntrip, 1969).

As the child develops, he or she may be shaped by external forces into behaving appropriately on an interpersonal level, but his internalized bad objects, if left uncorrected, can emerge during times of distress. We have all seen children whose "inner-outer" conflicts are obvious. An externally passive boy gives way to an explosive boy when he is feeling vulnerable. Winnicott (1965) has even described a process, the "false self," that is an apt descriptor of many abused children who have become precociously mature superficially, almost always in the service of an adult's needs, but who feel empty internally. The false self is typically seen more often and more eloquently in adolescents and adults (Elliott, 1994), but it has its origins in very young children.

The last conceptualization about specific self-issues that are related to sexual abuse comes from Linehan (1993), who described four broad domains central to her cognitive-behavioral approach with individuals diagnosed with borderline personality disorder. Sexual abuse is an increasingly frequent apparent etiologic factor in the lives of individuals with borderline personality disorders. Consequently, a number of sexually abused boys might share both behaviors and self-representations that are similar to other primitively organized, personality-disordered individuals. Linehan (1993) has described four basic skills that are lacking in individuals with this diagnosis: mindfulness, interpersonal affectiveness, emotion regulation, and distress tolerance. Her concept of mindfulness is particularly relevant to this chapter. Mindfulness reflects the degree to which the individual can think about who he is and the degree to which he can think about his thinking and the effect of his behaviors on other people. Self-development is also about the internalization of the perceptions of other people. What if these personifications, as Sullivan (1953) described the perceptions of other people, are inaccurate or discordant?

WESTEN'S SCHEMA OF SELF AND SEXUAL ABUSE

The previous section represents a distillation of common themes that can guide our therapy. Recently, a new schema was published, one that integrates multiple levels of self and memory. It deserves a brief mention here. Westen (1994) reports that child sexual abuse can affect self-representations in at least five ways. The first effect shows up in bodily representations. He also states that sexual abuse can have a second effect, or a disruption of episodic memories, which may be marked by periods of amnesia. This will lead to sexual abuse victims having no memory of entire periods of their lives. As a result, sexual abuse can sometimes lead to a severing of the link between generalized self-knowledge and particular episodes of abuse.

A third impact of childhood sexual abuse is that it renders many currently active self-representations inaccessible to the consciousness. The content in different representations can be too painful or terrifying; this leads to thoughts, emotions, or actions that the person cannot understand or acknowledge.

The fourth effect of sexual abuse on self-representations is the manner in which self-attributional processes are disrupted. Westen (1994) describes this as a shutting down of the capacity to think about one's own thoughts and behaviors. Finally, sexual abuse experiences often disrupt normal developmental processes associated with self-representation. For example, in the normal course of events, children's representations become more abstract, differentiated, subtle, and increasingly focused on internal states and qualities. For individuals who lack access to salient aspects of themselves (especially aspects that are affectively highly charged) because of their trauma, integration of the different aspects of self is very difficult.

❏ Symptoms Reflecting Problems With Self

Problems in self-perception are usually not as overtly apparent as difficulties with attachment or dysregulation. This is particularly true with young children, whose sense of self is immature and whose capacity to describe internal feelings is reduced. The reduced sense of efficacy that the child experiences as a result of abuse may simply manifest itself as avoidance or withdrawal. Many families would view that as a positive behavior, however, because avoidant and withdrawn children require less energy and effort.

Children who have difficulty talking about their feelings may manifest their distress with somatic symptoms. This likely reflects the abused child being focused on the integrity of his physical self (Friedrich & Schafer, in press) and having an unfounded sense of his body as ill or weak (Cole & Putnam, 1992). Extremely pertinent to self-issues would be helping the victim learn about his body, something suggested in movement therapy (Linden, 1988, 1990). However, disadvantaged children of all ages are likely to have more than the usual difficulties identifying their feelings or talking about their self-perceptions. Thus this phenomenon is not unique to sexually abused children. It may be that a symptom focus is less important than creating a therapy context in which the child can develop a greater sense of both efficacy and personal integrity, along with opportunities to develop his capacity to accurately discuss his thoughts and feelings (Noam, 1992).

However, in keeping with the practical, symptom-focused approach of this book, a number of psychological consequences and attendant symptoms will be identified in this section. I will borrow from the four distilled themes identified in Table 10.2 to organize a discussion of these symptoms.

The boy with a *decreased sense of power and control* over his life may be avoidant or withdrawn on the one hand, or he may act in ways that make him vulnerable to external forces (including authority, further victimization, or situations that are dangerous and can result in self-harm). I am reminded of the lack of exploration in the playroom that the ambivalently attached, abused child exhibits. The world is just not as interesting, it takes more to get the boy excited about something, and his emotional energies seem to be depleted. Rather than a classic depression, however, this seems to be more an atypical form of depression, reflecting a type of learned helplessness and sense of inadequacy.

The second theme of *differentness* also would promote isolative behavior. The disadvantage is that the child removes himself from the

Table 10.2 Prior Attempts at Describing Self-Issues in Sexual Abuse Victims and Initial Attempt at Deriving Common Themes

Prior conceptualization	Common distilled themes
Finkelhor & Browne (1985)	
1. Stigmatization	
2. Powerlessness	Decreased Power and Control
	1. Powerlessness
Wolfe et al. (1991)	2. Empowerment
1. Self-blame and guilt	3. Dangerous world
2. Empowerment	4. Vulnerability
3. Dangerous world	5. Perceived vulnerability
4. Vulnerability	6. Cognitive distortions
Mannarino & Cohen (1994)	Differentness
1. Feeling different from peers	1. Stigmatization
2. Perceived vulnerability	2. Feeling different from peers
3. Self-blame	
	Guilt and Shame
Briere & Runtz (1993)	1. Self-blame and guilt
1. Cognitive distortions	2. Self-blame
2. Impaired self-reference	
	Self-Integrity
Winnicott (1965)	1. Impaired self-reference
1. False self	2. False self
	3. Mindfulness
Linehan (1993)	
1. Mindfulness	

opportunities for corrective emotional experiences that could enable his obtaining a more accurate view of self, with less of a sense of stigmatization.

The third theme of *guilt and shame* also has a number of very subtle but pernicious manifestations. Fossum and Mason (1986) define shame as "an inner sense of being completely diminished or insufficient as a person" (p. 5). Individuals with a pervasive sense of shame will operate under the premise that they are fundamentally bad, defective, and not fully valid as humans.

It is useful to distinguish between the terms *guilt* and *shame*. Guilt is developmentally more mature. Although painful, it does not reflect directly on one's identity, nor does it diminish one's sense of personal worth. Rather, it reflects an internalized conscience or set of values or both. The possibility of repair exists for guilt, and the individual can come to view the incident accurately and to move forward.

It is much more difficult to alter shame. Shame is part of the person's very fiber of being. Examining shame does not result in freeing the person to move on and behave differently the next time the situation rolls around. Rather, addressing shame opens the individual up to a repeated sense of basic inadequacy. Fossum and Mason (1986) describe a "shame-bound cycle" in which the abuse behavior of one family member becomes the victimization and induction into shame of another. People within the family system swap places in this cycle of shame, and very often one finds the "perfect child" as well as the "black sheep" operating in the same system. The polarity between good and bad speaks to the primitive nature of shame.

Finally, symptoms will reflect the absence of *self-integrity*. This could reflect the incongruity between the boy's outer behavior and his inner feelings of emptiness. It could also pertain more directly to what Linehan (1993) describes as "reduced mindfulness." Not only is the child incapable of observing himself accurately (or the behavior of other people accurately as well), he is prone to behaving in ways that are incongruous and unpredictable. It is from these behavioral instances that the therapist has the opportunity to expose the hidden, internalized feelings of inadequacy that populate the boy's personal interior.

How does the clinician move from these general distilled themes to the specific symptoms listed in Table 10.3? A number of the disorders listed will take some time to emerge and present most fully in late adolescence and early adulthood. Although I have not had the opportunity to follow any sexually abused boys as they transition into young adulthood, I have had that opportunity with two sexually abused girls, both of whom have received a variety of diagnoses along the way, including major depression, posttraumatic stress disorder, and, more recently, borderline personality disorder. The profound difficulties they had with forming a coherent and integrated sense of self was reflected when they were still latency-aged children. Behaviors that they exhibited included suicide attempts, being part of a victimizing relationship, and vegetative difficulties suggestive of depression.

Table 10.3 Specific Symptoms Reflecting Self-Issues

1. Unstable sense of self

2. Marked identity problems

3. Multiple personality disorder

4. Somatization disorder

5. Distorted body image

6. Reduced self-efficacy

7. Atypical depression

8. Borderline features

However, one can see that decreased power and/or control can be manifested in dependency and a reduced sense of efficacy and potency, and it can contribute to a variable presentation from one day to the next. A sense of differentness is most directly reflected in a distorted body image along with identity problems, including gender dysphoria and issues of sexual identity. Guilt and/or shame is most likely to show up in symptoms that are in the affective disorder cluster, most typically depression. Self-integrity is reflected in an unstable sense of self, multiple personality disorder, and somatization disorders. It is as if one part of the child does not know what the other part is doing. This perpetuates the overuse of denial and dissociation, as with children who are inarticulate about talking about feelings or who dissociate automatically. Such children have been rendered more vulnerable to the emergence of more clearly crystalized dissociative states, which would be precursors to multiple personality disorder.

❏ **Assessment of the Self**

In keeping with a focus on careful assessment, I have suggested a number of measures that can assess different aspects of self. These are listed in Table 10.4 and include parent-, teacher-, and child-completed measures. The measures are both generic and abuse-specific.

Table 10.4 Psychological Assessment of Self-Issues

I. Parent-Completed Measures
  A. Generic
    1. MMPI (Friedrich, 1991b)
    2. Intelligence
  B. Abuse-Specific
    1. Trauma Symptom Inventory (Briere, 1994)

II. Teacher-Completed Measures
  A. Teacher Report Form (Achenbach & Edelbrock, 1986)

III. Child-Completed Measures
  A. Generic
    1. Body perception
    2. Child Behavior Checklist (Achenbach & Edelbrock, 1983)
      a. Somatic complaints
    3. Human figure drawing
    4. Sentence completion (Loevinger & Wessler, 1970)
    5. Intelligence
    6. Children's Assessment Schedule (Hodges, McKnew, Cytryn, Stern, & Kline, 1982)
    7. Perceived Competence Scale for Children (Harter, 1982)
  B. Abuse-Specific
    1. CITES–R (Wolfe et al., 1991)
      a. Self-blame and guilt
      b. Dangerous world
      c. Empowerment
      d. Personal vulnerability
    2. Children's Attributions and Perceptions Scale (CAPS) (Mannarino et al., 1994)
    3. Sexual Meaning Scale (Maddock, 1988)

General measures of self-esteem have been frequently used in studies of sexually abused children (Kendall-Tackett et al., 1993) but with very inconsistent findings. Most likely this is due to the inability of young children to accurately think about themselves in relationship to another person. It would be very important to include abuse-specific measures in your assessment. Both the CITES–R (Wolfe et al., 1991) and the CAPS (Mannarino et al., 1994) have empirical validation of their utility. In addition, they assess the majority of the common distilled themes that are presented in Table 10.2.

11

Self-Theory: Individual Therapy

The small seed of despair cracks open and sends experimental tendrils upward to the fragile skin of calm holding him together.

—Guest, 1976, p. 2

I have other images relative to self-issues in sexually abused boys. One is of dams: big, thick, packed dirt barriers, erected to hold back an enormous amount of roiling, hot, tormented water. Sometimes I feel that, despite all the inner turmoil, the boy's distress is unreachable and he remains untouched in the therapeutic encounter. At times I am haunted by images of what he might be like as an adult. I fear for whoever is in the way when the dams burst, spewing forth material from years past.

Individual therapy designed to enhance and correct the boy's sense of self is based on the therapist having an accurate understanding of the boy's view of himself and his world (Santostefano & Calicchia, 1992). There needs to be both a common language and a synchronicity between the therapist and the child. As mentioned earlier, blanket reassurances (e.g., it was not your fault) to the child are misguided. These statements are often confusing and unbelievable to the child, and their repeated use undermines the boy's sense of connection to his therapist.

171

For example, a child who is physiologically aroused during the victimization and appreciated some of the attention and support that the abuser provided may not understand the therapist's focus on the negative aspects of the abuse, particularly if this focus characterizes the initial stage of the therapy.

Individual therapy must assist the child in correcting his immature and inaccurate self-perceptions. A central technique would be the boy's learning how to understand and describe his contradictory feelings. This can be facilitated through a number of exercises aimed at understanding feelings, including the use of a feelings list, "feelings basket," (James, 1989, p. 192), or other feelings exercises described by James (1989). Other techniques suggested in this chapter are summarized in Table 11.1.

There are several uses of the boy's new ability to label feelings. For example, differential affect training teaches children to identify their own feelings, to identify the feelings in other people, to express their own feelings, and to reflect the feelings of other people (Craighead, Meyers, & Craighead, 1985).

Harter (1977) has described an excellent technique to confront the extreme and contradictory self-perspectives that the victimized child often has. The child gradually makes progressive approximations to a more accurate perception of himself as having a combination of positive, neutral, and negative features. These extreme perspectives are multidimensional emotions in a unidimensional mind (e.g., "all happy" or "all mad") (Harter, 1983a). The child needs to learn how to conceptualize two emotions simultaneously, even those of opposite valence.

It is also important to increase a child's sense of self-efficacy. For example, the therapist could contract with the child for increased competency. Through the use of goal setting, the sexually reactive child can be placed "in charge of his penis" or contract for more self-control with masturbation. A brief list of possible goals I have created with boys include the following:

1. Take initiative with friends or teachers
2. Complete homework/assigned tasks
3. Interrupt negative, self-defeating thoughts about self
4. Behave assertively
5. Reduce victim behavior

Table 11.1 Techniques

1. Learn to identify and process feelings
2. Contract with the child for competency
3. Externalize the problem
4. Confront the child's all-or-nothing thinking about his or her capabilities
   a. circle drawings
   b. bifurcated balloons
5. Correct inappropriate cognitions
6. Actively construct a more positive view of self
7. Examine sexual self

Older children, particularly those who are better at describing their feelings, may benefit from learning how to "externalize the problem" (White, 1989). This actually has a unique developmental sensitivity for a number of reasons. Children are egocentric, and they assume blame for numerous things that happen to them. Sexually abused children might view themselves as bad, duplicitous, and guilty of the abuse. It is helpful for the child to learn how to externalize (and not internalize) the problem. The child can begin to think about these self-defeating thoughts as separate from himself: The thoughts "sneak up on him when he is unaware." This allows the child to see himself differently. For example, he now has the potential for a more active role in keeping negative feelings outside and in learning to cope better with those times when he is more vulnerable to negative thoughts.

In addition, a maltreated child may be quite self-critical, and this creates the potential for depression and impaired motivation. Older latency-aged and adolescent victims can be aided in the development of a "personal fable." This is in regard to some unique aspect of themselves that has assisted their overcoming the abuse. This can be done in a cognitive therapy format, complete with a blackboard to facilitate the child's visual perception of the important concept that thoughts create feelings and also direct behavior. For example, Cunningham and McFarlane (1990) have written about the role of "vulture thoughts" in the thinking of sexually aggressive children. This concept of "vulture thoughts" is a way to make meaningful to children a basic tenet of cognitive therapy.

Finally, in keeping with Harter's (1983a) suggestion, the therapist would do well to avoid focusing on insight in the boy. Rather, the therapist can concentrate on a developmentally simpler task—namely, to increase the accuracy of the child's self-perception and to include in this self-perception a greater sense of efficacy. Young children are highly egocentric, and their self-assumptions often reflect wishes rather than accuracy. Presumably, greater integration brings more accuracy. If the boy is given a mechanism whereby he can now think more accurately, hopefully he can use the technique to confront the resurgence of inappropriate/inaccurate cognitions at later life cycle/ developmental transitions.

Harter (1983b) points out that environmental changes, including trauma, can produce inaccuracies in the judgment of one's abilities. In addition, she writes that children who consistently view themselves inaccurately, either by overestimating or by underestimating their competence, expose themselves to less challenging problems. The use of avoidant coping strategies is a manifestation of this.

There are some very interesting clinical implications for this finding. Supportive therapists who want to enhance an abused child's self-esteem should concentrate on the accuracy of the self-perception, not necessarily on the optimism of the perception. In fact, Harter (1983b) states that "a strategy . . . undoubtedly doomed to failure involves . . . categorically asserting . . . 'you are not dumb, you know, you really are quite smart' " (p. 135).

Numerous contributors to inaccurate self-perception exist in the world of the maltreated child. Examples of these inaccuracies include all-or-none thinking, overgeneralizations, and shifts from one extreme self-precept to the other (Lipovsky, 1992). In the presence of increased stress and reduced support, an abused child is more likely to remain stuck at an immature level of self-perception than another child without this history.

Harter (1977) presents several clinical examples of all-or-none thinking. She describes a case of a girl who saw herself as dumb. She used a circle-drawing technique to increase the accuracy of the girl's self-perception. In some ways, this approach mimics cognitive therapy but it is more developmentally appropriate and simultaneously focuses on affect as well as thinking. She has suggested the use of "bifurcated balloons" as well (Harter, 1983a). These are drawn over the heads of drawings of two people talking. The use of two balloons over each person allows the child to identify multiple feelings about the same person in the conversation.

Another phenomenon in the area of self-perception pertains to stability, or conservation of self, across settings and in the face of contradictions. Children vary in whether changes are attributed to internal versus external forces. Internally focused children and adolescents are not as likely to be bothered by these fluctuations (Harter, 1988). Because maltreatment is an external force, the child has to exert a significant effort to not blame him- or herself.

Despite the centrality of self-perception in the establishment of the self, it may come as a surprise to beginning child therapists that children usually have little interest in self-examination. Given the fact that children are so deeply embedded in the family matrix, they most naturally will externalize their problems (Kegan, 1982). In fact, the therapist may find it more fruitful to alter the family influences on self-development than to work on helping the child develop insight. Harter (1988) goes so far as to suggest that there are developmental reasons that promote the use of more didactic techniques and argue against attempts at insight with children. This suggestion would support the types of psychoeducational interventions reported elsewhere (Mandell & Damon, 1989) that are focused on self-issues.

❏ Treatment Foci

Four distilled themes were identified in the previous chapter (see Table 10.2). These were derived from the research literature examining self-issues with adults and children. They include (a) decreased power and/or control and its effect on the boy's sense of potency, (b) differentness, (c) guilt and/or shame and the boy's assumption of responsibility for the abuse, and (d) self-integrity. Another issue that will be discussed here is the boy's notions of his sexual self. An overarching treatment focus can be best summarized as creating a self-perception that blends accuracy with appropriate subjectivity.

DECREASED POWER AND CONTROL

The boy's sense of his efficacy is a central element of his overall self-perception. He may have no practice in thinking about himself, or his self-perception may be very negative and, consequently, he pushes it out of awareness. Both of these speak to a common, underlying deficiency—the absence of dialogue or language about the self. The lack of capacity to talk about self is common in maltreated children (Beeghly & Cicchetti, 1994). This unique need is best addressed in individual therapy or group therapy.

Because these boys usually are not very proficient at talking about themselves, the therapist needs to assist this process by introducing a framework for the conversation. Cognitive therapy with adults relies on the verbal adult to articulate the self-defeating, irrational thoughts. Cognitive therapy with children often needs to start with giving them a language to present their thoughts about themselves. Questions in the CITES–R (Wolfe et al., 1991) and CAPS (Mannarino et al., 1994) present a very usable therapy framework. For example, the CAPS item, "I am weaker than other children (boys) my age" can be the basis of very useful discussion. For boys who answer "No," you might ask them to help you list ways in which they are stronger, ways they are equally strong, and ways they might feel weaker. By presenting this format, you are already expanding their capacity to think more maturely about themselves.

If the boy is still reluctant to admit any feelings of weakness, ask him how another sexually abused boy might answer that question. This lets him practice taking the perspective of another, an important developmental process.

The reader might ask whether the therapist should interfere with the boy's youthful, albeit defensive, grandiosity. Shouldn't you let him think those positive thoughts? In actuality, grandiose thoughts should be the norm of all preschool children and extend up through age 7 years or so (Shirk & Saiz, 1992). "I am the best soccer player on the team" and "I scored all of the goals" stated by a 6-year-old boy are developmentally appropriate and should not be challenged, even if there is contrary evidence. This type of lying is not malicious but a common phenomenon at this age.

If a 6-year-old boy denies that he feels less capable or more worried after having been molested, I typically do not confront this thinking. I allow him these thoughts and tell him about the range of feelings and thoughts another child might have. With older boys, I figure out ways to keep coming back to the issue, using graduated steps to help them identify any feelings of inadequacy that persist. Here again, circle drawings and bifurcated balloons are helpful (Harter, 1977, 1983a).

A good assessment can be of enormous help here. Let me present an example where an assessment was able to guide decision making as to whether a boy was in need of some gentle confronting of his inaccurate perceptions. The boy in question was a close-mouthed, 9-year-old boy who had been molested to an indeterminate degree by a teenage girl. The boy claimed everything was fine. The parents appeared reasonably supportive so I felt I could trust them to enhance his continued rebound. However, since the abuse, the parents reported on the Child Behavior Checklist (CBC) (Achenbach & Edelbrock, 1983) that the boy had sleep problems, nightmares, increased emotionality, and reduced involvement with friends. All of these symptoms pointed to distress and alienation. In addition, the boy refused to give an answer to Card 15 from the Roberts Apperception Test for Children (McArthur & Roberts, 1982), a card that often pulls for sexual content in sexually abused children (Friedrich & Share, in press).

Even an evaluation as cursory as the above tells you several things that can guide your treatment. These include (a) unspoken distress (i.e., sleep problems and nightmares, from the CBC); (b) feelings of alienation and possibly differentness (i.e., reduced peer involvement, from the CBC); and (c) an inability to talk about topics that are reminiscent of the abuse (i.e., Card 15 refusal). These argue for continued therapy; whether it is focused on the boy, the parents, or some combination will be up to you. But you would be less able to proceed unless you obtained some information in an organized, objective manner, something that psychological assessment is uniquely able to do.

Older boys and teenagers can also benefit from structured conversations that focus on the future and how to counter negative self-evaluations down the line. It is very helpful to make the situations very concrete and, whenever possible, to use role play (e.g., scripted conversations, story stems) (Buchsbaum, Toth, Clyman, Cicchetti, &

Emde, 1992), and projective stories (McCrone, Egeland, Kalkoske, & Carlson, 1994).

Passivity or reduced initiative is another manifestation of decreased sense of efficacy. We tend to think of troubled boys as behaving in an externalizing manner, with passivity being a less common feature. However, I think there are probably as many troubled boys who behave in an avoidant-defended or passive manner as behave in a more exaggerated and aggressive manner. Sometimes the passivity is punctuated by explosive outbursts, but the overall behavior is best characterized as passive, often including some very noticeable dependent features. It makes sense to think of passivity as related to the powerlessness that the boy might experience because of the abuse. If the boy cannot have control over his body, then how can he believe he is in control over his schoolwork or in taking the initiative to complete projects that are expected of him? Usually, however, passivity and dependency take a fair amount of time to develop, and in addition to the powerlessness inherent in the sexual abuse, there is often powerlessness that is part of the parent-child relationship. By itself, this can give rise to a more avoidant style of attachment. This treatment area lends itself to goal setting in individual therapy. I would recommend that the therapist identify with older boys those areas in which they could behave more competently or exhibit more initiative. If they are motivated to make some changes and contracting in this way will not simply lead to more frustration, then one or more goals could be identified on a goal attainment scale specific to the boy.

DIFFERENTNESS

This is also a concept that requires some level of cognitive developmental sophistication to truly grapple with in a therapeutically useful way. Very young children, particularly those less than 6 years old, may not be very secure in their mastery of self-other representations (Harter, 1983b). Highly egocentric thinking does not allow a boy to be able to engage in dialogue about feelings that are broken or damaged. The boy does not understand that concept, even if he is feeling that way. The early primary-grade boy does have more cognitive facility to think about how two people are different, but he still has difficulty thinking about his internal workings and how they might be different from those of another boy or how another boy might perceive him (Harter, 1988). However, his negative self-perceptions might be there in the drawings you ask him to make of himself. For example, they could show up in human figure distortions or other indicators that could reflect feeling different or separate from people.

At the age of 8 years and younger, simply having the boy draw two pictures of himself, before and after the abuse, can be quite helpful and give him a vehicle to present the contrasting feelings. I wait to decide the contrast until I have seen his first human figure drawing, something I get in the first or second session. If there are some clear emotional indicators (i.e., reduced size, absent limbs, shading) in the first drawing, I then ask the boy to draw another one based on how he must have looked before all this happened.

Because of the multiple ways we develop our sense of self, the child's therapist is wise to use more than simply language or drawings. The motoric level of self-representation shows up in children feeling their bodies are now different. Sometimes this is heard most eloquently from teenagers, who have an exaggerated sense of other people observing them. However, such feelings are also present when the boy is younger. James (1989) describes movement components of her therapy that can be quite useful for examining how accurately the boy views himself.

Again, as is the case with the decreased potency described in the previous section, it is often helpful to employ "another boy." You can get at your patient's perceptions about himself by commenting on the thoughts, feelings, and drawings of "another boy" who also experienced sexual abuse. Are you now putting words in the head of the boy in your office or contaminating the accuracy of his recall (Ceci & Brunk, 1993) or taking away from his experience? These are necessary concerns—what the boy might do with such suggestions about his feelings—but I do not think it is a given one way or the other. The hope is to initiate discussion so that some correction can occur.

GUILT AND SHAME

In order to reduce feelings of guilt and shame, these need to be brought out into the open. Each of these concepts has developmental qualities, both with regard to their formation and with regard to the boy's ability to discuss them (Damon, 1988).

Shame is difficult to address (Fossum & Mason, 1986). It is maintained by being secretive, and it is also very difficult and very painful for the boy to articulate. It is the psychic equivalent of walking around naked all day, next to someone more handsome and more muscular than oneself. Older latency-aged and adolescent boys are capable of talking about shame, though they are never truly willing to do so. Even boys who inappropriately disclose and have no boundaries often are unable to talk about this feeling.

We have a natural instinct, when we see shame in a sexually abused boy, to provide support and reassurances. We do so in an effort to eliminate the shame that permeates all other aspects of himself, making him feel different and less capable.

A better way to provide support is to make it more meaningful—to add language to the experience of support. For example, most boys will work hard not to think about their abuse. They may never think about whether they feel guilty, and their behavioral reactivity is the only indication that they are overwhelmed by feelings of shame and inadequacy. Statements to these boys of the following type are likely to be unheard and unincorporated: "Lots of kids think it is their fault that they were molested. But it's not your fault," "You didn't ask for it to happen," "Grownups shouldn't treat kids that way," and "If he would have asked you for permission you would have said 'no.' "

I think repeated dialogue that goes something like the following is more helpful, particularly with latency-aged and adolescent boys. The boy here is Steve, a 13-year-old. Both Steve and his 8-year-old sister, Molly, were molested by a stepuncle, Harold. The first knowledge of the abuse came from Steve, who told another relative. The abuse of Steve's sister only emerged later.

Therapist It's typical that kids have mixed feelings about what happened. They can feel mad at themselves, that's blaming yourself, or they can feel mad at whoever did it, and even more have feelings like confusion over why it happened, sadness about what it all means about themselves. Some kids even tell me they feel so ashamed they don't want other people to ever see them again because they're sure they know all about it and will think they're stupid. Do you recognize any of those feelings in yourself?

Steve I don't know. You said a lot of them.

Therapist I'm sorry. You're right. Let's see, I said sad, anxious, anger at themselves, anger at the other person, and then the biggie— ashamed.

Steve I'm supposed to choose one?

Therapist Most boys have more than one.

Steve I think I have all of them.

Therapist You have all of them and maybe even ones I didn't even say.

Steve Probably.

Therapist So what makes you mad at yourself?

Steve I was stupid.

Therapist How were you stupid?

Steve Going with him and all.

Therapist You were stupid because you went with Harold?

Steve Well, he had molested my sister.

Therapist You knew he had done that before you went with him?

Steve Well, no, but I should have.

Therapist Man, you're blaming yourself for not knowing something no one would know.

Steve Well, I feel stupid.

Therapist But I want to make sure you feel stupid only about things you could have done something about. Not for things you couldn't have known.

Steve Molly told Mom after I told my aunt.

Therapist Now that's something to feel proud about. Your telling your aunt let Molly get it off her chest.

Steve Yeah, he was going to do it to her again.

Therapist I dare you to feel stupid about protecting your sister.

It is important sometimes that the therapist examine the self-blame in as minute a manner as possible. This can help open up the boy to hearing alternative interpretations and let him accept cognitions that are affirming, not self-defeating. It is also critical to realize that working and reworking the same self-defeating thoughts is usually important. Children are usually polite to adults and will say the things we want to hear, not necessarily what is true.

Dealing with guilt and shame can also be a goal-directed therapeutic process. The therapist can develop a number of goals pertaining to negative and self-defeating thoughts that the child agrees to counter. Through dialogue, the therapist can identify ways in which the boy behaves in a victim type of manner (e.g., "How do kids pick on you at school?") or in a manner that reflects his perception that he is "bad." Both the negative thoughts and victim behavior can be made foci of the treatment, with goals established on how to behave differently at home, in school, or with friends.

SELF-INTEGRITY

Self-integrity is an advanced concept similar to guilt and shame, primarily because it requires a level of self-perception that does not occur until late in the concrete operations stage of cognitive development. Because of that, I prefer not to think about techniques per se but rather about creating a therapeutic holding environment that enables the boy to think about himself in all his diversity (e.g., broken, unbroken, normal, not normal, gay, straight).

No young boy will know how to respond to you if you ask him an arcane question about self-integrity. However, he will know what you are talking about if you approach it from the angle of alienation. Alienation can include alienation from self as well as alienation from others. As the boy moves into adolescence, he becomes able to talk more clearly about being in touch with his feelings, knowing how his feelings and thoughts are interconnected, and whether or not he feels as if he is "inside his body" at that moment. These issues are some of the self-issues that also pertain to dissociation (Putnam, 1993).

The most practical way to address issues of self-integrity with a sexually abused boy or adolescent would be to help him develop a greater sense of connection between his thoughts, feelings, and behaviors. This is directly counter to both alienation and dissociation. For example, Steve's mother reported that after a visit to his father, Steve exploded at his younger sister, Molly. When she confronted him, Steve had no idea why he had behaved in that way, and the mother was worried that he was not appropriately contrite. When Steve talks, he seems both embarrassed and indifferent about the situation, and he has a difficult time talking about it or recalling the event.

Therapist Now we're at the part of doing therapy that I really hate. I get to be the heavy for your Mom.

Steve You mean about Molly? I don't want to talk about it.

Therapist Who does? I don't want to bring it up and you wish it'd just go away.

Steve So let's just leave it alone.

Therapist Part of me wants to leave it alone and another part of me thinks we should use this as a way to learn how to make you into the kid you want to be.

Steve What do you mean by that?

Therapist Well, Harold was an asshole to you. I don't think you ever want to be an asshole to Molly.

Steve I don't.

Therapist That's right. You're not mean. You just explode and feel like shit afterwards.

Steve I know I do. I hate that feeling.

Therapist And rather than spread the shitty feeling around, you clam up. Don't want to talk about it.

Steve She was crying.

Therapist Molly was crying. She felt hurt by you.

Steve Yeah.

Therapist How many people knew you were crying on the inside?

Steve No one. But I was.

Therapist You think you were mad at her?

Steve No. I don't know why I did it.

Therapist Anything make you mad earlier in the day?

Steve My dad's such an ass.

Therapist So he made you feel mad.

Steve Frustrated.

Therapist Frustrated. So frustrated you exploded and Molly was in the way?

Steve Yeah.

Therapist That happens all the time after you're with your dad.

Steve This is the first time I hit Molly.

Therapist I'm sorry. I wasn't clear. This is the first time you hit Molly, but your Dad always makes you frustrated.

Steve Always.

Therapist And so frustration at Dad leads to explosions at home and then you feel like shit because that's not how you wanted to be.

Steve Yeah.

Therapist What gets you so frustrated at his house?

Steve He just ignores me. Acts like I'm not there. Spends all the time with his new wife.

Therapist Now that's helpful. He doesn't only make you frustrated. You also feel hurt. Ignored. Like you're not important.

Steve Exactly.

From this point, I was able to help Steve identify more accurately the various feelings he had and, over the next several sessions, help him understand how these feelings and thoughts got played out. Although anger management strategies are not based in self-theory, they do have a positive effect on overall self-integrity.

SEXUAL SELF

Problems in this area are frequent and expected. This is true even if no one is reporting overt sexual behavioral manifestations. Again, the guiding principle is articulation of an accurate self-perspective and integrating an aberrant sexual self into an authentic self. I have found it useful to use the items from the sexual concerns scale of the TSC–C (Briere, 1989b) as a lead-in. These include questions related to sexual feelings and sexual urges. However, it is even more useful to make the dialogue about sexual feelings and thoughts as personally relevant as possible: "Why did he choose to moleste me?" "Does this mean I'm gay?" "What do other kids think?" "What will I tell my girlfriend and what will she think about me when she hears about it?" The therapist needs to ask questions of this type and, for many boys, model a range of responses as well. The aim is not to be provocative but to allow the boy to open up the often split-off part of himself and thus enable corrective thinking.

I have learned from Paul Gerber to step boldly in asking questions and to expect that a significant history of sexual abuse will have some sexuality-specific outcomes. He has developed lists of questions that he uses in his work as Clinical Director at Hennepin County Home School. These are designed to provide openings to discussion and include frank questioning about sexual behaviors that duplicate the abuse. He and I both agree that use of these questions must be judicious.

Zach had originally told me to quit asking him about what he had done to his younger sister. This 12-year-old could talk about what his stepfather had done to him, but he needed to see how his abuse and victimizing were connected. At the beginning of a session, I told him we had some tough work to do, but I was not going to spend too much time on it and he only had to read what I wrote, listed below:

What Happened	What I Think	What I Feel	How I Act
Stepdad touched → my privates	I'm bad; He's stupid	→ Sad, alone	→ Pretend it did not affect me
I touch my sister's privates	→ I'm bad; I'm stupid	→ No one understands	→ Do not talk; get mad if asked
Dr. Friedrich asks about what I did to my sister	→ Doesn't he know I can't talk about it?	→ Sad, alone, hurt	→ Get mad

I had written this down on a sheet of paper. The contents were bits and pieces of what the boy had told me, as well as some inferences from his responses to several tests. Once the chart was in front of him, I reread each of the three events, going from left to right. I also pointed out that he felt alone or misunderstood after each of these three things. By talking about it, I was helping him feel less alone. I think the chart was not as overwhelming to him as questioning him directly. In addition, the chart represented in some ways a "gift" to the boy because of my work on it. The issues were finally on the table and could be addressed.

12

Self-Theory: Group Therapy

The man is speaking to the boy, who is wanting, who is wary.
—Caddy, 1989, p. 47

This chapter will focus exclusively on pair therapy (Selman & Schultz, 1990) and its modification for use with sexually abused boys. Pair therapy could legitimately be presented in the group therapy chapters for attachment, dysregulation, or self-issues. But the original reason I began to see sexually abused boys in dyads was not because of attachment concerns. Rather it made more sense to manage the frequent dyscontrol that occurs in a boys group by limiting the number of boys. In addition, the more I appreciate its utility, the more I realize that the self of the sexually abused boy is enhanced and corrected via interpersonal processes, with small groups being an excellent vehicle for developing therapeutic interpersonal contexts.

There are a variety of reasons why it is excellent clinical practice to see boys in dyads. A primary rationale that is in keeping with a dyadic focus is the fact that smaller groups are less likely to overly arouse boys who are already too easily dysregulated. Dyads also lend themselves to greater control and structure of the group process. A boy in a dyad can only be rejected by one other boy, not by a group of five or six. The greater control and structure that are available with dyads are absolutely essential when your focus is on creating a consistently corrective and positive relationship.

Secondary reasons are that in many locales the number of boys available for group therapy is small. Many of us think about groups being most appropriate when there is a critical mass (e.g., five to eight group members) (Yalom, 1975). But what if you have three boys in your agency who need therapy? If you adhere to conventional group practice directives, you will have to work with them individually or not at all. Another scenario is that the five boys on your caseload are split fairly evenly between those with more of a victim stance and those who are more the victimizer. I think that any time victimizing boys exceed a 1:4 ratio with victimized boys, the therapist will have group management problems. Structured, short-term psychoeducational groups can handle a smaller ratio but not if the group process is more critical.

The dyad is the basic unit of human interaction. Many latency-aged boys have yet to master successful dyadic interaction or communication, much less communication with a larger group. Their play with you is parallel at best, even though they are clearly of the age at which they could play interactively. I once heard that the resolution of the Oedipal complex was about resolving one's ability to have a relationship with more than one person simultaneously (i.e., with both mother and father). The rather primitive and disorganized quality (i.e., pre-Oedipal) that is characteristic of the interpersonal dynamics of many sexually abused boys would suggest that a dyad is the place to start. The boys simply are not ready for a triad.

A dyad also lends itself to better screening and selection of group members. Typical group process works best with reasonably verbal, mature boys who have some capacity for self-regulation. I believe dyads make for better use of group process. Two boys who are reasonably similar, albeit immature and reactive, can still work with each other and not get lost in a group of more capable boys.

A frequent reason for my use of pair therapy is that I often only have two similarly aged boys at a time, not five to six as is recommended. Or I have four boys, two of whom are balanced more on the victim end and two boys who are more offender based in their styles. A group of those four boys is not going to work as effectively as two pairs. In addition, you typically will have to focus less on policing the victimizing boys if they are in a dyad by themselves.

Learning self-control and countering dysregulation is also related to predictability. Pair therapy allows you to work with a consistent set of players and reduce the disruptions that come with large, open-ended groups. The boys that I see in pairs do not benefit very much from a psychoeducational approach to therapy. The metaphor of learning disabilities is useful here. Emotionally disturbed boys are learning disabled when it comes to processing emotions and generalizing their experiences. They need to practice, with a lot of role play, the opportunities they could not get as part of a group of seven to eight boys completing a 12- to 15-week program. Although this type of psychoeducational approach will be useful for a number of boys, I do not think agitated, sexually reactive and aggressive boys are going to be helped.

❑ Theoretical Framework

The developmental theory that is the basis of pair therapy is quite compelling and definitely is directed at how children and adolescents become more complex interpersonal beings. Robert Selman has spent much of his career studying how children negotiate with each other, how they form friendships, and how they share experiences. A basic premise is that social interaction becomes more mature as the child learns how to integrate and balance two related developmental tasks—intimacy and autonomy (Selman & Schultz, 1990). These are also the same developmental lines suggested by Kegan (1982) and discussed briefly in Chapter 10. Intimacy involves the sharing of experience, whereas autonomy requires some capacity to negotiate interpersonal conflict. Both of these tasks are critical to the formation of any relationship, as well as to dyadic therapy. In addition, they comprise the essential dialectic in all individuals.

Of particular relevance to the development of sexual abuse victims is the fact that they were treated without empathy; hence, they will have to work extra hard to learn empathy. Pair therapy appears particularly useful at helping victims learn how to treat each other with empathy (Nakkula & Selman, 1991). The dilemmas encountered in dyadic interaction enable the boys to develop a repertoire of interpersonal ethics. Pair therapy encourages a boy to treat his counterpart more fairly than he himself was treated in his own primary relationships.

According to Selman and Schultz (1990), the development of both intimacy and autonomy proceeds in stages. The most primitive developmental level is labeled the *egocentric-impulsive* level. Experiences are shared (intimacy) via unreflective, even contagious, imitation (e.g., mutual burping and farting among boys), whereas negotiation (autonomy) is equally impulsive and not thought through (e.g., physically or verbally striking out, leaving the room when the stress level gets too high). The next developmental level is called *unilateral one-way*. Experiences are now shared through expressive enthusiasm but without a true concern for reciprocity (e.g., excitement in a group member over another boy's toy that he brings to group but not making eye contact or doing anything that indicates true engagement). At this level, autonomy is reflected in one-way orders or through automatic passivity/compliance (e.g., stereotypical roles in dyads with a leader and follower whose roles reflect those taken in their own victimization and family experiences).

For purposes of elaboration, think of a typical opening group strategy in which you have each boy describe the events of the week or his feelings about some issue or event. Boys at the egocentric-impulsive level are likely to blurt out something that may or may not be related to what another boy said. It may even be completely irrelevant to the group. If one boy starts swinging his legs, another boy might also. A spontaneous and highly sensitive revelation by one might be ignored or responded to inappropriately by another. Give and take, even at a basic level, is not a given. Imagine having five or six boys like that. Distress frequently creates regression in social situations. Imagine now that all of the boys are at the egocentric-impulsive level. How do you do group work, or build on mutual, reciprocal sharing and cooperation? You cannot. You could be left doing day care for 60 to 90 minutes.

Although there are two more levels, *reciprocal-reflective* and *mutual third-person* (see Table 12.1), a reasonable goal for therapists working in pairs with child or adolescent male victims is to approximate the

Table 12.1 Interpersonal Developmental Levels

Intimacy Function	Level	Autonomy Function
Contagious imitation	Egocentric-impulsive	Impulsive fight or flight
Expressive enthusiasm but no reciprocity	Unilateral one-way	Use of one-way commands or automatic obedience
Joint reflection on similar perceptions/ experiences	Reciprocal-reflective	Cooperation via persuasion or deference
Collaborative, empathic reflection	Mutual third-person	Collaborative strategies integrating needs of both parties

SOURCE: Adapted from *Making a Friend in Youth: Developmental Theory in Pair Therapy* (p. 29), by R. L. Selman and L. H. Schultz (1990). Chicago: University of Chicago Press. Copyright © 1990 University of Chicago Press. Adapted with permission.

reciprocal-reflective level. This is the stuff of true group interaction, with one group member saying or sharing something, and the other boy responding with something similar, but not in a dismissive or competitive way. This can lead to true intimacy. Autonomy is promulgated at this level through the use of cooperative strategies that are designed to either persuade or appease. However, both boys are able to use each of these styles and their roles are not so clearly fixed.

To illustrate the reciprocal-reflective level, consider this scene between two sexually abused 13-year-old boys with whom I worked as a dyad during their hospitalizations following suicide attempts. Although each boy was relatively closed off when talking individually to his resident, putting them together was quite helpful. One was led to talk about his feelings prior to his suicide attempt. He revealed that once he made the decision, he felt "completely calm, like nothing could touch me." The other boy said that he got the same feeling "just before I punched someone." This led to a discussion about anger and how suicide was an angry act. Each boy was then able to talk about who he most wanted to get back at with his suicide. Rather than the suicide being a disembodied, unprocessed event, it now had been articulated, and each boy had to think before trying it again.

In addition to these four developmental levels in the child's capacity to coordinate the perspectives of autonomy and intimacy, Selman and Schulz (1990) introduce another concept regarding interpersonal negotiation strategies. These strategies can be either other- or self-transforming. The self/other distinction is quite pertinent to group work with sexual abuse victims. In fact, Elliott (1994) describes other-directedness as a common interpersonal stance, even in high-functioning adult female sexual abuse victims.

The self/other transforming styles get worked out interpersonally in groups of sexually abused boys by the assumption of victim/ victimizer roles and strategies. For example, at the unilateral one-way level, other-transforming interpersonal negotiation strategies consist of one-way orders to control the other boy for his own gratification (e.g., "give me your popcorn"). The boy who is a self-transformer may then comply as part of his routine submission to another boy's wishes. Flexibility among these roles is very appropriate. It suggests more maturity when boys can move between self- and other-transforming strategies.

Typically, pair therapy facilitators are not very active or directive. Their role is to monitor group process and provide an adult suppressant (Selman & Schultz, 1990). However, I believe that pair therapists need to be more active with sexually abused boys. This is true not only because of the unique needs of sexually abused boys, but also because the model of therapy that I am presenting demands a more direct approach.

❏ Strategies

SCREENING

Pair therapy will succeed if you choose two boys who are at very similar developmental levels. Deviation by one developmental level, as described by Selman and Schultz (1990) in Table 12.1, is too much. For example, if you place a boy who is primarily egocentric-impulsive with one who is unilateral one-way, the more mature child will pursue a relationship with you and not with his peer.

Although the case material that I will present is with two extremely disturbed boys, pair therapy should not be relegated only to the most troubled children. Latency-aged boys at either the egocentric-impulsive or unilateral one-way levels can work together. Even two teenage boys who have the capacity for reciprocity in their relationship can be combined, with the dyadic experience being as effective as one they could have in a larger group.

In addition to developmental level, other important screening considerations include the following: similarity in victimization experiences; similar intelligence and language capacities; and, typically, a similar age, although chronological age and developmental level are certainly not a perfect correlation.

TECHNIQUES

The methods described attempt to create a context for self-development. Structure and predictability form the basis of the early pair therapy groups until the boys can learn to tolerate more ambiguity or until they have internalized the group's structure (see Table 12.2).

These activities involve an opening ritual that includes a weekly check-in and a snack. The check-in includes a review of any homework assignments (given to more competent boys), as well as revisiting any salient issues raised in the prior group meeting.

The snack and check-in both "feed" the boys as well as provide an opportunity to integrate their therapy experience into a more coherent whole. Severely disturbed boys do not integrate. Their lives are a series of fragmentary occurrences. A review helps to counter continued fragmentation by tying their week to a predictable event. Because a focus on the positive is critical to this model, the weekly check-in includes a review of a range of urges, including helpful ones.

Goals are traditionally established early on, usually in two broad areas: self-control and relationships. For example, one boy may have three goals that are monitored weekly and that persist over the duration of the dyad. They could include reducing the number of fights by using several strategies: removing himself from the scene or expressing feelings; using imagery to counter intrusive thoughts; and increasing the number and length of positive exchanges with foster parents.

Table 12.2 Typical Pair Therapy Structure

---

1. Opening Ritual
2. Snack
3. Weekly check-in
   a. Helpful urges
   b. Hurtful urges
   c. Sexual urges
4. Weekly goal review—two broad sets of goals traditionally established early on
   a. Self-control
   b. Relationships
5. Review of homework (assigned to more competent boys who have integrated the pair process)
6. Receive rewards—in session/group home
7. Shared activity (therapeutic games, drawings, collages)
8. Role play
   a. Problem solving
   b. Feelings exchange
9. Process events of the group's session/Receive rewards
10. Closing ritual

Homework related to the goals is regularly assigned. Written confirmation that it was accomplished results in rewards given both in the therapy session and in the home setting. Homework is not assigned to boys at the egocentric-impulsive level because it is not realistic to expect them to comply.

The meat of the session, and the portion that allows for some marvelous interchanges and the emergence of group process, is contained in the shared activity. It is best to select activities that invite reciprocity and taking turns. Through the use of therapeutic games, either generic or specific to sexual abuse, the boys learn how to disclose, talk about a broad range of feelings, exhibit concern and respect for the other's experiences, and do all of this in a manner such that they do not become overwhelmed or lose control. Frequently, the shared activity can naturally give rise to role plays that can lead to more effective problem solving or reciprocal sharing of feelings.

For example, in response to a question in a relational game, "Tell me about a time when you were really scared?" an 11-year-old boy, Adam, told his 12-year-old peer, Ben, "You'll laugh at me." There was truth in his statement, based on eight prior sessions. Ben was taken aback and did not know how to respond. The therapist set up a demonstration in which Adam disclosed first to him and then to Ben, after Ben had agreed to imitate the therapist.

The shared activities are not only sexual abuse related but deal with other issues of family violence, rejection by peers and parents, and loneliness. Through the use of props, pictures, or constructional activities, including structured opportunities for shared disclosure, the boys in the dyads begin to learn that relationships can be positive, reciprocal, and nonexploitative. I realize that the efficacy of group approaches to social skill training has been disputed (Beelman, Pfingsten, & Losel, 1994). Furthermore, there are no empirical outcome data on pair therapy with sexually abused boys. However, I am convinced that the intimacy and longer-term work allowed with pairs make the type of social skill training/support provided more likely to be efficacious and generalizable.

The sharing of the abuse experience bears more elaboration. For primitively organized boys, this needs to occur more than two or three times during the course of the group. This can be done through an activity called "Bad Things That Happened to Me" (illustrated in Table 12.3) in which the therapist acts as a recorder to provide more formality to the process and to establish a written record of what is said. (A video camera, especially if pornography is not an issue for the boy, can add to the boy's ability to integrate a disembodied voice with his image of himself.)

The group ends with a recontracting for goals, assigning homework (to then be shared with the boys' caregivers), and a closing ritual, sometimes the same as the opening ritual. The pair session lasts from 45 to 80 minutes, depending on the maturity of the boys. I think that the rituals serve to sandwich the experience, thus marking it in a way that makes it both more tolerable and more likely to be integrated into the boys' overall self-representation.

In fact, the supportive, nurturing posture that can be promulgated when working with only two boys, as opposed to a larger number, is a key feature and makes growth possible. As you can see in Table 12.2,

Table 12.3 Bad Things That Happened to Me

Time 1 (highly reactive to each other)	
Jason	*Joe*
1. Butt-fucked	1. Butt-fucked hundreds of times
2. Butt-fucked millions of times	2. Spit out come
3. Ate come	3. Took dirty picture of me
4. Tied me up with tape and took porno	4. Made me have sex with other guys
5. Burned my butt	5. Mean to me

Time 2 (more depressed and ashamed)	
1. They left me all alone	1. They never come to see me
	2. They must think I'm bad

Time 3 (still depressed but more articulate)	
1. I lost my mom	1. No one comes to see me anymore
2. I asked him to stop and he never would	2. Made me think I'm gay
	3. Sometimes I think about them when I don't want to

I suggest generosity with snacks and rewards. But I have seen difficult little boys who automatically provoke rejection, start to anticipate the sessions, view the other boy as a friend, and become more likeable to the therapist. I am reminded here of Sullivan's (1953) emphasis on the overwhelming importance of a "chum" for latency-aged boys. Watching these boys begin to get eager to spend time with each other and even try some new self-transforming or other-transforming approaches informs you that you are onto something. Pair work is messier and more trying than briefer, structured, larger groups, but change can occur on multiple levels, not only on the cognitive level. I believe that the following case material will illustrate this contention.

❑ Case Presentation

Quite by accident, I met two very similar boys at close to the same time. Each had experienced a remarkable level of sexual abuse, loss, and deprivation. Each was a tremendous management problem in both outpatient and inpatient settings. Both boys desperately needed corrective emotional experiences, but they could not even begin to tolerate individual therapy. In fact, throughout my first several, individual sessions with each of these boys, I felt completely disconnected from them and had the eerie experience of interacting with boys who were fragments of a complete self. I would see different pieces of the same boy and usually these pieces were fleeting and difficult for me to tolerate.

Jason was 6 years old when I met him. He came into the hospital because of aggressive and sexualized behavior in his kindergarten setting. He had lived with his grandfather for the prior 2 years because his mother had found him to be unmanageable. Over the course of my involvement with this boy, I found out that the grandfather had molested all of his sisters and daughters. His one son had committed suicide at the age of 15, and the family lore was that he had been a sexual abuse victim of the grandfather as well.

Jason reported that he had watched pornography with his grandfather, and, on these occasions, mutual masturbation and fellatio occurred. He was very bothered by cameras of all types and reported having been filmed while engaging in sexual acts with another boy. A subsequent search of the grandfather's house did turn up a large quantity of pornography, both commercial and homemade. Jason appeared in some of the pornography.

When he was first hospitalized, Jason was extremely provocative. He was one of those boys who instantly activated a very negative and defensive counterreaction in staff members. He was sexual with all staff, male and female, and grossly inappropriate socially. He could not focus in class for more than a few minutes and was significantly behind in acquiring the basic skills needed at the kindergarten level. However, he did have near average intelligence overall as measured by the Wechsler Intelligence Scale for Children–Revised (Wechsler, 1974).

As soon as our suspicion turned to the grandfather, he and Jason's mother stopped visits to the hospital. Jason became nondisclosive for several weeks afterwards. However, this was an extremely unpredictable boy, and he resumed blurting out different aspects of his life in impulsive ways and in ways that I now more clearly see reflecting a dissociative-like process.

Joe was chronologically a first grader and about 7 months older than Jason when he was admitted to the hospital 2 weeks after Jason. However, he was in a self-contained setting with two other boys and a teacher's aide. The net effect of Joe's admission to the hospital was an extremely challenged inpatient unit that resorted at times to moderately punitive interactions with both boys. However, both Joe and Jason were somewhat willing to work for privileges based on an ever-evolving and creative point system. As is the case with almost every point system that I have used with very troubled children, the targeted behaviors rarely seem to either generalize or get internalized.

Joe was the youngest of several siblings removed from their parents because of severe abuse and neglect. He was adopted at the age of 3 years by a family that had several other adoptive and foster children. Joe was molested over a 2-year period by two of his male siblings in the home, as well as by a relative of his adoptive father. This hospital admission was his second, and his adoptive parents took steps to revoke his adoption shortly after his admission. Psychological testing completed at admission was not valid, but it suggested that Joe's intellectual abilities, under the best of circumstances, were at least average. (See Table 12.4 for intelligence and academic achievement results administered 16 months apart, with the first administration at the time each boy came into the hospital.)

I met with each boy individually shortly after he came into the hospital. My subjective experience was that both were wildly reactive and clearly bothered by the intensity of being alone in a small room with a male. I quickly realized that they were very immature socially. For example, when I asked Joe a question about how many classmates he had at school before he came into the hospital, he responded with a story about a nurse who had cheated him out of a snack. He never made eye contact with me, moved the upper part of his body up and down while talking to me, and broke off halfway through the story. I was able to figure out what he was trying to say to me only because I had heard that scenario from another staff member in morning rounds. What had actually happened was that Joe had stolen the snacks of two other children and had been caught. He was unable to get out of the moment long enough to respond to me about something else.

Table 12.4 Changes Over Time in Psychological Test Results

Jason	Time 1	Time 2
WISC–R (Wechsler, 1974)		
VIQ	84	101
PIQ	100	95
FSIQ	90	98
WRAT–R (Jastak & Wilkinson, 1984)		
Reading	81	92
Math	85	93
Spelling	77	86
Joe		
WISC–R (Wechsler, 1974)		
VIQ	90	98
PIQ	96	102
FSIQ	92	102
WRAT–R (Jastak & Wilkinson, 1984)		
Reading	94	91
Math	88	98
Spelling	89	94

NOTE: Expressed in standard scores ($x = 100$, $SD = 15$).

Several strands came together to push me into seeing both of these boys as a dyad. First, one of my former students and a wonderful friend, Bill Luecke, had introduced me to the work of Robert Selman (Selman, 1980). Second, more out of desperation than any brilliant therapeutic move on my part, I assumed that the adage of the whole being greater than the sum of its parts might prove to be true with these two boys. I hoped that I could add essentially one third of an ego with one third of an ego and come up with something closer to having an entire boy in the room at one time. Finally, I enjoy challenges—even ones that seem insurmountable. I am sure that I come by this honestly because of my father, a Lutheran missionary to staunchly Catholic, Hispanic, migrant farm workers in south Texas.

In the next section, I will summarize a number of sessions over the course of my therapy with these two boys, including some follow-up information. Therapy notes are edited to highlight key developmental features.

SYNOPSIS OF SESSIONS

Session 1. We met in the hospital group therapy room and, on the way in, Joe and Jason were wiping mucus on each other. They immediately tore into the popcorn treats that I had brought and then fought over the video game controls, even though there were two. Joe shoved Jason four times during this exchange, and Jason reciprocated twice. They started and abandoned checkers, foosball, and Sorry. In drawing, Joe's squiggle was a breast (see Winnicott, 1965). Joe and Jason both cupped their hands over their chests and strutted around the room in this manner, repeatedly bumping into me where I was sitting on the floor. I ended the session after 35 minutes. At the next morning's staff meeting, it was reported that Joe had to be placed into seclusion for the first time that week.

Session 2. Once in the unit group room, both boys began to fly around the room like pretend airplanes, bumping into me and each other. I separated them, giving them separate drawing activities at either side of the room with the direction to draw something they could then talk about at the end. Joe said he was going to draw a penis, and Jason said he was going to draw a butthole. Despite my efforts at redirection, I gave in and each boy had a partially completed drawing to talk about. As Jason began to show his picture, Joe hit him. Jason then fell on the floor and began to cry inconsolably. I ended the session after 29 minutes. Both Joe and Jason were placed in seclusion later that day.

Session 3. Both boys again fought over the video game. I then alternated playing foosball with each boy while the other was playing the video game. Their drawings were again of sexual details, and both Joe and Jason grabbed their crotches after this. I implemented a point system with points for sharing, doing things together, nonsexual drawings, and nonsexual behavior. They were fined for aggression toward me or each other. The session ended after 40 minutes. Neither boy was placed in seclusion.

Session 8. The boys finished a collaborative family drawing on 3 foot × 3 foot paper for which they both received points. Jason drew his grandfather naked. Joe drew his biological mother as a witch but did not include his adoptive parents. He did add the head of one of his perpetrators. Each boy marked on each other an equal number of times with felt tip markers. Reciprocity was beginning. The session ended after 50 minutes.

Session 9. The point system for cooperation and respect for the other appeared to be working. Each boy completed the "Bad Things That Happen to Me" exercise (see Table 12.3). I stopped it after each boy clearly was becoming out of control. Video game collaboration took on a sexualized tone, and the session was ended at 32 minutes. Both boys were placed in seclusion shortly after return to unit.

Session 11. The session involved a shared drawing activity where both boys drew feelings of loneliness, sadness, happiness, and anger. Again, the boys marked on each other an equal number of times with the markers. The point system was again working, and the session ended at 52 minutes. Jason was placed in seclusion.

Session 13. After two foosball games, I returned to the boys' first lists about "bad things that happened to me." This triggered both boys hitting each other, a farting contest, and Joe slapping Jason on the butt. Jason grabbed at Joe's crotch, missed, and fell on the floor. He cried for approximately 30 seconds, seemingly unrelated to the fall. Both boys tolerated 3 minutes of time-out and returned to foosball. I planned their reentry to unit and contracted for compliance. The session ended at 50 minutes. Neither boy was placed in seclusion.

Session 14. I initiated a ritual of "high fives" at the beginning of the session. Jason joined Joe in criticizing the popcorn for being boring. In an effort to prompt their internalizing of me, we took Polaroid pictures of each boy standing next to me. Joe asked Jason to play foosball. The session ended after 50 minutes. At rounds the next morning, the nurse said that Joe had his picture of me sitting on his dresser. Jason's picture could not be found.

Session 19. Jason was discharged to a therapeutic foster home setting but now comes back to the unit for the therapy with Joe. The boys' relationship seemed to suffer. Joe said, "It's not fair" and would not share the video game. He then was able to state that he missed having Jason out of the hospital. The session ended at 55 minutes.

Session 21. Both boys were in therapeutic foster homes. Each boy was able to discuss feelings about his foster parents and his respite parents; the conversation focused on the food eaten in each family. The boys made lists of the foods they had eaten in their different homes. This had Jason idealizing his mother's food. I brought in the foster mothers at end of the session, and each boy introduced the other boy to his foster mother. Joe asked for a high five at the end of the session. The session lasted 60 minutes.

Session 28. Joe expressed concern that Jason was absent due to an illness. He agreed to brainstorm with me about how to express his concern, but he did not cooperate in making a card and he refused to do a high five. The session was over at 43 minutes. Subsequently, Joe's foster mother called to say that "the honeymoon is clearly over."

Session 35. I refocused both boys on the purpose of the group after Joe came in stating that his foster mother was upset with him for "mooning" another boy in the home. We began the second "Bad Things That Happen to Me" (listed in Table 12.3). Unlike the first one, which began to get fantastical, this time both boys seemed inhibited with each other, rather shy, clearly sad, and even ashamed. The themes predominantly echoed loneliness and abandonment—issues clearly significant in both boys' lives. We contracted around behavior at the foster homes and, following the session, shared this with the foster mothers. The session ended at 55 minutes.

Session 43. Jason shared a piece of gum with Joe and asked why he had missed the previous session, expressing that "it wasn't as much fun." The boys were able to complete an entire game of Sorry with minimal rule violation. Joe spontaneously talked about having shoved another boy in school. This led to some problem solving around Joe's behavior with the other boy. Each of the boys participated in a role play; this was stopped and started three times before we could complete it. Each boy took home a picture of the other boy. The session ended at 53 minutes. As they were walking out the door, Jason told Joe, "You better be here next week."

Session 46. Joe had broken his arm in the intervening week, and Jason inhibited, on two separate occasions, an urge to hit Joe's cast. He finally gave in during a game of Sorry and then tolerated time-out. Another Polaroid picture was sent home. The session ended at 55 minutes.

Session 51. Jason was absent because he had the stomach flu. Joe was concerned. He demanded to call Jason at his foster home but instead agreed to write a letter.

Session 63. The rules appeared to be working, and the point system had now been dropped. Each boy agreed to goals on cooperating in the group and taking turns. We began work on a third "Bad Things That Happen to Me" (see Table 12.3) and took Polaroids of me for each boy and one of both boys together. The boys agreed to look at them during the week if they started getting upset. The session ended at 55 minutes.

Session 64. Both boys were reluctant to be more specific in the "Bad Things That Happen to Me," but they were able to articulate more clearly their loneliness and feelings of abandonment. Joe began to cry and focused on how he missed his adoptive family. Jason was able to tolerate his tears. The session ended at 60 minutes.

Session 69. It appeared that Jason would be moving to a long-term foster placement with the potential for adoption. Joe described horror stories from his adoptive home and was able to talk coherently, although somewhat automatically, about his sexual abuse by his adoptive brothers while his adoptive mother ignored what was going on. He then got angry with Jason and stated that he should be adopted before Jason because he was older. Each of the boys participated in an activity in which they talked about good points and bad points of adoption. I began to teach the boys strategies for dealing with intrusive thoughts. The session ended after 70 minutes.

Session 77. The session involved structured disclosure around victimization prompted by Joe's foster mother reporting his increasing masturbation. Disclosure was facilitated by the use of a tape recorder. The boys frequently checked each other's reaction as they spoke, and they were able to respect the other. Jason talked about his own masturbation and how he even would put his finger in his rectum. Joe agreed that he did the same. The session ended at 70 minutes.

Session 88. Jason had grabbed two girls in school the previous week. This seemed to be related to his accidentally running into his grandfather and mother at Social Services. His foster mother sent along a note wanting both boys to discuss this and problem solve. Jason alternated being angry, rejecting, defensive, and shutting down. Joe wanted to know more of what Jason had done and talked about his own sexual touching of children. He mentioned that children were afraid of him at school. This led to both boys participating in a joint activity about sexual feelings, urges, wishes, and fears. The boys even occasionally offered some relevant comments to each other, with Joe, for example, stating, "I stay on the other side of the playground from the kindergarten kids." Each of them agreed to help the other control their urges. The session ended after 70 minutes.

Session 97. Preparations were under way for Jason to move out of town with his long-term foster family. His weekend visits with them had gone well. Joe came in with a broken arm, wearing a cast that extended to the middle of his upper arm. He had fallen from the porch of his foster home. He gave two different versions of the story and finally settled on the one that I had heard earlier from his foster mother. Jason then showed him several scars on his hands and knees, clearly feeling one-upped by Joe's cast. Three different times he showed self-restraint at not hitting Joe's cast and was praised each time. We had group activity on how both boys should treat a hurt dog, a hurt cat, or a hurt friend. Jason wrote a get well card for Joe and we both signed his cast. Joe's only other signature prior to that was from his foster mother. The session ended at 70 minutes.

Session 103. This was the last joint session with both boys. Jason was settling into his new home and clearly was less interested in both Joe and myself. Joe responded by acting hurt, grabbing more of the snack, but then apologizing with my prompt. Each boy took a final group picture.

CONCLUSIONS

Although initial sessions occurred as often as twice a week while both boys were in the hospital, the duration of the therapy extended over a 26-month period. Each boy exhibited qualitative changes, including more appropriate behavior in the foster home, greater control over sexual behavior, and increased willingness to talk about feelings. In addition, each boy was able to exhibit greater reciprocity and even mutuality with the other. The fact that Jason was viewed as adoptable and Joe was still in the same foster home are also qualitative markers of success.

The only measures that I had available both at hospital admission and then 16 to 17 months later were results from the WISC–R (Wechsler, 1974) and the Wide Range Achievement Tests–Revised (WRAT–R) (Jastak & Wilkinson, 1984). The time elapsed between initial testing and retesting was sufficient enough to ensure that any practice effect was minimal. Both boys showed improvement in terms of overall intellectual abilities and in selected achievement test scores. The most parsimonious explanation of this improvement is that each was capable of tolerating and cooperating with one-on-one adult-child interaction at the time of the second testing. I would also like to think that both boys were increasingly more organized and coherent and thus could independently have some motivation to do well. Both boys continued to be elevated, at termination, on four to six subscales from the Child Behavior Checklist (Achenbach & Edelbrock, 1983).

Other pair therapy work I have done has neither lasted as long nor been with boys who have been so seriously problematic. Long-term follow-up is not available on either Joe or Jason, although each boy did receive some additional therapy at the end of the pair therapy they had with me. However, a reading of the edited session comments suggests greater tolerance for the other's distress, more self-control, greater reciprocity, and a more integrated way of behaving.

13

Self-Theory: Family Therapy

Even the helpless victim of a hopeless situation, facing a fate he cannot change, may rise above himself, may grow beyond himself and by so doing change himself.

—Frankl, 1992, p. 147

It is a bit strange for me, whose primary theoretical identification is with family systems theory, to talk about self-issues and family therapy. Traditionally, issues of the self have been thought to be better dealt with through intensive individual therapy. However, by this time in the book, you are appreciative of the fact that the attachment-derived internal working model comprises a portion of the self of the developing child. This internal model becomes incorporated into the adult self as well. From early on, I was drawn to interpersonal perspectives and to the theoreticians who discussed interpersonal issues in the formulation of the self. These include the ego psychologists Harry Stack Sullivan (1953), Karen Horney (1950), and Eric Erickson (1950), and object relations theorists, Guntrip (1969) and Winnicott (1965). In fact, Horney (1950) described three resolutions to interpersonal conflict that are prototypes of the three basic attachment types of secure, avoidant, and resistant. She said that people learn over time to move away from (avoidant), move against (resistant), or move toward other people. An approach that flexibly combines all three styles is the most healthy resolution, with moving toward other people, in moderation, a mark of security.

Two very large questions organize this chapter. The first question pertains to how family therapy can help a sexually abused boy feel less shameful and be more accurate in understanding himself and the sexual abuse experience. In addition, can family therapy help him behave in a more mature and integrated fashion that includes more self-control than is typically seen in sexually abused boys?

The second question pertains to the self of the parents. By self of the parents, I mean those primarily individual issues that drive the parents' view of themselves as capable, effective, and as loving their child. For example, how can family therapy empower a mother to behave more appropriately with a son who treats her like her ex-husband, the same man who molested this boy? Her son hits her, locks her out of the house, and on at least one occasion urinated on her while she was sleeping. How can the therapist help her derive a more optimistic view of her possibilities with this boy so that she can try out new strategies while managing her depression better because she can view the origins of it more accurately?

In a manner more specific to issues of self-development but still similar to some of the strategies described in Chapter 5, the therapist who works with this boy and his family wants to help the parents step back and see themselves as more competent and capable individuals. Possibly because I live in the upper midwest, I have heard, at least four times in the past 2 years, parents state something like the following: "I have this fear that some TV camera is going to come to my door and the newsman is going to ask me if I am aware that I am the mother of the next Jeffrey Dahmer?" That is a profoundly negative and pessimistic view of self as a parent.

Driving many of the strategies that I will talk about in this chapter are the perspectives that both reality and the perception of one's self is a creative, constructionistic process (White & Epston, 1990). Helping a patient appreciate his complexity is a far better outcome than his simply adhering to a rather grimly simplistic view of self as "a bad parent" or a "bad child." I am also firmly convinced that articulation, expression, and elaboration are critical to self-development. No one ever grows unless he is talking about who he is and all his various and sundry, hidden, dark and negative perspectives.

❏ **Enhancing the Child's Self-Development via Family Therapy**

A delightful piece of family therapy is a videotape with Salvador Minuchin requesting that the acting-out boy behave in a similar manner right there in the office. The boy refused and shrank back in his chair. He suddenly seemed to be much less powerful and was then capable of self-control. This appreciation that the boy could choose whether or not he acted out had an initially subtle but eventually powerful effect on the family's perception of the child. There is no therapeutic milieu that carries more potential for the parents to quickly see their child in a more positive manner than family therapy. The obverse is also true, I realize. But although some therapists may anticipate that family sessions will fall apart and that the status quo will persist, I think it is very important to maintain a hopeful, activist stance.

There are a number of ways you can help parents see their child as having more competence. Timing is a key feature here and putting child and parent together in the same room will backfire unless the abuse is acknowledged, the parents supportive, and there is a commitment by the parents to the child.

Children can role-play their mature and less mature sides, and, once the child is in the room, the parents have an in vivo opportunity to practice their parenting. The therapist can talk to the parents, in front of the child, about the child's competence in the individual or group therapy in which he has participated up to that point. A range of techniques are suggested in Table 13.1.

Table 13.1 Techniques

1. Get unacceptable feelings out in the open and normalize them

2. Examine parental attributions regarding their child, their parenting, etc.

3. Examine the process of parenting

4. Externalize the problem

5. Explore parents' projection and feelings of betrayal

6. Create new stories about the child

7. Appeal to parents' complexity

8. Goal setting

❑ **Enhancing the Parents'
Self-Development via Family Therapy**

GETTING UNACCEPTABLE FEELINGS OUT IN THE OPEN

Here is an example of when articulation of the problem can be helpful. The shameful mother is ambivalent about expressing the fact that
she finds her son's behavior disgusting. In fact, she wants as little to
do with him as possible. These thoughts are driving her behavior toward him, but casual questioning of her only reveals the fact that "yes,
he's challenging, but after all, he's my son." As someone who is trained
in observing human behavior, you are clearly aware of the tension and
distance that exists between the members of this dyad. Somewhere
along the line—not in front of the boy of course—the mother should
have some sense that you are aware of those true feelings. This can
happen in several ways. You could suggest that those feelings are quite
likely given the situation and you expect her to have them and be struggling with them, or you can give her an opportunity to articulate that
distress out of earshot of the boy.

Once you have helped the parents identify that there really are aspects of themselves that dislike the child intensely, you are then in a
position in which you can help the parents identify parts of themselves
that are committed to the child, that behave competently with the

child, and that remain open and hopeful for future growth in their boy (Schwartz, 1987).

EXAMINING PARENTAL ATTRIBUTIONS

Nonoffending parents who have been victimized in the past and who now have a child who has been sexually abused may blame the child. However, they are also most likely to view themselves as inept. Countering that perspective will be very difficult, but family therapy is an appropriate arena to confront that parental perception. This may be done by empowering the parents and allowing them to see their effectiveness with small, easily attainable goals that are set in terms of their ability to parent their child.

Some of the same "all-or-nothing" thinking that the child has about himself will be found in the parents regarding their perception of the child. The parents can be encouraged to externalize their negative projections of the child. For example, it is rare for parents to "always hate their child." However, there are times when their "dislike for the child gets the better of them." Dialoguing between the parents and the child about these specific instances can go a long way toward developing a more positive sense of connection between the parents and the child.

When I discuss self issues of parents, I am speaking specifically to the parents' perceptions of themselves as capable, competent parents. I am not addressing personality change or turning someone with a sadistic personality disorder into someone who no longer terrorizes his or her child. Although the task of altering parental perceptions is easier than creating personality change, it is no mean feat, nevertheless. But I think it can be done with many parents via a combination of support for change, creating alternatives, empowering the parents, and helping them learn new skills.

Traditionally, we speak about the role of cognitive therapy to examine the parents' attitudes about their competence or the behavior of their child. Essentially, the view is that the attributions held by the parents are pessimistic, not valid, and self-defeating. At times, however, a more traditional cognitive approach can sound like something that could be charitably described as coercion. Consider the following example.

Mom Why didn't I pick up on what he was doing to Tim? I just kick myself about it.

Therapist You figure that you should have protected Tim if you had known what to look for.

Mom Yeah, the other moms in the group all picked up on it. Their kids told them right away.

Therapist If other moms picked up on it, you're really beating on yourself because you didn't.

Mom Exactly. I really feel like shit. (Starts to cry)

Therapist Well let's take a look at how realistic it is for you to think that you could have detected it. Basically, you're saying anyone but Janice could have caught it.

Mom That's what I'm saying.

Therapist You're the only person in the world who could have missed it.

Mom Feels like that to me.

Therapist You were home every minute of the day. You could have caught it.

Mom No, I wasn't, but I should have been.

Therapist But Ralph made you get a job.

Mom I shouldn't have listened to him. Look where it got me.

Therapist Ralph is slick. Look at what you've found out. He made your kids not trust you. He did it to other kids and got away with it. I think it's unrealistic for you to think you could have stopped him or picked up on what was going on right away.

Mom Look at what I did to him. I don't care what it is. Realistic or whatever (Begins to cry again).

Therapist (After a pause). But as soon as you got wind of it, you kicked Ralph out and got Tim in to see me.

Mom I know what you're trying to do. You're trying to make me feel better. But it's not working. Sex abuse is on TV all the time. You'd think it'd get through my thick head.

Although a parent who assumes responsibility is better than one who shirks responsibility, this mom was not only resisting my efforts at getting her to see herself more optimistically, but she was also underfunctioning at home because of her guilt and depression. This also made her less available in a nurturing or consoling way. Consequently, Tim was suffering a triple loss: his sexual abuse, lack of structure and guidance from mom, and marked decline in the mother's attention and support.

Thus I decided to try a different approach, one that did not absolve the mother of the guilt she was determined to hang on to, but one that let her have the guilt as long as she reactivated some of her competent self. This is, in some ways, a version of the "parts" therapy described by Schwartz (1987). Each individual contains an internal family system consisting of a number of characters/players. For most parents and children with whom I use this technique, I talk about "parts."

Mom He just stood there and sassed me. Swore at me. I know he feels mad at me. I have to let him get that out, don't I?

Therapist So you've decided, I screwed up. I've got to take all the crap Tim dishes out. As long as he needs to dump crap on me I need to take it since I screwed up by not picking up on it sooner.

Mom Well I don't like it.

Therapist Of course you don't like it. There's the sensitive part of you that is willing to do whatever you think he needs. Isn't that true?

Mom Well, I try.

Therapist And then there's the part that says, the more he acts like this, the more he's sounding like my dad or his father and I don't want to see that happen.

Mom He does sound just like his dad. Gets his face all that way.

Therapist So let's do your future daughter-in-law a favor at least. She'll thank you if we can get that good mom part going again and you put your foot down.

Mom How?

Therapist Just because you are sensitive on the one hand doesn't mean you can't put your foot down on the other.

Mom I don't know.

Therapist You want to be more than just a garbage can for all his crap, don't you?

Mom That was my mom. No, I can't let that happen again. All it got her was an early grave.

Therapist And your dad never had to apologize and never learned his lesson.

Mom He never did. The creep. Poor mom. (Starting to cry again)

Therapist (After a pause). Let's do something in honor of your mother. Something that lets her know she's got a daughter who can take a stand.

Mom How's that?

Therapist (Drawing a circle on a piece of paper). The circle is you, Janice. If all you do is take crap you're just a wimp. All of you is a wimp. A garbage can for crap. But you want to be more than that. Don't you?

Mom Yeah. I really do.

Therapist You are more than that. Part of you got Tim to therapy. Another part of you knows Tim needs you to put your foot down. Another part of you is soft, not like a wimp, but like a mother should be. (The circle is now divided into four pieces; see Figure 13.1.)

Mom But what do I do?

Therapist If you sit in this wimp part, you roll over and play dead. You say, "I ruined his life. Shoot me."

Mom But then he'd be like his dad.

Therapist Right. You got the point. So what if we kick in some of your other parts. The sensitive part that still can read him a story at night because he's afraid of his bedroom.

Mom Did I ever tell you I used to do that?

Therapist Yes, you did, and you can again. Particularly if we get this strong part of you going. The one that needs to reteach him right from wrong.

Mom He just flares at me now. Just goes off.

Therapist But you used to be able to control Tim.

Mom Before all this.

Therapist You're sounding like the wimpy part. You're more than just a wimp. If you were just a wimp, you couldn't love him like you do.

The use of this "parts" approach allows you to help the parents see some of themselves as positive. They cannot hear all positive, but if it is in the context of some good, some not so good, it is more tolerable to people who hate themselves. I have never seen this approach contribute to dissociation either, which has been raised as a concern.

EXAMINING THE PROCESS OF PARENTING

When you were never given permission to be a parent and when all the expectations were that you would do a lousy job, a typical response is to operate rather blindly. These parents sometimes seem as if they never stop to think about the what or why of parenting. The results

Figure 13.1. Therapeutic Drawing

are random parenting acts or parents who gradually slide into less helpful stances with their child, including avoidant/tolerant or avoidant/punitive.

If you simply take a skill-deficit perspective, you are out there trying to teach new strategies to ill-prepared people. Skills are not enough. These parents' behavior outside of my office is sometimes a complete mystery to me. Webster-Stratton's (1991) review of the treatment of conduct-disordered children indicated that a parent-based approach is most effective, but programs that expand their focus to include depression, marital discord, stress, and lack of support in the parents are needed to improve overall success.

It is important to find out whether or not the parents that you see were ever given permission by their family of origin either to get married or to parent children. Talking about permission giving for parenting is also a way for the therapist to exhibit the necessary compassion that is in such short supply in these individual's lives. Frequently, their "head is down," they are "plodding" along, and they are fearful to stop and examine what is going on around them for fear that they will never get started again. For you to be a voice of concern and compassion at this time in their lives can begin the process of altering their internal working model.

EXTERNALIZING THE PROBLEM

This is a phenomenon that comes from White (1989) and is a several-stage process. For example, let us consider a boy who compulsively masturbates. This creates rejection by his older sister and aggravates his mother's already somewhat hostile relationship with him. The first step in taking action around this would be to ask questions that are labeled "relative influence questions" (White, 1989, p. 8). Questions are asked that encourage people who live with a child to describe different ways in which the problem has influenced their lives and their relationships. These first questions would encourage the mother and the sister to map out the influence of the problem in their lives and in their relationship with the boy. A second set of questions encourages the mother and the daughter, as well as the son, to talk about how they have influenced the problem of compulsive masturbation. Often the therapist and parents can be surprised at different, albeit small, ways that family members have influenced the problem and have been effective in dealing with it. This might be identified, for example, when a mother, in a fit of pique, threatens not to let the boy watch the TV until he agrees not to masturbate. She could be able to recall that she actually had some influence over the course of the problem for a few days.

The next step in the process of externalization would be to define the problem that will be externalized. The details of the effects of the problem or the nature of the problem are always unique and need to be sought out. Generic questions are not that useful. For example, it is important to know when the boy masturbates. A mutually acceptable definition of the problem is then created. The masturbation problem, for example, can be described as an entity, and through the use of language, parents and siblings can be asked about the degree to which they cooperate with the maintenance of the problem (i.e., get angry at the boy, say insulting words to him) or whether they defy the influence of the problem and turn their back on the behaviors that maintain it. This treating the problem as an entity unto itself is extremely useful. Not only does it allow the family members to gain some perspective on how they interact with the problem, it lends itself to altering their perspective on the boy. For example, with a boy who is compulsively masturbating, it was useful to identify the fact that the mother and sister could have some influence on whether or not the boy masturbated, and he could go along with the idea that the problem was an entity, outside himself, that was getting in the way of his enjoyment (e.g., with his friends). In this way he could take a stance in turning his back on the problem.

DISCUSSING BETRAYAL BY THE CHILD

To truly accept a child, you need to accept all parts of him, the good and the bad. This is why acceptance of the boy as a victim is more than sympathy for what has happened (see Chapter 3). A complex picture expands your therapy opportunities. The parents also need to be viewed as complex and likely to have a full range of feelings about their son, including resentment about the fact that he has been victimized and has made them feel inept. I strongly believe that the majority of the parents that I work with, despite frequently having significant psychological problems, sincerely wish to do a better job with their children. Often, however, they are not very capable of more mature and complex psychological processing. Their internal working model may be fairly simplistic, so that people are constructed in terms of black and white, with very few shades of gray in between. In an effort to get these parents to be more positive to their son, you may collude in ignoring the fact that they feel extremely hurt and even betrayed by his victimization. His sexual abuse has pointed out their failure as parents. They may be very hurt because their son did not disclose the abuse early on.

Exploring betrayal and hatred is not something that can be done in front of the boy. But if the parent is reasonably capable, I believe it is important for the therapist to provide the parent with an opportunity to talk about these feelings of hurt and even betrayal. Parents need to ask, "Why did it happen to me?" in an effort to begin to address the pent-up frustration and hurt that accompanies their son's victimization. Discussing betrayal is also a way to address some of the shame and guilt that they experience and that gets in the way of a fuller connection to their son. This is not a strategy that is useful with primitive or primarily rejecting parents. They think he is a "little shit" and talking about betrayal only solidifies their beliefs.

However, this strategy can be useful when you see parents who, week in and week out, try to do the right thing for their son. They are being dutiful and keeping a stiff upper lip and, in general, have remained positive. These are the parents who have both the psychological resources and the resilience that will let them benefit from discussion of the broad range of feelings they have for their son. Other parents who have worked hard in their own therapy may be aided in having a chance to give voice to their feelings of betrayal. This strategy works because it promotes integration of the disparate, seemingly conflicted aspects of the parent. For example, a committed mother, who vacillated from week to week in being able to deal with her son, was thrilled when I said, "You know, you can really hate him from time to time. You'd be honest if you did. If you hate him every now and then, you can love him better at other times."

CREATING NEW STORIES ABOUT THE CHILD

This again comes from the constructionist approach to family therapy (White & Epston, 1990). It extends the reframing of the boy's behavior into a larger and more future-oriented sphere. The reality of the day-to-day life of many of the boys and their parents is often quite grim. They have a hard time thinking about the future, and when they do, their future perspective is not very positive. Their view of their son is that he is "problem saturated" not "solution saturated." Projecting the boy into the future and thinking out loud about his being a capable and competent son, providing grandchildren, and correcting the wrongs of the sexual abuse can be empowering to all parties. It can create a broader picture of a boy to whom the parents can commit themselves. Included in this is the concept of a unique, hopeful outcome.

APPEAL TO THE PARENTS' COMPLEXITY

Sometimes I think about this technique as being the "therapeutic use for shame and guilt induction." Some parents are overly critical and hostile toward their boy and seem to show very little flexibility or alternative, more positive behaviors. How can you get them to treat the boy more positively? Reframes and positive connotations are seemingly ignored.

I worked with a mother who had some mental health training. Despite this area of expertise, she was an extremely brittle, almost constantly angry and negativistic parent. Sessions with her and her son were always painful and left me feeling quite bloodied and pessimistic. An opening came in my work with her, however, after she received a fairly critical annual review by her supervisor. The feedback session had included suggestions that she had "borderline features." She knew how negative this diagnosis was, and her anxiety about being considered as having such a pathological personality disorder was evident when she came into the session and brought up her personnel rating early in the session.

She asked me whether or not I thought she had borderline features or a borderline personality disorder. I could see that she looked apprehensive at what I might say. Because of my underlying strategy of looking for the positive in every patient I work with, my reply was that "You're far too complicated to be borderline." This allowed me to work with her in terms of thinking about the different ways in which she was both positive and negative with her son, along with doing some of the more neutral and mundane aspects of parenting. We even set it up so that she agreed to do a number of more positive things with her son as a way to prove to her employer that she was not as bad a person as her boss had decided. This allowed a type of interesting therapeutic triangulation (Bowen, 1978), which worked for this mother and her son. This speaks again to the almost always present

Table 13.2 Self-Representation-Related Goal Setting

	Goal 1	Goal 2
Optimal Outcome (+2)	I do not blame myself and affirm my good parenting	Think about Ned's behavior without automatically thinking about his father
Acceptable Outcome (0)	When I blame myself, I counter it rationally	Realize Ned is like me and like his father—he is going to have positives and negatives
Current Level (–2)	Blame myself whenever I think about it	Everything Ned does makes me think about his father and hate him

wish by parents, even those parents with significant abuse histories, to be better parents to their son and to improve that aspect of self that includes parenting.

GOAL SETTING

Using the format outlined in Table 5.2, therapist and parent arrive at a number of positively worded goals—that is, to increase the frequency of behaviors designed to enhance their self-perspective and their view of their son's competence. Germane to self-perception are goals that pertain to the following:

1. Interrupting self-critical thoughts about their parenting
2. Interrupting pejorative thoughts about their son
3. Increasing the congruency of their statements, feelings, and actions toward the son
4. Parenting from their most loving "part"

We revisit Ned and his mother, Joyce, regarding two goals that were set up about self-development. These are listed in Table 13.2 and include attributions that Joyce made about her failure as a wife and mother and her ability to see Ned with increasingly positive accuracy, rather than to see him as potentially dangerous and hurtful to her.

❏ **Concluding Remarks**

Writing this book has been invigorating—most of the time. The integrated model presented here is stimulating to me intellectually and makes a great deal of sense clinically. I believe it distills some of the "head" and "heart" central to good, informed, and compassionate clinical work. Now we need to turn our attention to documenting the effectiveness of an approach of this type—for both boys and girls and their families.

Appendix A
Child Sexual Behavior Inventory: Version 3

Please answer all questions regarding the child, ages 2 to 12 years, you are bringing to the clinic today.

For office use only	
	Today's Date
5-10	__ __ – __ __ – 19__ __
11-12	_____ Child's age at last birthday
	Child's Sex (Check one)
13	_____ 1. Male
	_____ 2. Female
	Child's Race (Check one)
14	_____ 1. White
	_____ 2. Black
	_____ 3. Hispanic

For office
use only

_____   4. Asian

_____   5. Native American

_____   6. Other

The child's *primary female caregiver must complete this item.* Who
is completing this questionnaire? (Check one)

15   _____   1. Natural mother

_____   2. Adoptive mother

_____   3. Stepmother

_____   4. Foster mother

16-17   _____   Total number of children in family (include this child
and all biological, step-, and adoptive children who
are a brother or sister to this child).

Marital Status (Check one)

18   _____   1. Single, never married, not living with a partner

_____   2. Single, never married, living with a partner

_____   3. Married

_____   4. Separated

_____   5. Divorced, not remarried, not living with a partner

_____   6. Divorced but remarried or living with a partner

_____   7. Widowed

_____   8. Widowed but remarried or living with a partner

Education

How many years did the father go to school (Circle one
number; 12 = high school graduate or GED)

19-20   3 4 5 6 7 8 9 10 11 12 13 14 15 16 17 18 19 20 21 22 23 24

How many years did the mother go to school (Circle one
number; 12 = high school graduate or GED)

21-22   3 4 5 6 7 8 9 10 11 12 13 14 15 16 17 18 19 20 21 22 23 24

For office use only	

Family's Total Income Each Year (Check one)

23

_____ 1. Less than $10,000

_____ 2. $10,001 through $15,000

_____ 3. $15,001 through $25,000

_____ 4. $25,001 through $35,000

_____ 5. $35,001 through $45,000

_____ 6. $45,001 through $60,000

_____ 7. $60,001 through $80,000

_____ 8. $80,001 and above

Please answer two questions about your child's friends.
How many close friends does your child have? (Check one)

24

_____ 0. None

_____ 1. 1

_____ 2. 2

_____ 3. 3 or more

How well does your child get along with his or her friends?

25

_____ 1. Better than average

_____ 2. Average

_____ 3. Worse than average

Day Care

26-27   In the past 6 months, how many hours per week has your child been cared for out of the home by an adult caregiver? _____

Life Events

Please check all events listed below that have *ever* happened to your child. Please be frank. Answers are confidential.

28   _____   Either parent has been hospitalized

29   _____   Either parent died

30   _____   Parents divorced

31   _____   Parents separated

For office use only			
32	_____		Other deaths in the immediate family
33	_____		Child was physically abused
34	_____		Child was *suspected of having been sexually abused* by an adolescent or adult

Check whether any of the following have happened to your child.

35-37	_____		Child was *sexually abused*, and this was determined by social services
38	_____		Child was in foster care
39	_____		Child was adopted
40	_____		Child required more than one day of hospitalization
41	_____		Parents hit, slapped, or shoved each other
42	_____		Either parent arrested

General Questions About Your Child
(Circle Yes or No for each statement)

43	Yes	No	My child has had counseling in the past 6 months
44	Yes	No	My child has a physical handicap
45	Yes	No	My child is mentally retarded
46	Yes	No	My child can watch any TV or movies he or she wants
47	Yes	No	My child has seen naked adults on TV or in a movie
48	Yes	No	My child has seen adults having sex on TV or in a movie
49	Yes	No	My child has seen his or her parents having sex
50	Yes	No	We have magazines at home with nude pictures in them
51	Yes	No	If my child wants, he or she can sleep all or part of the night with his or her parents
52	Yes	No	My child has seen me or another adult naked in the past 6 months
53	Yes	No	My child has showered or bathed with an adult in the past 6 months

For office use only					

Questions About Your Child's Behavior

Please circle the number that tells how often your child has shown the following behaviors *recently or in the last 6 months:*

0 = Never
1 = Less than 1 time per month
2 = 1 to 3 times per month
3 = At least 1 time per week

54	0	1	2	3	Dresses like the opposite sex
55	0	1	2	3	Stands too close to people
56	0	1	2	3	Talks about wanting to be the opposite sex
57	0	1	2	3	Touches sex (private) parts when in public places
58	0	1	2	3	Masturbates with hand
59	0	1	2	3	Draws sex parts when drawing pictures of people
60	0	1	2	3	Touches or tries to touch his or her mother's or other women's breasts
61	0	1	2	3	Masturbates with toy or object (blanket, pillow, etc.)
62	0	1	2	3	Plays with a friend
63	0	1	2	3	Touches another child's sex (private) parts
64	0	1	2	3	Tries to have sexual intercourse with another child or adult
65	0	1	2	3	Puts mouth on another child's or adult's sex parts
66	0	1	2	3	Touches sex (private) parts when at home
67	0	1	2	3	Touches an adult's sex (private) parts
68	0	1	2	3	Touches animals' sexual parts
69	0	1	2	3	Makes sexual sounds (sighs, moans, heavy breathing, etc.)
70	0	1	2	3	Asks others to engage in sexual acts with him or her
71	0	1	2	3	Rubs body against people or furniture
72	0	1	2	3	Puts objects in vagina or rectum
73	0	1	2	3	Tries to look at people when they are nude or undressing
74	0	1	2	3	Pretends that dolls or stuffed animals are having sex
75	0	1	2	3	Shows sex (private) parts to adults
76	0	1	2	3	Tries to look at pictures of nude or partially dressed people
77	0	1	2	3	Talks about sexual acts
78	0	1	2	3	Kisses adults he or she does not know well
79	0	1	2	3	Gets upset when adults are kissing or hugging

For office use only					
80	0	1	2	3	Overly friendly with men he or she does not know well
81	0	1	2	3	Kisses other children he or she does not know well
82	0	1	2	3	Talks flirtatiously
83	0	1	2	3	Tries to undress other children against their will (opening pants, shirt, etc.)
84	0	1	2	3	Eats breakfast
85	0	1	2	3	Wants to watch TV or movies that show nudity or sex
86	0	1	2	3	When kissing, tries to put his or her tongue in other person's mouth
87	0	1	2	3	Hugs adults he or she does not know well
88	0	1	2	3	Shows sex (private) parts to children
89	0	1	2	3	Tries to undress adults against their will (opening pants, shirt, etc.)
90	0	1	2	3	Is very interested in the opposite sex
91	0	1	2	3	Puts his or her mouth on mother's or other women's breasts
92	0	1	2	3	Knows more about sex than other children the same age
93	0	1	2	3	Other sexual behaviors (please describe)

A. _____

B. _____

For these last questions, think about your child's *entire life, not just* the past 6 months.

Circle One

94	True	False	I have seen my child touch his or her private parts, even in the privacy of his or her home.
95	True	False	My child has shown sexual behavior.
96	True	False	It is normal for children to have sexual feelings and curiosity.

107-109	0 1 D

Appendix B
Goal Attainment Scaling

	Goal 1	Goal 2	Goal 3	Goal 4	Goal 5	Goal 6

Optimal
level of
change
(+2)

Acceptable
level of
change
(0)

Current
level of
behavior
(–2)

References

Achenbach, T. M., & Edelbrock, C. (1983). *Manual for the Child Behavior Checklist and the revised Child Behavior Profile.* Burlington: University of Vermont, Department of Psychiatry.

Achenbach, T. M., & Edelbrock, C. (1986). *Manual for the Teacher Report Form and teacher version of the Child Behavior Profile.* Burlington: University of Vermont, Department of Psychiatry.

Ainsworth, M. D. S. (1989). Attachments beyond infancy. *American Psychologist, 44,* 709-716.

Ainsworth, M. D. S., Blehar, M. C., Waters, E., & Wall, S. (1978). *Patterns of attachment: A psychological study of the strange situation.* Hillsdale, NJ: Lawrence Erlbaum.

Alexander, P. C. (1992). Application of attachment theory to the study of sexual abuse. *Journal of Consulting and Clinical Psychology, 60,* 185-195.

Alexander, P. C. (1993). The differential effects of abuse characteristics and attachment in the prediction of long-term effects of sexual abuse. *Journal of Interpersonal Violence, 8,* 346-362.

American Psychiatric Association. (1994). *Diagnostic and statistical manual of mental disorders* (4th ed.). Washington, DC: Author.

Anastopoulos, A. D., & Barkley, R. A. (1992). Attention deficit-hyperactivity disorder. In C. E. Walker & M. C. Roberts (Eds.), *Handbook of clinical child psychology* (2nd ed., pp. 413-430). New York: John Wiley.

Armstrong, J., Putnam, F. W., & Carlson, E. (1993). *Adolescent–Dissociative Experiences Schedule* (Version 1.0). Unpublished test.

Auster, P. (1989). *Moon palace.* New York: Penguin.

227

Barkley, R. A. (1987). *Defiant children: Parent-teacher assignments*. New York: Guilford.

Bath, H. I., & Haapala, D. A. (1993). Intensive family preservation services with abused and neglected children: An examination of group differences. *Child Abuse and Neglect, 17*, 213-225.

Beeghly, M., & Cicchetti, D. (1994). Child maltreatment, attachment, and the self system: Emergence of an internal state lexicon in toddlers at high social risk. *Development and Psychopathology, 6*, 5-30.

Beelman, A., Pfingsten, U., & Losel, F. (1994). Effects of training social competence in children: A meta-analysis of recent evaluation studies. *Journal of Clinical Child Psychology, 23*, 260-271.

Belsky, J., Youngblade, L., & Pensky, E. (1989). Child rearing history, marital quality, and maternal affect: Intergenerational transmission in a low-risk sample. *Development and Psychopathology, 1*, 291-304.

Bene, E., & Anthony, E. J. (1976). *Manual for the children's version of the Family Relations Test*. Windsor, UK: NFER.

Benedict, L. L. W., & Zantra, A. A. J. (1993). Family environmental characteristics as risk factors for childhood sexual abuse. *Journal of Clinical Child Psychology, 22*, 365-374.

Benjamin, L. (1993). Every psychopathology is a gift of love. *Psychotherapy Research, 3*, 1-24.

Bentovim, A. (1992). *Trauma organized systems: Physical and sexual abuse in families*. London: Karnac.

Berliner, L. (1991). Therapy with victimized children and their families. *New Directions for Mental Health Services, 51*, 29-46.

Bernstein, E. M., & Putnam, F. W. (1986). Development, reliability, and validity of dissociation scale. *Journal of Nervous and Mental Disease, 174*, 727-735.

Bolton, F. G., Morris, L. A., & MacEachron, A. E. (1989). *Males at risk: The other side of sexual abuse*. Newbury Park, CA: Sage.

Bowen, M. (1978). *Family therapy in clinical practice*. New York: Jason Aronson.

Bowlby, J. (1969). *Attachment and loss: Vol. 1. Attachment*. New York: Basic Books.

Bowlby, J. (1973). *Attachment and loss: Vol. 2. Separation*. New York: Basic Books.

Bowlby, J. (1980). *Attachment and loss: Vol. 3. Loss*. New York: Basic Books.

Bowlby, J. (1984). Violence in the family as a disorder of the attachment and caregiving systems. *American Journal of Psychoanalysis, 44*, 9-28.

Brady, C., & Friedrich, W. N. (1982). Levels of intervention: A model for training in play therapy. *Journal of Clinical Child Psychology, 11*, 39-43.

Braun, B. G. (1988). The BASK model of dissociation. *Dissociation, 1*, 4-23.

Bretherton, I., Ridgeway, D., & Cassidy, J. (1990). Assessing internal working models of the attachment relationship: An attachment story completion task for 3-year-olds. In M. T. Grunberg, D. Cicchetti, & E. M. Cummings (Eds.), *Attachment in the preschool years* (pp. 273-308). Chicago: University of Chicago Press.

Bretherton, I., & Waters, E. (1986). Growing points of attachment theory and research. *Monographs of the Society for Research in Child Development, 50*, 1-290.

Bridges, G. L. (1990). Lisa's ritual, age 10. In D. Keenan & R. Lloyd (Eds.), *Looking for home* (pp. 193-194). Minneapolis, MN: Milkweed.

Briere, J. (1989a). *Therapy for adults molested as children: Beyond survival*. New York: Springer.

Briere, J. (1989b). *Trauma Symptom Checklist–Children.* Los Angeles: Department of Psychiatry, University of Southern California School of Medicine.

Briere, J. (1992). *Child abuse trauma: Theory and treatment of lasting effects.* Newbury Park, CA: Sage.

Briere, J. (1994). *Trauma Symptom Inventory.* Odessa, FL: Psychological Assessment Resources.

Briere, J., & Elliott, D. M. (1993). Sexual abuse, family environment, and psychological symptoms: On the validity of statistical control. *Journal of Consulting and Clinical Psychology, 61,* 284-288.

Briere, J., & Runtz, M. (1989). The Trauma Symptom Checklist (TSC–33): Early data on a new scale. *Journal of Interpersonal Violence, 4,* 151-163.

Briere, J., & Runtz, M. (1993). Childhood sexual abuse: Long-term sequelae and implications for psychological assessment. *Journal of Interpersonal Violence, 8,* 312-330.

Buchsbaum, H. K., Toth, S. L., Clyman, R. B., Cicchetti, D., & Emde, R. N. (1992). The use of a narrative story stem technique with maltreated children: Implications for theory and practice. *Development and Psychopathology, 4,* 603-625.

Burgess, A. W., Hartman, C. R., & McCormack, A. (1987). Abused to abuser: Antecedents of socially deviant behaviors. *American Journal of Psychiatry, 144,* 1431-1436.

Burkett, L. P. (1991). Parenting behaviors of women who were sexually abused in their families of origin. *Family Process, 30,* 421-434.

Burns, R. C., & Kaufman, S. M. (1972). *Actions, styles and symbols in Kinetic Family Drawing* (K-F-D). New York: Brunner/Mazel.

Caddy, J. (1989). *The color of mesabi bones.* Minneapolis, MN: Milkweed.

Calverly, R. M., Fischer, K. W., & Ayoub, C. (1994). Complex splitting of self-representations in sexually abused adolescent girls. *Development and Psychopathology, 6,* 195-213.

Carlson, V., Cicchetti, D., Barnett, D., & Braunwald, K. (1989). Disorganized/disoriented attachment relationships in maltreated infants. *Developmental Psychology, 25,* 525-531.

Caron, C., & Rutter, M. (1991). Comorbidity in child psychopathology: Concepts, issues, and research strategies. *Journal of Child Psychology and Psychiatry, 32,* 1063-1080.

Ceci, S. J., & Brunk, M. (1993). Suggestibility of the child witness: A historical review and synthesis. *Psychological Bulletin, 113,* 403-439.

Chodorow, N. (1978). *The reproduction of mothering.* Berkeley: University of California Press.

Cicchetti, D. (1989). How research on child maltreatment has informed the study of child development: Perspectives from developmental psychopathology. In D. Cicchetti & V. Carlson (Eds.), *Child maltreatment* (pp. 377-431). Cambridge, UK: Cambridge University Press.

Cicchetti, D., Cummings, E. M., Greenberg, M. T., & Marvin, R. S. (1990). An organizational perspective on attachment beyond infancy. In M. T. Greenberg, D. Cicchetti, & E. M. Cummings (Eds.), *Attachment in the preschool years* (pp. 3-50). Chicago: University of Chicago Press.

Cicchetti, D., Ganiban, J., & Barnett, D. (1991). Contributions from the study of high risk populations to understanding the development of emotion regulation. In J. Garber & K. A. Dodge (Eds.), *The development of emotion regulation and dysregulation* (pp. 15-48). New York: Cambridge University Press.

Cicchetti, D., Toth, S., & Bush, M. (1988). Developmental psychopathology and incompetence in childhood: Suggestions for intervention. In B. B. Lahey & A. E. Kazdin (Eds.), *Advances in clinical child psychology* (Vol. 11, pp. 1-77). New York: Plenum.

Cole, P. M., & Putnam, F. W. (1992). Effect of incest on self and social functioning: A developmental psychopathology perspective. *Journal of Consulting and Clinical Psychology, 60,* 174-184.

Craighead, W. E., Meyers, A. W., & Craighead, L. W. (1985). A conceptual model for cognitive-behavior therapy with children. *Journal of Abnormal Child Psychology, 13,* 331-342.

Crittenden, P. M. (1992). Treatment of anxious attachment in infancy and early childhood. *Development and Psychopathology, 4,* 575-602.

Crittenden, P. M. (1994). Peering into the black box: An exploratory treatise on the development of self in young children. In D. Cicchetti & S. L. Toth (Eds.), *Disorders and dysfunctions of the self* (pp. 79-148). Rochester, NY: University of Rochester Press.

Crittenden, P. M., & Ainsworth, M. D. S. (1989). Child maltreatment and attachment theory. In D. Cicchetti & V. Carlson (Eds.), *Child maltreatment* (pp. 432-463). Cambridge, UK: Cambridge University Press.

Crittenden, P. M., & Dilalla, D. L. (1988). Compulsive compliance: The development of an inhibitory coping strategy in infancy. *Journal of Abnormal Child Psychology, 16,* 585-599.

Cunningham, C., & MacFarlane, K. (1990). *When children molest children.* Orwell, VT: Safer Society Press.

Damon, W. (1988). *The moral child.* New York: Free Press.

Day, L., & Reznikoff, M. (1980). Preparation of children and parents for treatment at a children's psychiatric clinic through videotaped modeling. *Journal of Consulting and Clinical Psychology, 48,* 303-304.

Deblinger, E., McLeer, S. V., & Henry, D. (1990). Cognitive behavioral treatment for sexually abused children suffering post-traumatic stress: Preliminary findings. *Journal of the American Academy of Child and Adolescent Psychiatry, 29,* 747-752.

De Jong, A. R. (1989). Sexual interactions among siblings and cousins: Experimentation or exploration? *Child Abuse and Neglect, 13,* 271-279.

DeLozier, P. P. (1982). Attachment theory and child abuse. In C. M. Parkes & J. Stevenson-Hinde (Eds.), *The place of attachment in human behavior* (pp. 95-117). New York: Basic Books.

DeSalvo, L. (1989). *Virginia Woolf.* Boston: Beacon.

Dodge, K., & Garber, J. (1992). Domains of emotion regulation. In J. Garber & K. A. Dodge (Eds.), *The development of emotion regulation and dysregulation* (pp. 3-11). New York: Cambridge University Press.

Donovan, D. M., & McIntyre, D. (1990). *Healing the hurt child.* New York: Norton.

Downey, G., & Coyne, J. (1992). Children of depressed parents. *Psychological Bulletin, 108,* 50-76.

Durrant, M., & White, C. (1990). *Ideas for therapy with sexual abuse.* Adelaide, South Australia: Dulwich Centre Publications.

Eckenrode, J., Laird, M., & Doris, J. (1993). School performance and disciplinary problems among abused and neglected children. *Developmental Psychology, 29,* 53-62.

Egeland, B. (1994, October). *Mediators of the effects of child maltreatment on development adaptation in adolescence.* Paper presented at the 8th Annual Rochester Symposium on Developmental Psychopathology, Rochester, NY.

Egeland, B., & Erickson, M. F. (1983, August). *Psychologically unavailable caregiving: The effects on development of young children and the implications for intervention.* Paper presented at the International Conference on Psychological Abuse, Indianapolis, IN.

Egeland, B., Jacobvitz, D., & Sroufe, L. A. (1988). Breaking the cycle of abuse. *Child Development, 59,* 1080-1088.

Egeland, B., Sroufe, L. A., & Erickson, M. (1983). The developmental consequence of different patterns of maltreatment. *International Journal of Child Abuse and Neglect, 7,* 459-469.

Einbender, A. J., & Friedrich, W. N. (1989). Psychological functioning and behavior of sexually abused girls. *Journal of Consulting and Clinical Psychology, 57,* 155-157.

Elicker, J., Englund, M., & Sroufe, L. A. (1992). Predicting peer competence peer relationships in childhood from early parent-child relationships. In R. Ponks & G. Ladd (Eds.), *Family-peer relationships: Modes of linkage.* Hillsdale, NJ: Lawrence Erlbaum.

Elliott, D. M. (1994). Impaired object relations in professional women molested as children. *Psychotherapy, 31,* 79-86.

Elliott, D. M., & Briere, J. (1992). The sexually abused boy: Problems in manhood. *Medical Aspects of Human Sexuality, 26,* 68-71.

Erickson, E. (1950). *Childhood and society.* New York: Norton.

Eth, S., & Pynoos, R. S. (1985). Psychiatric intervention with children traumatized by violence. In E. Benedek & D. Schetky (Eds.), *Emerging issues in child psychiatry and the law* (pp. 285-319). New York: Brunner/Mazel.

Everson, M. D., Hunter, W. M., Runyon, D. K., Edelsohn, G. A., & Coulter, M. L. (1989). Maternal support following disclosure of incest. *American Journal of Orthopsychiatry, 59,* 197-207.

Exner, J. E. (1974). *The Rorschach: A comprehensive system.* New York: Wiley-Interscience.

Faller, K. C. (1988). *Child sexual abuse: An interdisciplinary manual for diagnosis, case management, and treatment.* New York: Columbia University Press.

Famularo, R., Fenton, T., Kinscherff, R., Ayoub, C., & Barnum, R. (1994). Maternal and child post-traumatic stress disorder in cases of child maltreatment. *Child Abuse and Neglect, 18,* 27-36.

Field, T. (1985). Attachment as psychobiological attunement: Being on the same wave length. In M. Reite, & T. Field (Eds.), *The psychobiology of attachment and separation* (pp. 415-450). Orlando, FL: Academic Press.

Finkelhor, D. (1984). Boys as victims: Review of the evidence. In D. Finkelhor (Ed.), *Child sexual abuse: New theory and research* (pp. 150-170). New York: Free Press.

Finkelhor, D., & Browne, A. (1985). The traumatic impact of child sexual abuse: A conceptualization. *American Journal of Orthopsychiatry, 55,* 530-541.

Fischer, S., & Greenberg, R. P. (Eds.). (1989). *The limits of biological treatments for psychological distress: Comparisons with psychotherapy and placebo.* Hillsdale, NJ: Lawrence Erlbaum.

Fossum, M. A., & Mason, M. J. (1986). *Facing shame.* New York: Norton.

Fox, N. (1994, October). *Conceptual and methodological issues in the study of children's responses to violence.* Paper presented at the 8th Annual Symposium on Developmental Psychopathology, Rochester, NY.

Fraiberg, S., Adelson, E., & Shapiro, V. (1975). Ghosts in the nursery: A psychoanalytic approach to the problems of impaired infant-mother relationships. *Journal of the American Academy of Child Psychiatry, 14,* 387-421.

Frankl, V. (1992). *Man's search for meaning*. Boston: Beacon.

Freud, A. (1963). The concept of developmental lines. *Psychoanalytic Study of the Child, 18*, 245-268.

Friedrich, W. N. (1988). Behavior problems in sexually abused children: An adaptational perspective. In G. E. Wyatt & G. J. Powell (Eds.), *Lasting effects of child sexual abuse* (pp. 171-191). Newbury Park: Sage.

Friedrich, W. N. (1990). *Psychotherapy of sexually abused children and their families*. New York: Norton.

Friedrich, W. N. (1991a). *Casebook of sexual abuse treatment*. New York: Norton.

Friedrich, W. N. (1991b). Mothers of sexually abused children: An MMPI study. *Journal of Clinical Psychology, 47*, 778-783.

Friedrich, W. N. (1991c, August). *New research with the Trauma Symptom Checklist–Children*. Paper presented at the annual meeting of the American Psychological Association, San Francisco.

Friedrich, W. N., Beilke, R. L., & Urquiza, A. J. (1987). Children from sexually abusive families: A behavioral comparison. *Journal of Interpersonal Violence, 2*, 391-402.

Friedrich, W. N., Beilke, R. L., & Urquiza, A. J. (1988). Behavior problems in young sexually abused boys: A comparison study. *Journal of Interpersonal Violence, 3*, 21-28.

Friedrich, W. N., Berliner, L., Urquiza, A. J., & Beilke, R. L. (1988). Brief diagnostic group treatment of sexually abused boys. *Journal of Interpersonal Violence, 3*, 331-343.

Friedrich, W. N., Einbender, A. J., & Luecke, W. J. (1983). Cognitive and behavioral characteristics of physically abused children. *Journal of Consulting and Clinical Psychology, 51*, 313-314.

Friedrich, W. N., Grambsch, P., Damon, L., Hewitt, S., Koverola, C., Lang, R., Wolfe, V., & Broughton, D. (1992). The Child Sexual Behavior Inventory: Normative and clinical contrasts. *Psychological Assessment, 4*, 303-311.

Friedrich, W. N., Jaworski, T. M., Huxsahl, J., & Bengston, B. (in press). *Sexual concerns and dissociation in sexually abused children and adolescents*. Manuscript submitted for publication.

Friedrich, W. N., & Luecke, W. J. (1988). Young school-age sexually aggressive children. *Professional Psychology, 19*, 155-164.

Friedrich, W. N., Luecke, W. J., Beilke, R. L., & Place, V. (1992). Psychotherapy outcome of sexually abused boys: An agency study. *Journal of Interpersonal Violence, 7*, 396-409.

Friedrich, W. N., & Reams, R. A. (1994). Parentification of children scale. Unpublished manuscript available from W. N. Friedrich, Mayo Clinic, Rochester, MN 55905.

Friedrich, W. N., & Schafer, L. C. (in press). Somatization in sexually abused children. *Journal of Pediatric Psychology*.

Friedrich, W. N., & Share, M. (in press). *Responses of sexually abused and nonabused children to the Roberts Apperception Test*. Manuscript under review for publication.

Friedrich, W. N., Tyler, J. D., & Clark, J. A. (1985). Personality and psychophysiological variables in abusive, neglectful, and low income control mothers. *Journal of Nervous and Mental Disease, 173*, 1-12.

Friedrich, W. N., Urquiza, A. J., & Beilke, R. L. (1986). Behavior problems in sexually abused young children. *Journal of Pediatric Psychology, 11*, 47-57.

Froderberg, A., Friedrich, W. N., Suman, V., & Houston, M. (1994). *Sexual abuse and kinesthetic recall*. Manuscript in preparation.

Gavey, N., Florence, J., Pezano, S., & Tan, J. (1990). Mother-blaming, the perfect alibi: Family therapy and the mothers of incest survivors. *Journal of Feminist Family Therapy, 2,* 1-25.

George, C., Kaplan, N., & Main, M. (1985). *The adult attachment interview.* Unpublished manuscript, University of California at Berkeley.

Gil, E. (1991). *The healing power of play: Working with abused children.* New York: Guilford.

Gil, E., & Johnson, T. C. (1993). *Sexualized children.* Rockville, MD: Launch Press.

Gilgun, J. F. (1989, November). *The sexual development of men sexually abused as children.* Paper presented at the annual conference of the National Committee on Family Relations, New Orleans, LA.

Gilligan, C. (1982). *In a different voice: Psychological theory and women's development.* Cambridge, MA: Harvard University Press.

Goodman, G. S., & Clarke-Stewart, A. (1991). Suggestibility in children's testimony: Implications for child sexual abuse investigations. In J. L. Doris (Ed.), *The suggestibility of children's recollections* (pp. 92-105). Washington, DC: American Psychological Association.

Gottman, J. M. (1994). *Why marriages succeed or fail.* New York: Simon & Schuster.

Greenberg, M. T., Speltz, M. L., & DeKleyen, M. (1993). The role of attachment in the early development of disruptive behavior problems. *Development and Psychopathology, 5,* 191-213.

Guest, J. (1976). *Ordinary people.* New York: Ballantine.

Guntrip, H. (1969). *Schizoid phenomena, object-relations, and the self.* New York: International Universities Press.

Harter, S. (1977). A cognitive-developmental approach to children's expression of conflicting feelings and a technique to facilitate such expression in play therapy. *Journal of Consulting and Clinical Psychology, 45,* 417-432.

Harter, S. (1982). The perceived competence scale for children. *Child Development, 53,* 87-97.

Harter, S. (1983a). Cognitive-developmental considerations in the conduct of play therapy. In C. E. Schaefer & K. J. O'Connor (Eds.), *Handbook of play therapy* (pp. 95-127). New York: John Wiley.

Harter, S. (1983b). Developmental perspectives on the self-system. In E. M. Hetherington (Ed.), *Handbook of child psychology: Socialization, personality, and social development* (4th ed., pp. 275-386). New York: John Wiley.

Harter, S. (1988). Developmental and dynamic changes in the nature of the self concept. In S. R. Shirk (Ed.), *Cognitive development and child psychotherapy.* New York: Plenum.

Harter, S., Alexander, P. C., & Niemeyer, R. A. (1988). Long-term effects of incestuous child abuse in college women: Social adjustment, social cognition, and family characteristics. *Journal of Consulting and Clinical Psychology, 56,* 5-8.

Hartman, C. R., & Burgess, A. W. (1993). Information processing of trauma. *Child Abuse and Neglect, 17,* 47-58.

Herman, J. L. (1992). *Trauma and recovery.* New York: Basic Books.

Herndon, A. D., & Law, J. G. (1986). Post-traumatic stress and the family: A multimethod approach to counseling. In C. R. Figley (Ed.), *Trauma and its wake. Vol. II: Traumatic stress theory, research, and intervention.* New York: Brunner/Mazel.

Hewitt, S. K., & Friedrich, W. N. (1991). Effects of probable sexual abuse on preschool children. In M. Q. Patton (Ed.), *Family sexual abuse: Front line research and evaluation* (pp. 57-74). Newbury Park, CA: Sage.

Hodges, K., McKnew, D., Cytryn, L., Stern, L., & Kline, J. (1982). The Child Assessment Schedule (CAS) diagnostic interview: A report on reliability and validity. *Journal of the American Academy of Child Psychiatry, 21,* 468-473.

Holub, M., Bauer, S., & Friedrich, W. N. (in press). Correlates of suicidal behavior and ideation in an adolescent psychiatric sample. *Journal of the American Academy of Child and Adolescent Psychiatry.*

Horney, K. (1950). *Neurosis and human growth.* New York: Norton.

Hunter, M. (1989). *Abused boys: The neglected victims of sexual abuse.* Lexington, MA: Lexington Books.

Hussey, D. L., Strom, G., & Singer, M. I. (1992). Male victims of sexual abuse: An analysis of adolescent psychiatric inpatients. *Child and Adolescent Social Work Journal, 9,* 491-503.

Jacobvitz, D., & Sroufe, L. A. (1987). The early caregiver-child relationship and attention-deficit disorder with hyperactivity in kindergarten: A prospective study. *Child Development, 58,* 1488-1495.

James, B. (1989). *Treating traumatized children.* Lexington, MA: Lexington Books.

Jastak, S., & Wilkinson, G. S. (1984). *Wide Range Achievement Test—Revised administration manual.* Wilmington, DE: Jastak Associates.

Jensen, J. B., Pease, J. J., ten Bensel, R., & Garfinkel, B. (1991). Growth hormone response patterns in sexually or physically abused boys. *Journal of the American Academy of Child and Adolescent Psychiatry, 30,* 784-790.

Jinich, S., & Salkas, A. (1994, January). *Group therapy for sexually abused boys.* Paper presented at the Conference on Responding to Child Maltreatment, San Diego, CA.

Johnson, T. C. (1991). Treatment of a sexually reactive girl. In W. N. Friedrich (Ed.), *Casebook of sexual abuse treatment* (pp. 270-290). New York: Norton.

Johnson, T. C., & Berry, C. (1989). Children who molest: A treatment program. *Journal of Interpersonal Violence, 4,* 185-203.

Jones, D. P. (1987). The untreatable family. *Child Abuse and Neglect, 11,* 409-420.

Jones, J. C., & Barlow, D. H. (1990). The etiology of post-traumatic stress disorder. *Clinical Psychology Review, 10,* 299-328.

Kamsler, A. (1990). Her-story in the making: Therapy with women who were sexually abused in childhood. In M. Durrant & C. White (Eds.), *Ideas for therapy with sexual abuse* (pp. 9-36). Adelaide, South Australia: Dulwich Centre Publications.

Karen, R. (1994). *Becoming attached.* New York: Warner Books.

Kegan, R. (1982). *The evolving self.* Cambridge, MA: Harvard University Press.

Kendall, P. C., & Braswell, L. (1985). *Cognitive behavior therapy for impulsive children.* New York: Guilford.

Kendall-Tackett, K. A., Williams, L. M., & Finkelhor, D. (1993). The impact of sexual abuse on children: A review and synthesis of recent empirical studies. *Psychological Bulletin, 113,* 164-180.

Kihlstrom, J. F., Glisky, M. F., & Anguilo, M. J. (1994). Dissociative tendencies and dissociative disorders. *Journal of Abnormal Psychology, 103,* 117-124.

Kinney, J., Haapala, D., & Booth, C. (1991). *Keeping families together: The HOME-BUILDERS model.* New York: Aldine de Gruyter.

Kiresuk, T. J., & Sherman, R. E. (1968). Goal attainment scaling: A general method for evaluating comprehensive mental health programs. *Community Mental Health Journal, 4,* 443-453.

Klaus, M. H., & Kennel, J. H. (1976). *Maternal-infant bonding.* St. Louis, MO: C. J. Mosby.

Kohlberg, L. (1984). *The psychology of moral development.* San Francisco: Harper & Row.

Kovacs, M. (1991). *Child Depression Inventory.* North Tonawanda, NY: Multihealth Systems, Inc.

Lanktree, C., & Briere, J. (1992, August). *Therapy for sexually abused children: Treatment outcome using the TSC–C.* Paper presented at the annual meeting of the American Psychological Association, Washington, DC.

Larson, N., & Maddock, W. (1986). Structural and functional variables in incest family systems: Implications for assessment and treatment. In T. Trepper & M. J. Barrett (Eds.), *Treating incest: A multiple systems perspective* (pp. 27-44). New York: Haworth.

Lazarus, A. (1993). Tailoring the therapeutic relationship, or being an authentic chameleon. *Psychotherapy, Research and Practice, 30,* 404-407.

Levang, C. A. (1989). Interactional communication patterns in father/daughter incest families. *Journal of Psychology and Human Sexuality, 1,* 53-68.

Linden, P. (1988). Being in movement: Intention as a somatic meditation. *Somatics, 7,* 54-59.

Linden, P. (1990). Applications of being in movement in working with incest survivors. *Somatics, 9,* 38-47.

Linehan, M. M. (1993). *Skills training manual for treating borderline personality disorders.* New York: Guilford.

Lipovsky, J. A. (1992). Assessment and treatment of post-traumatic stress disorder in child survivors of sexual assault. In D. W. Foy (Ed.), *Treating PTSD: Cognitive-behavioral strategies* (pp. 127-164). New York: Guilford.

Lipovsky, J. A., Saunders, B. E., & Murphy, S. M. (1989). Depression, anxiety, and behavior problems among victims of father-child sexual assault and nonabused siblings. *Journal of Interpersonal Violence, 4,* 452-468.

Loevinger, J., & Wessler, R. (1970). *Measuring ego development* (Vol. 1). San Francisco: Jossey-Bass.

Maccoby, E. E. (1980). *Social development.* New York: Harcourt, Brace & Jovanovich.

Maccoby, E. E., & Jacklin, C. N. (1974). *The psychology of sex differences.* Stanford, CA: Stanford University Press.

Maddock, J. (1988, July). *The Sexual Meaning Scale: Development of a semantic differential.* Paper presented at the annual conference of the National Council on Family Relations, Philadelphia, PA.

Main, M. (1990). Cross cultural studies of attachment organization: Recent studies, changing methodologies, and the concept of conditional strategies. *Human Development, 33,* 48-61.

Main, M., & George, C. (1985). Responses of abused and disadvantaged toddlers to distress in age mates: A study in the day care setting. *Developmental Psychology, 21,* 407-412.

Main, M., Kaplan, N., & Cassidy, J. (1985). Security in infancy, childhood, and adulthood: A move to the level of representation. *Monographs of the Society for Research in Child Development, 50,* 66-104.

Main, M., & Solomon, J. (1990). Procedures for identifying infants as disorganized/disoriented during the Ainsworth strange situation. In M. Greenberg, D. Cicchetti, & M. Cummings (Eds.), *Attachment in the preschool years* (pp. 121-160). Chicago: University of Chicago Press.

Main, M., & Weston, D. (1981). The quality of the toddler's relationship to mother and father: Related to conflict behavior and readiness to establish new relationships. *Child Development, 52,* 932-940.

Mandell, J. G., & Damon, L. (1989). *Group treatment for sexually abused children*. New York: Guilford.

Mannarino, A. P., & Cohen, J. A. (1994). *The psychological impact of child sexual abuse. Final Program Report*. Grant #90-CA-1460. Washington, DC: National Center on Child Abuse and Neglect.

Mannarino, A. P., Cohen, J. A., & Berman, S. R. (1994). The Children's Attributions and Perceptions Scale: A new measure of sexual abuse related factors. *Journal of Clinical Child Psychology, 23*, 204-211.

McArthur, D. S., & Roberts, G. D. (1982). *Roberts Apperception Test for Children*. Los Angeles: Western Psychological Services.

McCrone, E. R., Egeland, B., Kalkoske, M., & Carlson, E. A. (1994). Relations between early maltreatment and mental representations of relationships assessed with projective storytelling in middle childhood. *Development and Psychopathology, 6*, 99-120.

McGuinness, D. (1989). Attention deficit disorder: The emperor's clothes, animal "pharm," and other fiction. In S. Fischer & R. P. Greenberg (Eds.), *The limits of biological treatments for psychological distress: Comparisons with psychotherapy and placebo* (pp. 151-187). Hillsdale, NJ: Lawrence Erlbaum.

McLeer, S., Deblinger, E., Atkins, M., Foa, E., & Ralphe, D. (1988). Post-traumatic stress disorder in sexually abused children. *Journal of American Academy of Child and Adolescent Psychiatry, 27*, 650-654.

Meichenbaum, D. (1977). *Cognitive-behavior modification*. New York: Plenum.

Miller, A. (1983). *For your own good*. New York: Farrar, Straus & Giroux.

Millon, T. (1992). *Millon Clinical Multiaxial Inventory–II (MCMI–II)*. Minneapolis, MN: National Computer Systems.

Minuchin, S. (1974). *Families and family therapy*. Cambridge, MA: Harvard University Press.

Minuchin, S., Rosman, B. L., & Baker, L. (1978). *Psychosomatic families*. Cambridge, MA: Harvard University Press.

Moos, R. (1979). *Family environment scale*. Palo Alto, CA: Consulting Psychologists.

Morgan, R. F. (1990, April). *Behavioral problems of children likely to parallel sleep difficulties*. Paper presented at the Southeastern Psychological Association Conference, Atlanta, GA.

Morris, R. J., & Kratochwill, T. R. (1983). *Treating children's fears and phobias*. New York: Pergamon.

Mufson, L., Moreau, D. Weissman, M. W., & Klerman, G. L. (1993). *Interpersonal psychotherapy for depressed adolescents*. New York: Guilford.

Mura, D. (1985). Male grief: Notes on pornography and addiction. *Utne Reader*, October-November, 46-54.

Mussen, P. (1975). Communication and the development of prosocial behavior. *American Speech and Hearing Association, 17*, 324-330.

Nakkula, M., & Selman, R. (1991). How people "treat" each other: Pair therapy as a context for the development of interpersonal ethnics. In W. N. Kurtines & J. L. Gewirtz (Eds.), *Handbook of moral development and behavior* (pp. 179-211). Hillsdale, NJ: Lawrence Erlbaum.

Newberger, C. M., Gremy, I. M., Waternaux, C. M., & Newberger, E. H. (1993). Mothers of sexually abused children: Trauma and repair in longitudinal perspective. *American Journal of Orthopsychiatry, 63*, 92-102.

Noam, G. G. (1992). Development as the aim of clinical intervention. *Development and Psychopathology, 4*, 679-696.

Oliver, M. B., & Hyde, J. S. (1993). Gender differences in sexuality: A meta-analysis. *Psychological Bulletin, 114*, 29-51.

Ollendick, T. H., Mattis, S. G., & King, N. J. (1994). Panic in children and adolescents: A review. *Journal of Child Psychiatry and Psychology, 35*, 113-134.

Parker, H., & Parker, S. (1986). Father-daughter sexual abuse: An emerging perspective. *American Journal of Orthopsychiatry, 56*, 531-549.

Patterson, G. R. (1993). Orderly change in a stable world: The antisocial trait as a chimera. *Journal of Consulting and Clinical Psychology, 61*, 203-224.

Patterson, G. R., Reid, J. B., Jones, R. R., & Conger, R. E. (1975). *A social learning approach to family intervention: Vol. 1: Families with aggressive children*. Eugene, OR: Castalia.

Paveza, G. J. (1988). Risk factors in father-daughter child sexual abuse: A case control study. *Journal of Interpersonal Violence, 3*, 290-306.

Perez, C. M., & Widom, C. S. (1994). Childhood victimization and long-term intellectual and academic outcomes. *Child Abuse and Neglect, 18*, 617-633.

Perry, B. D. (1993a). Neurodevelopment and the neurophysiology of trauma, I: Conceptual considerations for clinical work with maltreated children. *APSAC Advisor, 6*(1), 14-18.

Perry, B. D. (1993b). Neurodevelopment and the neurophysiology of trauma, II: Conceptual considerations for clinical work with maltreated children. *APSAC Advisor, 6*(2), 14-20.

Pescosolido, F. J. (1993). Clinical considerations related to victimization dynamics and post-traumatic stress in the group treatment of sexually abused boys. *Journal of Child and Adolescent Group Therapy, 3*, 49-73.

Peters, S. D. (1988). Child sexual abuse and later psychological problems. In G. E. Wyatt & G. J. Powell (Eds.), *Lasting effects of child sexual abuse* (pp. 101-117). Newbury Park, CA: Sage.

Peterson, R. F., Basta, S. M., & Dykstra, T. A. (1993). Mothers of molested children: Some comparisons of personality characteristics. *Child Abuse and Neglect, 17*, 409-418.

Pfeffer, C. R. (1986). *The suicidal child*. New York: Guilford.

Porter, E. (1986). *Treating the young male victim of sexual abuse*. Orwell, VT: Safer Society Press.

Putnam, F. W. (1991, October). *Behavioral and psychophysiological correlates of sexual abuse*. Paper presented at the annual meeting of the American Academy of Child and Adolescent Psychiatry, San Francisco.

Putnam, F. W. (1993). Dissociative disorders in children: Behavioral profiles and problems. *Child Abuse and Neglect, 17*, 39-45.

Putnam, F. W., Helmers, K., & Trickett, P. K. (1993). Development, reliability, and validity of a child dissociation scale. *Child Abuse and Neglect, 17*, 731-742.

Reams, R. A., & Friedrich, W. N. (1994). The efficacy of time-limited play therapy with maltreated preschoolers. *Journal of Clinical Psychology, 50*, 889-899.

Rhodes, R. (1990). *A hole in the world*. New York: Simon & Schuster.

Rolf, J., Masten, A. S., Cicchetti, D., Nuechterlein, K. H., & Weintraub, S. (1990). *Risk and protective factors in the development of psychopathology*. Cambridge, UK: Cambridge University Press.

Root, M. P. P., Fallon, P., & Friedrich, W. N. (1986). *Bulimia: A systems approach to treatment*. New York: Norton.

Rosen, K. S., & Rothbaum, F. (1993). Quality of parental caregiving and security of attachment. *Developmental Psychology, 29*, 358-367.

Rosenhan, D. L., & Seligman, M. E. (1984). *Abnormal psychology.* New York: Norton.

Russell, D. E. H. (1986). *The secret trauma: Incest in the lives of girls and women.* New York: Basic Books.

Sameroff, A. J., Seifer, R., Barocas, R., Zax, M., & Greenspan, S. (1987). IQ scores of 4-year-old children: Social environmental risk factors. *Pediatrics, 79,* 343-350.

Santostefano, S., & Calicchia, J. A. (1992). Body image, relational psychoanalysis, and the construction of meaning: Implications for treating aggressive children. *Development and Psychopathology, 4,* 655-678.

Schroeder, C. S., & Gordon, B. N. (1991). *Assessment and treatment of childhood problems: A clinician's guide.* New York: Guilford.

Schwartz, D., Dodge, K. A., & Coie, J. D. (1993). The emergence of chronic peer victimization in boy play groups. *Child Development, 64,* 1755-1772.

Schwartz, R. (1987). Our multiple selves. *Family Therapy Networker, 11,* 25-31.

Scott, R. L., & Stone, D. A. (1986). MMPI profile constellations in incest families. *Journal of Consulting and Clinical Psychology, 54,* 364-368.

Scott, W. (1992). Group therapy with sexually abused boys: Notes toward managing behavior. *Clinical Social Work Journal, 20,* 395-409.

Selman, R. L. (1980). *The growth of interpersonal understanding.* New York: Academic Press.

Selman, R. L., & Schultz, L. H. (1990). *Making a friend in youth: Developmental theory in pair therapy.* Chicago: University of Chicago Press.

Selvini-Palazzolli, M., Boscolo, L., Cecchin, G., & Prata, G. (1978). *Paradox and counter paradox.* New York: Aronson.

Shirk, S. R. (Ed.). (1988). *Cognitive development and child psychotherapy.* New York: Plenum.

Shirk, S. R., & Saiz, C. C. (1992). Clinical, empirical, and developmental perspectives on the therapeutic relationship in child psychotherapy. *Development and Psychopathology, 4,* 713-728.

Silverstein, O., & Rashbaum, B. (1994). *The courage to raise good men.* New York: Viking Penguin.

Smiley, J. (1989). *Ordinary love and good will.* New York: Alfred A. Knopf.

Smith, D., & Saunders, B. (1994, January). *Personality characteristics of father/perpetrators and non-offending mothers in incest families: Individual and dyadic analyses.* Paper presented at the annual Responding to Child Maltreatment Conference, San Diego, CA.

Smyrnios, K. X., & Kirkby, R. J. (1993). Long-term comparisons of brief versus unlimited psychodynamic treatments with children and their parents. *Journal of Consulting and Clinical Psychology, 61,* 1020-1027.

Speltz, N. L. (1990). The treatment of preschool conduct problems: An integration of behavioral and attachment concepts. In M. T. Greenberg, D. Cicchetti, & E. E. Cumming (Eds.), *Attachment in the preschool years* (pp. 399-426). Chicago: University of Chicago Press.

Springs, F. E., & Friedrich, W. N. (1992). Health risk behaviors and medical sequelae of chilldhood sexual abuse. *Mayo Clinic Proceedings, 67,* 527-532.

Sroufe, L. A. (1988). The role of infant-caregiver attachment in development. In J. Belsky & T. Nezworski (Eds.), *Clinical implications of attachment* (pp. 18-38). Hillsdale, NJ: Lawrence Erlbaum.

Sroufe, L. A. (1989). Pathways to adaptation and maladaptation: Psychopathology as developmental deviation. In D. Cicchetti (Ed.), *The emergence of a discipline: Roches-*

ter symposium on developmental psychopathology (Vol. 1, pp. 13-40). Hillsdale, NJ: Lawrence Erlbaum.

Sroufe, L. A., & Fleeson, J. (1986). Attachment and the construction of relationships. In W. Hartup & Z. Rubin (Eds.), *Relationships and development* (pp. 51-71). Hillsdale, NJ: Lawrence Erlbaum.

Sroufe, L. A., Jacobvitz, D., Mangelsdorf, S., DeAngelo, E., & Ward, M. J. (1985). Generational boundary dissolution between mothers and their preschool children: A relationship systems approach. *Child Development, 56,* 317-325.

Sroufe, L. A., & Ward, M. J. (1980). Seductive behavior of mothers of toddlers: Occurrence, correlates, and family origins. *Child Development, 56,* 317-325.

Stark, K. D., Rouse, L. W., & Livingston, R. (1991). Treatment of depression during childhood and adolescence: Cognitive-behavioral procedures for the individual and family. In P. C. Kendall (Ed.), *Child and adolescent therapy: Cognitive-behavioral procedures* (pp. 165-206). New York: Guilford.

Steinglass, P., Bennett, L. A., Wolin, S. J., & Riess, D. (1987). *The alcoholic family.* New York: Basic Books.

Strayer, J. (1980). A naturalistic study of emphatic behaviors and their relation to affective states and perspective-taking skills in preschool children. *Child Development, 51,* 815-822.

Stricker, R. (1990). Island. In D. Keenan & R. Lloyd (Eds.), *Looking for home* (pp. 273-274). Minneapolis, MN: Milkweed.

Strupp, H. H., & Binder, J. L. (1984). *Psychotherapy in a new key.* New York: Basic Books.

Struve, J. (1990). Dancing with the patriarchy: The politics of sexual abuse. In M. Hunter (Ed.), *The sexually abused male* (Vol. 1, pp. 3-46). Lexington, MA: Lexington Books.

Sullivan, H. S. (1953). *The interpersonal theory of psychiatry.* New York: Norton.

Tannen, D. (1990). Gender differences in topical coherence: Creating involvement in best friends' talk. *Discourse Processes, 13,* 73-90.

Taylor, S. E. (1983). Adjustment to threatening events: A theory of cognitive adaptation. *American Psychologist, 38,* 1161-1173.

Terr, L. C. (1981). Forbidden games: Post-traumatic child's play. *American Journal of Orthopsychiatry, 20,* 740-759.

Terr, L. C. (1990). *Too scared to try.* New York: Harper Collins.

Terr, L. C. (1991). Childhood traumas: An outline and overview. *American Journal of Psychiatry, 148,* 10-20.

Trepper, T. S., & Barrett, M. J. (1989). *Systemic treatment of incest.* New York: Brunner/Mazel.

Trickett, P. K., McBride-Chang, C., & Putnam, F. W. (1994). The classroom performance and behavior of sexually abused females. *Development and Psychopathology, 6,* 183-194.

Uherek, A. M. (1991). Treatment of a ritually abused preschooler. In W. N. Friedrich (Ed.), *Casebook of sexual abuse treatment* (pp. 70-92). New York: Norton.

van der Kolk, B. A. (1988). The trauma spectrum: The interaction of biological and social events in the genesis of the trauma response. *Journal of Traumatic Stress, 1,* 273-290.

van der Kolk, B. A. (1994, October). *Disorders of extreme stress.* Paper presented at the 8th Annual Rochester Symposium on Developmental Psychopathology, Rochester, NY.

Walsh, F. (1978). Concurrent grandparent death and birth of schizophrenic offspring: An intriguing finding. *Family Process, 17,* 457-463.

Walters, M., Carter, B., Papp, P., & Silverstein, O. (1988). *The invisible web.* New York: Guilford.

Watkins, B., & Bentovim, A. (1992). The sexual abuse of male children and adolescents: A review of current research. *Journal of Child Psychology and Psychiatry, 33,* 197-248.

Webster-Stratton, C. (1991). Strategies for helping families with conduct-disordered children. *Journal of Child Psychology and Psychiatry, 32,* 1047-1062.

Wechsler, D. (1974). *Manual for the Wechsler Intelligence Scale for Children–Revised.* New York: Psychological Corporation.

Werner, H. (1948). *Comparative psychology of mental development.* New York: International Universities Press.

Westen, D. (1994). The impact of sexual abuse on self structure. In D. Cicchetti & S. L. Toth (Eds.), *Disorders and dysfunctions of the self* (pp. 223-249). Rochester, NY: University of Rochester Press.

Wexler, D. B. (1991). *The PRISM Workbook: A program for innovative self-management.* New York: Norton.

White, M. (1989). *Selected papers.* Adelaide, South Australia: Dulwich Center Publications.

White, M., & Epston, D. (1990). *Narrative means to therapeutic ends.* New York: Norton.

Williams, L. M., & Finkelhor, D. (1992). *The characteristics of incestuous fathers.* Family Research Laboratory, University of New Hampshire.

Winnicott, D. W. (1965). *Maturational processes and the facilitating environment.* New York: International Universities Press.

Wolfe, D. A., Sas, L., & Wekerle, C. (1994). Factors associated with the development of post-traumatic stress disorder among child victims of sexual abuse. *Child Abuse & Neglect, 18,* 37-50.

Wolfe, V. V., Gentile, C., Michienzi, T., Sas, L., & Wolfe, D. A. (1991). The Children's Impact of Traumatic Events Scale–Revised: A measure of post-sexual-abuse PTSD symptoms. *Behavioral Assessment, 13,* 359-383.

Yalom, I. (1975). *The theory and practice of group psychotherapy* (2nd ed.). New York: Basic Books.

Zahn-Waxler, C., Cole, P. M., & Barrett, K. C. (1992). Guilt and empathy: Sex differences and implications for the development of depression. In J. Garber & K. A. Dodge (Eds.), *The development of emotion regulation and dysregulation* (pp. 243-272). New York: Cambridge University Press.

Zimbardo, P. G., LaBerge, S., & Butler, L. D. (1993). Psychophysiological consequence of unexplained arousal: A post-hypnotic suggestion paradigm. *Journal of Abnormal Psychology, 102,* 466-473.

Index

About the Author

William N. Friedrich, PhD, ABPP, is Professor and Consultant in the Department of Psychiatry and Psychology at the Mayo Clinic and the Mayo Medical School in Rochester, Minnesota. His position at Mayo includes clinical practice, as well as teaching, consultation, and training. Prior to moving to the Mayo Clinic, he was a faculty member at the University of Washington in the Department of Psychology. He is a Diplomate with the American Board of Professional Psychology in both clinical psychology and family psychology. He has authored over 100 publications, including three books. He has also written over a dozen published short stories. Two of his books are directly related to sexual abuse—*Psychotherapy of Sexually Abused Children and Their Families* and *Casebook of Sexual Abuse Treatment.* He and his wife have two teenage children.